Miniatures

Miniatures

Views of Islamic and
Middle Eastern Politics

Daniel Pipes

Transaction Publishers
New Brunswick (U.S.A.) and London (U.K.)

Library of Congress Catalog Number: 2003065033
ISBN: 0-7658-0215-5
Printed in the United States of America

Library of Congress Cataloging-in-Publication Data

Pipes, Daniel, 1949-
    Miniatures : views of Islamic and Middle Eastern politics / Daniel Pipes.
        p. cm.
    Includes bibliographical references (p.) and index.
    ISBN 0-7658-0215-5 (alk. paper)
        1. Islam and politics—Middle East. 2. Middle East—Politics and
    government.   I. Title: Views of Islamic and Middle Eastern politics.
    II. Title.

BP173.7 .P565 2004
909'.097670825—dc22   2003065033

For Nina Rosenwald, in Friendship

Contents

INTRODUCTION

The German philosopher Georg W. F. Hegel wrote in 1837 about Muslim states: "In its spread Mahometanism founded many kingdoms and dynasties. On this boundless sea there is a continual onward movement, nothing abides firm."* This emphasis on the volatility of Muslim politics is as true for the twenty-first century as it was in the seventh or the nineteenth. Indeed, at present, Hegel's perception of "continual onward movement" has become *the* preoccupation of world politics—and at the central concern of the roughly hundred essays that follow.

These essays represent a crossover: I have a Ph.D. in the medieval history of Islam, yet much of my writing in recent years takes the shape of a weekly column that appears in newspapers and on websites. I endeavor to bring my specialized knowledge to a general audience via miniature research essays; thus the name of this volume.

This undertaking is made possible by the acute interest in the topics I cover; indeed, no single region of the world has quite dominated American and Western public discourse as does the Middle East today. This results mainly but not exclusively from the attacks of September 11 and the ensuing war on terrorism. Other prominent topics include militant Islam, Muslims in the West, the Arab-Israeli conflict, Iraq, Saudi Arabia, the price of oil and gas, and intra-Western debates over these issues.

Miniatures' sections closely reflect those themes.

Part 1 covers the war on terror. I argue (in chapter 1) that terror's war against Americans began not with the destruction of the World Trade Center in 2001 but with the double assault on U.S. embassies in November 1979. Many of the pre-9/11 essays manifest my frustration that so few Westerners recognized the state of war that ex-

---

*Georg W.F. Hegel, *Vorlesungen über die Philosophie der Geschichte*, trans. J. Sibree as *Philosophy of History* (New York: Dover, 1956), p. 358.

1

isted. Over this twenty-two-year period, from November 1979 to September 2001, my writings leveled four main criticisms at U.S. government policy: its insistence that militant Islamic attacks on Americans were criminal incidents, not war; its unwillingness to destroy the enemy forces; its ignoring the ideology of militant Islam that motivated these attacks; and its reluctance to make the policy changes required to win the war.

After 9/11 (chapter 2), I gave the Bush administration mixed grades, praising it for addressing the first two mistakes and protesting against the continuation of the latter two. On the positive side, Washington did instantly shunt aside the criminal paradigm in favor of the military one ("*war* on terrorism"); the expeditionary force to Afghanistan, plus troops in such locations as the Philippines, Georgia, and Yemen, evidenced an intent to root out enemy forces.* On the negative side, with a few exceptions, officials continued to ignore the militant Islamic ideology that motivates the attacks ("war on *terrorism*"). And while some policy changes did occur (for example, in the areas of immigration, airline security, and police surveillance of places of worship), I found these inadequate. Two out of four is not good enough; I worry that unless politicians summon the courage to make all the necessary changes, there will be a heavy price to pay.

The politically correct interpretation of the Muslim world by the U.S. government, leading media, and academic specialists holds that militant Islamic violence is a "fringe form of Islamic extremism" repudiated by the overwhelmingly moderate Muslim majority, or even that it has nothing to do with Islam at all ("killers whose only faith is hate" was how the president described those behind a series of murderous attacks in Riyadh in May 2003).** In chapter 3, I report on developments in the Muslim world after 9/11—joy at the death of thousands of Americans, wide Muslim support for bin Laden and dismay at the fall of the Taliban regime, a Taliban-like movement growing in Saudi Arabia, the spread of militant Islam to areas far beyond the Middle East—by way of demonstrating that the establishment position offers political bromides, not serious analysis.

---

*I do not include the overthrow of Saddam Hussein as part of this undertaking, seeing his regime as basically unconnected to militant Islam.

**Wall Street Journal*, 14 May 2003.

Shifting focus, part 2 looks at some general issues concerning Islam and Muslims. I begin (in chapter 4) with a basic point, that today's international crisis concerns not Islam the religion but militant Islam the ideology. This argument has three happy implications:

- This is not a religious war between Christendom and the *umma* (community of Muslims);

- Moderate Muslims have a vital role in the fight against militant Islam; and

- It is possible to devise policy goals to defeat and marginalize militant Islam.

I then focus on some details of militant Islam, noting the moral failings of Islamists, establishing the terrible reality of *jihad*, and noting the near-absence of religious freedom in the Middle East.

In addition to the traditional regions of Muslim habitation, Islam has, in the past four decades, developed a presence in the West. These immigrants, converts, and their descendents have vast implications for both sides, the Muslim and the Western (chapter 5). I take up various questions about American Islam—the number of American Muslims, their division into moderates and militants, and the acute tensions between those two groups that come out most evidently when atheistic or even secular Muslims express themselves. Looking further away, I note some major developments in Australia and Denmark.

The growth of militant Islamic institutions in the United States and their bullying their way into the public square (chapter 6) is a particular concern of mine. The Islamists demand special consideration in everything from school textbooks to university commencement speeches to government-subsidized television—and often they get it. These organizations do so well in large part because they succeed at presenting themselves as moderates, letting their true views come out only behind closed doors or by implication. I show some aspects of their real, extremist nature.

Part 3 looks at various political conflicts in the Middle East, especially the Arab war against Israel. Chapters 7 and 8 look at the eras of "Oslo Diplomacy" (1993-2000) and "Oslo War" (2000-03). The reader can see the evolution of my writing, from a mild concern in the early years to an ever-increasing agitation that peaks in late 2000 and then, as the folly of the Oslo presumptions become more widely recognized, a return to relative calm.

Syria (chapter 9) has been a specialty of mine since 1985, with an emphasis on several themes: (1) how the sense of truncation gives Syrian politics a deep-seated expansionist edge; (2) how Westerners tend to reduce Syria to its relations with Israel, thereby missing the many other internal and external facets of that country; and (3) how Hafez al-Assad, ruler of Syria from 1970 until 2000, never intended to sign a peace treaty with Israel. I have devoted entire books to the first two subjects; here I provide interpretations over a seven-year period of Assad's policy vis-à-vis Israel, followed by a couple of posthumous reviews. I can claim to be the only analyst who predicted in January-March 2000 that Assad would not sign an agreement with Israel.

Iraq (chapter 10) has been a major problem since Saddam Hussein invaded Kuwait in 1990, but a problem many that Americans preferred to ignore after their victory of early 1991. I offer one provocation (arguing for Washington to pull back until asked by others to take on the Iraqi dictator) but otherwise support the view that the U.S. government has no choice but to take on this foul aggressor, and the sooner the better. I strongly supported the campaign to overthrow Saddam Hussein when it finally came in March-April 2003.

Part 4 deals with the American interpretation of the Middle East, concentrating on government and scholars. The section on policy (chapter 11) takes a running start by reviewing the nearly two-century-history of the Arabists who have so deeply affected U.S. government attitudes, then looks at such specifics as the rationale for the U.S. subvention of Israel, the fact that Republicans support Israel more consistently than Democrats, strange moments in U.S. relations with Israel and with Egypt, and the case for holding the Kingdom of Saudi Arabia accountable for 9/11. (The two articles urging the victims and victims' families to sue the Kingdom of Saudi Arabia had a key role in inspiring the $1 trillion case against Riyadh currently in preparation to go to trial.)

The final chapter (12) reports on scholarship, with an emphasis on revisionism. I report on the scholars who are turning early Islamic history upside down by throwing out the standard sources; on a historian who reverses the accepted understanding of the Ottoman Empire as a passive force; and an analyst (admittedly French, not American) who bucks all evidence to declare militant Islam a dying movement. The book rounds out with a review of the ironic role of nineteenth-century Jewish scholars and a remarkable study of contemporary Arab thought.

As these writings imply, I believe it useful for a specialist like myself to peer ahead, going on the record with predictions, and warning of dangers. In the past I took three stands that were then controversial and now widely accepted: warning of militant Islam's assault on the West, predicting Hafez al-Assad would not sign a peace treaty with Israel, and anticipating that the Oslo process would end in disaster.

I continue to make such statements, two in particular: the "war on terror" can be won only when militant Islam, not terrorism, is recognized as the enemy; and the Arab-Israeli conflict will wind down only after the Palestinians accept the existence of Israel.

Making such statements has rewards and costs. On the positive side, there is the after-the-fact recognition that comes with getting it right. Two days after 9/11, for example, the *Boston Globe* said I "saw what lay ahead and tried to sound the alarm"* and the *National Post* of Canada observed in 2002 that "If the world had acted on [my] warnings, September 11 might never have happened."** The experience of predicting is less pleasant, however, before vindication arrives, when one finds oneself the object of hostile op-eds and editorials, insults on national television, and websites detailing one's alleged phobias and unsavory motivations. It can, in short, be painful to foresee developments, and then endure the waiting period for the world to catch up.

I thank Irving Louis Horowitz, editorial chairman and president emeritus of Transaction Publishers, for suggesting that I bring together in book form what I consider my best and most enduring short essays of recent years. I likewise thank those others on the Transaction staff—Mary Curtis especially—for turning this idea into the reality of cloth, paper, and ink.

I was not a columnist born, and I wish to thank those individuals who helped me become one. David Makovsky gave me my start as columnist in 1999, during his tenure as editor-in-chief of the *Jerusalem Post*, when he came to me with the unexpected and slightly

---

*Jeff Jacoby, "Our Enemies Mean What They Say," *Boston Globe*, 13 September 2001.
**Jonathan Kay, "Has Islamism Hit Its High-Water Mark?" *National Post*, 31 December 2002.

intoxicating invitation to write a column every two weeks. Thomas A. Rose, publisher and CEO of the *Jerusalem Post*, then urged me to take the column weekly, which I did in mid-2001. Robert McManus and Mark Cunningham invited me to write for the *New York Post* shortly after 9/11. I would also like to thank those editors at other papers—especially Natasha Hassan of the *National Post*, Steven Huntley of the *Chicago Sun-Times*, Thomas Winter of *Human Events*, and N. Richard Greenfield of the *Connecticut Jewish Ledger*—who see fit to publish my columns with some frequency.

My columns benefit from the help of many others. My co-authors (Steven Emerson, Lars Hedegaard, Zachary Rentz, Jonathan Schanzer, Alexander T. Stillman, Mimi Stillman, Tonya Ugoretz) helped make the articles here worth reading. Cynthia Dachowitz provides fast, focused research that gives many of my columns a factual base they would otherwise lack. Patrick Chisholm capably handles the column's syndication. Grayson Levy spurred me in early 2001 to put together a personal website, www.DanielPipes.org, maintains it for me, and sends out my writings to the wide world. Jane Maestro and the staff at the Middle East Forum run the organization so well that I can play hooky each week long enough to write a column. The Forum's board and donors provide the perch from which I can opine. Nina Rosenwald took on a leadership role when the Forum was yet fledgling, helping us through some tough spots. And my family has graciously tolerated my absences since 9/11.

Daniel Pipes
Philadelphia
June 2003

PART 1
WAR ON TERRORISM

1

BEFORE 9/11

"DEATH TO AMERICA"

Terrorism's war on America did not begin in September 2001. It began in November 1979, not long after Ayatollah Khomeini rode the slogan "Death to America" to power—and sure enough, the attacks on Americans soon began. Militant Islamic mobs besieged two U.S. embassies that month.

- In Iran, a militant Islamic mob took over the U.S. embassy in the capital Tehran and held fifty-two Americans hostage for the next 444 days. The rescue team sent to free those hostages in April 1980 suffered eight fatalities.

- In Pakistan, false rumors that U.S. troops had helped seize the Great Mosque in Mecca led to an attack on the embassy in Islamabad and the American Cultural Center in Lahore. The Pakistani authorities' slow response gave the mobs time to burn both buildings, killing four persons in Islamabad, two of them Americans.

These were the first of what are by now nearly four thousand fatalities at the hands of militant Islam's assault on Americans.

The Islamists' initial major act of violence against Americans, killing sixty-three, took place in April 1983 when they attacked the U.S. Embassy in Beirut. As the analyst David Makovsky notes, Washington "beat a hasty exit, and Islamic militants saw this as a vindication that suicide bombing was... deadly effective."

Other attacks included:

October 1983: 241 dead at the U.S. Marine barracks in Beirut.

December 1983: five dead at the U.S. embassy in Kuwait.

January 1984: the president of the American University of Beirut killed.

April 1984: eighteen dead near a U.S. airbase in Spain.

September 1984: sixteen dead at the U.S. embassy in Beirut (again).

December 1984: Two dead on a plane hijacked to Tehran.

June 1985: One dead on a plane hijacked to Beirut.

After a let-up, the attacks then restarted: Five and nineteen dead in Saudi Arabia in 1995 and 1996, 224 dead at the U.S. embassies in Kenya and Tanzania in August 1998 and seventeen dead on the *USS Cole* in Yemen in October 2000.

Simultaneously, the murderous assault of militant Islam also took place on U.S. soil:

July 1980: an Iranian dissident killed in the Washington, D.C. area.

August 1983: a leader of the Ahmadiyya sect of Islam killed in Canton, Mich.

August 1984: three Indians killed in a suburb of Tacoma, Wash.

September 1986: a doctor killed in Augusta, Ga.

January 1990: an Egyptian freethinker killed in Tucson, Ariz.

November 1990: a Jewish leader killed in New York.

February 1991: an Egyptian Islamist killed in New York.

January 1993: two CIA staff killed outside agency headquarters in Langley, Va.

February 1993: six people killed at the World Trade Center.

March 1994: an Orthodox Jewish boy killed on the Brooklyn Bridge.

February 1997: a Danish tourist killed on the Empire State building.

October 1999: 217 passengers killed on an EgyptAir flight near New York City.

In all, 800 persons lost their lives in the course of attacks by militant Islam on Americans before September 2001—more than killed by any other enemy since the Vietnam War. (Further, this listing does not include the dozens more Americans in Israel killed by militant Islamic forces as well as further afield yet, including Americans killed in Pakistan, Kashmir, and the Philippines.)

And yet, these murders hardly registered. Washington threatened retribution ("You can run but you can't hide") for attacks against Americans, but hardly ever carried through. "Scandal" is how one Israeli pilot correctly describes the military's inability to protect the World Trade Center or the Pentagon. Only with the events of September 11, 2001, did Americans finally realize that "Death to America" truly is the battle cry of this era's most dangerous foe, militant Islam.

In retrospect, the mistake began when Iranians assaulted the U.S. embassy in Tehran and met with no resistance. Interestingly, a Marine sergeant present at the embassy that fateful day in November 1979 agrees with this assessment. As the militant Islamic mob invaded the embassy, Rodney V. Sickmann followed orders and protected neither himself nor the embassy. As a result, he was taken hostage and lived to tell the tale. (He now works for Anheuser-Busch.)

Looking back, he believes that passivity was a mistake. The Marines should have done their assigned duty, even if it cost their lives: "Had we opened fire on them, maybe we would only have lasted an hour." But had they done that, they "could have changed history." Standing their ground would have sent a powerful signal that the United States of America cannot be attacked with impunity. In contrast, the embassy's surrender sent the opposite signal—that it's open season on Americans. "If you look back, it started in 1979; it's just escalated," Sickmann correctly concludes.

To which one of the century's great geostrategist thinkers, Robert Strausz-Hupé, adds his assent. Just before passing away early in 2002 at the age of ninety-eight, Strausz-Hupé wrote his final words, and they were about the war on terrorism: "I have lived long enough to see good repeatedly win over evil, although at a much higher cost than need have been paid. This time we have already paid the price of victory. It remains for us to win it."

(8 September 2002)

KHOMEINI, BETWEEN THE S.U. AND U.S.

A year after the revolution of 1979, Iran appears to be drifting into the Soviet orbit. While the Ayatollah Ruhollah Khomeini has fulminated often and loudly against a satanic United States, he has rarely condemned the Soviet assault on Afghanistan. His support of the continued holding of the fifty-two American hostages has led Western countries to cut some economic ties with Iran, forcing that country to depend more on trade with the Soviet Union.

Why does Khomeini alienate the United States, the one country that can protect him from the Soviet Union? Westerners, unable to answer this question, throw up their hands in despair and declare Khomeini irrational. But this is glib. Khomeini is not crazy; rather, he represents the Islamic tradition in Iranian culture and his actions make sense in the context of that tradition.

In the Western view, the Soviet Union threatens Iran far more than does the United States: It looms across a long common border and espouses an atheistic doctrine incompatible with Islam and many other institutions of Iranian life, such as private property and the family unit as an ideal.

But for the Ayatollah, it is America that is more threatening. He believes that after 1953, the United States government controlled the Shah and his regime and the Iranian people; further, he believes that Washington is trying to overthrow him and regain its old power. The failed rescue mission confirmed this fear.

It is American, not Soviet culture, that pervades Iran and horrifies Ayatollah Khomeini by, in his view, endangering the Islamic way of life with its loose ways (alcohol, jeans, pop music, nightclubs, movies, dancing, mixed bathing, pornography), with its conspicuous consumption, and with foreign ideologies (such as nationalism and liberalism). He and his followers fervently want an Iran free of foreign domination. So long as they perceive America as the greatest threat to Iran, nothing prevents them from relying on the Soviet Union. Although we share with the Iranians a respect for religion, private property and the family unit, the Ayatollah's regime also shares much with the Marxists against the West.

For one thing, they both feel considerable antipathy toward the West. The Soviet government, like Khomeini, worries about the allure of Western culture and tries desperately to contain it.

In an odd parallel, Islam claims to replace Christianity as the final revelation from God, and communism claims to succeed capitalism as the final stage of economic evolution. The West infuriates both its would-be successors with its continued wealth and power. They respond by presenting the West with its most sustained opposition. Just as earlier in this century they led the attack on European imperialism, today the Soviet Union and Muslim members of the Organization of Petroleum Exporting Countries are mounting the main challenge to Western political and economic power. Both have revolutionary temperaments; claiming a monopoly on truth, why should either allow imperfect or evil ways to exist for another day? Each propagates its message with rhetorical shrillness, indoctrination, biased law courts, and firing squads. Both tend not to tolerate dissent and regard nonbelievers with suspicion, emphasizing the deep gulf between themselves and outsiders.

Activist Islam and Marxism emphasize international solidarity over nationalism, community needs over those of the individual, egalitarianism over freedom.

Both engage in social engineering—this is the most important consideration. Scorning the modest goals and realistic expectations of liberalism, activist Muslims and Marxists pursue noble-sounding yet unattainable standards for society. For example, Islam forbids interest on money, and communism denounces profits, yet commercial life requires both.

Finally, because activist Islam and Marxism touch on every aspect of life, their governments incline toward totalitarianism.

While Khomeini shares ideological elements with *both* the United States and the Soviet Union, as a devout Muslim he believes in the superiority of his own creed and execrates both alternatives.

In the end, however, ideologies cancel out and Khomeini aligns Iranian foreign relations in accordance with his hopes and fears, not on the basis of theoretical affinities.

At present, Khomeini fears the United States more than the Soviet Union: The Russians are near but for him America is already within Iran. Our culture, not the Russians', has been undermining the Muslim way of life in Iran for decades. So long as these fears remain paramount, Ayatollah Khomeini and his followers can be expected to veer Iran toward the Soviet Union, for its ideology appears no worse to him than does our own.

(27 May 1980)

THE NEW ENEMY

On their way to power in Iran in 1978 Islamists shouted "Death to America," and they haven't stopped in the twenty years since. With this cry they declared war on the United States. Now, in August 1998, in a stunning development, the U.S. finally responded. Let's hope that the missile attacks on Sudan and Afghanistan truly mark a turning point, as President Bill Clinton and his aides have promised.

By Islamists I don't mean traditional, pious Muslims who attend mosque and do their best to live by Islam's many laws. The Islamists are Muslims who practice a distinctly twentieth-century, politicized version of Islam. They have turned an ancient faith into a modern-style ideology. Rejecting the "isms" that have come out of the West, such as liberalism and communism, they have declared that their version of Islam is an all-encompassing political outlook superior to anything the West can produce.

A state of war exists between them and the West, mainly America, not because of the American response but because Islamists see themselves in a long-term conflict with Western values. When Hasan at-Turabi, the effective leader of Sudan and a leading Islamist thinker, explicitly states that the Muslim world is currently at war, "Against its attackers, led by the imperialist powers—chiefly the U.S. and Israel," it's not hard to miss the point.

A closer look reveals that these Islamists, despite their viciously anti-Western views, have in fact imbibed some Western ways wholesale, and often right at the source. It's hardly accidental that so many of them, whether leaders or terrorist operatives, are engineers. They pride themselves on having mastered some of the West's most privileged knowledge.

Why, then, do they see themselves in battle with the United States? To understand, it is best to see them in the framework of other twentieth-century revolutionaries that upheld totalitarian causes. Like fascists or Marxist-Leninists, they are absolutely convinced that they know how to achieve the just society (in this case, through the minute application of Islam's many laws in all spheres of life, including the political); they rely on the state to remake human beings; and they are prepared to destroy anyone who obstructs their path.

Also, like fascists and communists, they viscerally hate the United States. Americans—individualistic, hedonistic, and democratic—

challenge all they represent, and the United States stands as the single greatest obstacle to fulfilling their vision. They hate Americans for who they are, not for what they do; short of giving up the American way of life, the United States cannot please or appease them.

This is why "Death to America" is not empty rhetoric. Time and again, Islamists have assaulted American citizens and institutions; the total death toll from all these and dozens of other attacks numbers over 600. In other words, more Americans have been killed and injured by Middle Eastern-related terrorism than by any other hostile force since the end of the Vietnam War.

What to do about this threat? Unfortunately, the U.S. government until now has seen this violence not as the ideological war it is, but as a sequence of discrete criminal incidents. This approach turns the U.S. military into a sort of global police force and requires it to have an unrealistically high level of certainty before it can go into action. Basically, it must have proof of the sort that can stand up in a U.S. court of justice. When such evidence is lacking, as is usually the case, the terrorists get away with their savagery. This explains why last Thursday's retaliations against sites in Afghanistan and Sudan were only the second such action in twenty years, the last one being the April 1986 bombing of Libya. In the vast majority of cases, the criminal paradigm assures that the U.S. government does not respond and killers of Americans pay little or no price.

The paradigm needs to be shifted. Seeing acts of terror as battles, not crimes, changes and improves the whole approach. As in a conventional war, America's military should not need to know the names and specific actions of enemy soldiers before fighting them. When reasonable evidence points to Middle Eastern terrorists having harmed Americans, U.S. military force should be deployed. If the perpetrator is not precisely known, then punish those who are known to harbor terrorists. Go after governments and organizations that support terrorism, not just individuals.

What to target? Missile installations, airfields, navy ships, and terrorist camps. In every case, the punishment should be disproportionately greater than the attack, so that it stings. The U.S. has a military force far more powerful than any other in the world; why spend hundreds of billions of dollars a year on it and not deploy it to defend Americans, or spend tens of billions for intelligence services if they're not able to finger suspects?

The missile attacks on Sudanese and Afghan targets will have long-term significance only if they are not a one-time event, but the start of a new era in which the U.S. government establishes a newly fearsome reputation. From now on, anyone who harms Americans should know that retribution will be certain and nasty. This means that Washington must retaliate every single time terrorism harms an American.

To those who say this would start a cycle of violence, the answer is simple: That cycle already exists; Americans are murdered in acts of terrorism every few months. Further, American retaliation is far more likely to stop it than to spur it on. The Islamists and others, such as Saddam Hussein, despise Americans as morally flabby and militarily incompetent ("paper tigers" is what Osama bin Ladin calls them, borrowing Mao's words). Showing their teeth, Americans are far more likely to intimidate their enemies than to instigate further violence.

It will be a happy day when American embassies are again built in busy downtown intersections out of normal materials—and not, as they are now, bunkers located in distant lots surrounded by high fences. Such a change will only be possible when the safety of Americans depends not on walls, metal detectors, and Marine guards, but on the deterrence established by years of terrible retribution against anyone who so much as harms a single American citizen.

(27 August 1998)

A NEW WAY TO FIGHT TERRORISM

On May 13, 1996, seventeen-year-old David Boim, an American, was standing at a bus stop in the West Bank with fellow yeshiva students when two Palestinian terrorists drove by in a car, shot him in the head, and killed him.

This tragic event led to a sequence of legal moves which culminated with the filling of a $600 million civil suit in a Chicago federal court in May 2000 against several alleged U.S.-based Hamas front organizations. Here is the complex link between those two events, exactly four years apart:

- It all began in October 1992, with the passing of a U.S. law enabling victims of terrorism to sue for civil damages against their aggressors.

- In January 1995, the Clinton administration declared Hamas a terrorist group whose assets could be seized.

- In April 1996, a U.S. law passed deeming it illegal for Americans to send any money to terrorist groups—even if that money is ostensibly sent to support the "humanitarian" works (hospitals, schools) supported by those groups.

- One of Boim's two killers died in September 1997, in the course of a suicide attack in Jerusalem that killed five civilians and injured 192.

- In February 1998, the other killer confessed to murdering Boim and a Palestinian Authority court sentenced him to ten years in prison at hard labor.

- In June 1998, the FBI seized $1.4 million in assets (including bank accounts, a house, and a van) from Mohammad Salah, a Palestinian living in Bridgeview, Illinois, from someone already arrested for money-running for Hamas, and from the Quranic Literacy Institute (QLI), a Muslim organization based in Oak Lawn, Illinois. An FBI affidavit explained that Salah and QLI were suspected of having laundered money for Hamas: "QLI and QLI-related entities or individuals likely were a source of funds for Salah's Hamas-related expenditures." For example, bank records revealed that QLI's president made out three checks for $6,000 each to Salah on three consecutive days in October, 1991.

Putting all these elements together, Stanley and Joyce Boim, the parents of David, filed a civil suit on May 12, 2000, against their son's killers, Salah, QLI, a high-ranking official of Hamas named Mousa Abu Marzook, and "a network of front organizations" in the U.S. whom they identified as Hamas affiliates. These included:

- the United Association for Studies and Research, a think tank in Annandale, Virginia;

- the Holy Land Foundation for Relief and Development, a charity in Richardson, Texas; and

- the Islamic Association for Palestine, a nonprofit group also in Richardson, plus two of its affiliates.

The plaintiffs' intend to establish the existence only of a financial and communications link between the American organizations and the killers—not that those organizations specifically bought the weapons used to kill David Boim. The defendants deny any connection: Dalell Mohammed of the Holy Land Foundation asserts that HLF "is in the business of helping refugees and people in need. We don't condone any sort of violence as we are a humanitarian organization."

The plaintiffs have two goals. The more modest of them is simply to establish a precedent that any support for a designated terrorist organization makes a person legally liable for that group's actions. This could have a major effect deterring support for such organizations. Nathan Lewin, the celebrated lawyer who is handling the case for the Boims, says that a victory in this case "would put teeth into the anti-terrorism laws that the Clinton administration has so far been loath to apply."

The more ambitious goal is to win a judgment against the named organizations. If David's parents succeed at this, terrorism expert Steven Emerson points out, it would "potentially result in the defendants exposed as agents of terrorism, marginalizing them. Even more important, Hamas raises about one third of its funds in the United States, and this funding would pretty certainly dry up, reducing Hamas's terrorism capabilities."

Defunding QLI and the other groups has precedents and is not a quixotic dream: the Southern Poverty Law Center some years ago won a comparable civil judgment against the Ku Klux Klan, impoverishing that organization, thereby severely reducing its reach and appeal.

But were the Boims to lose on both scores, the defendants will be vindicated, Hamas will have had its American base legally certified, and the anti-terrorism legislation will be shown as hollow.

Much, therefore, hangs on this case in Chicago.*

(26 May 2000)

THE NEW GLOBAL THREAT

On April 6, 2001, a thirty-three-year-old Algerian Islamist named Ahmed Ressam achieved the possibly unique distinction of being sentenced on the same day in two courtrooms in two countries for roughly the same crime.

Early in the day, a court in Paris convicted Ressam in absentia for belonging to a network of Islamist terrorists and sentenced him to five years in prison. Hours later, a court in Los Angeles convicted him for an act of terror for which he could be sentenced to 130 years in prison.

---

*Which, as of September 2003, remains unresolved.

Ressam is hardly the only Islamist in trouble with the law. Some other prominent cases, all of which had major developments the same week as Ressam's two convictions, include the following:

- The government of Yemen announced the arrest of three Islamists in Aden in connection with last October's bombing of the destroyer *USS Cole* that left seventeen American sailors dead and thirty-nine wounded. These arrests brought the total charged with that crime to fifteen.

- The Jordanian military prosecutor named two Islamist suspects in a foiled plot to attack U.S. and Israeli installations; twenty-two other persons had already been sentenced for this attempt, six of them to death.

- A Turkish court sentenced an Islamist to death on charges of "attempting to change the constitutional order by use of arms"—that is, overthrowing the government.

- The Italian police arrested five Islamists from North Africa, all suspected of links to Osama bin Laden, and announced that it had thereby smashed the "nerve center" of a militant Islamic terrorist group intent on carrying out operations across Europe.

- An Islamist of Algerian origin was detained by police in Berlin following raids across Germany that led to the discovery of firearms and bomb materials.

- In New York, the prosecution rested its case against the four alleged perpetrators of the 1998 Kenya and Tanzania embassy bombings.

The news that same week also concerned actual terrorism.

- In Algeria, Islamist rebels on one day killed twelve people, including six government soldiers and five shepherds (the latter executed by having their throats slashed). The next day, the Islamists fired on a military convoy and over thirty soldiers were killed.

- In Kashmir, the Indian police announced seven deaths on one day and ten more two days later—just an average week in this militant Islamic insurgency.

- In Bangladesh, the local militant Islamic party killed two men from another faction during a gun battle.

- In the southern Philippines, the Abu Sayyaf terrorist group threatened to kill an American hostage (and send his head to the Filipino president) but let the deadline slip, hoping the hostage's American mother would pressure the government to call off military attacks against Abu

> Sayyaf. The ploy failed; instead, government troops killed three Islamists in its declared "all-out war" on the rebels.

- Islamic extremists last week also resorted to violence in Nigeria, Sudan, Afghanistan, and Indonesia.

Militant Islamic terrorism has a worldwide reach. Eleven of the twenty-nine groups deemed by the U.S. Department of State to be "foreign terrorist organizations" are militant Islamic. Likewise, fourteen of twenty-one groups outlawed by the British Home Office for links to terrorist activity abroad are militant Islamic.

Moreover, what once was the tool of rogue states is now a deeply rooted phenomenon, drawing most of its funding from ordinary Muslims. Stefano Dambruoso, an Italian magistrate who uncovered militant Islamic networks in his country, notes that "It may seem strange, but apart from proceeds from illegal activity such as drug trafficking, one of the main sources of income for the groups is contributions."

This means, Dambruoso explains, that "Islamic terrorism in Europe is a deeply rooted phenomenon that regenerates itself continuously." This far-reaching sponsorship adds greatly to the reach of militant Islamic violence.

A danger exists that Islamists will acquire weapons of mass destruction, with incalculably dangerous results. Indeed, Osama bin Laden may already possess enriched uranium, a vital component for exploding nuclear bombs.

Ironically, Muslim governments are far ahead of their non-Muslim counterparts in understanding the profound menace of radical action in the name of Islam. Leaders in Tunisia, Turkey, and elsewhere have taken serious steps to combat this latter-day totalitarianism.

The time has come for Westerners also to understand that militant Islam presents a truly global threat, and to devote the mental energy and material resources required to fight it.

(11 April 2001)

TERRORISM ON TRIAL

with Steven Emerson

On May 29, 2001, a federal jury in New York returned a guilty verdict against four defendants accused of plotting the terrorist bombing in August 1998 of the U.S. embassies in Kenya and Tanzania. The successful prosecution of these murderers represents a great victory for the United States, for the principle of justice, and for the rule of law. We are all in debt to the brave and capable prosecutors.

Unfortunately, the trial does almost nothing to enhance the safety of Americans. The Qaeda group, headed by the notorious Osama bin Laden, which perpetrated the outrages in East Africa, will barely notice the loss of four operatives. Indeed, recent information shows that Al-Qaeda is not only planning new attacks on the U.S. but is also expanding its operational range to countries such as Jordan and Israel.

In Israel, for example, bin Laden has begun to develop a network among the terrorists of the Hamas organization. Last year, Israel arrested a Hamas member named Nabil Aukel who was trained in Pakistan and then moved to Afghanistan and Kashmir to put that training into practice. He returned to Israel with well-honed skills in the remote detonation of bombs using cellular phones, and was detailed to carry out terrorist attacks in Israel.

Perhaps the real importance of the New York trial lies not in the guilty verdicts but in the extraordinary information made public through court exhibits and trial proceedings. These have given us a riveting view into the shadowy world of Al-Qaeda—though you'd never know from following the news media, for this information was barely reported. Tens of thousands of pages from the trial transcript provide a full and revealing picture of Al-Qaeda, showing it to be the most lethal terrorist organization anywhere in the world.

They demonstrate that Al-Qaeda sees the West in general, and the United States in particular, as the ultimate enemy of Islam. Inspired by their victory over the Soviet Union in Afghanistan in the 1980s, the leaders of Al-Qaeda aspire to a similar victory over America, hoping ultimately to bring militant Islamic rule here. Toward this end, they engaged in many attacks on American targets from 1993 to 1998.

One striking piece of information that came out in the trial was bin Laden's possible connection to the World Trade Center bombing in New York in 1993. A terrorist manual introduced as evidence was just an updated version of an earlier manual found in the possession of the World Trade Center defendants.

The court evidence shows how Al-Qaeda is an umbrella organization that includes a wide range of militant Islamic groups, including Hezbollah (Lebanon), Islamic Jihad (Egypt), the Armed Islamic Group (Algeria), as well as a raft of Iraqis, Sudanese, Pakistanis, Afghans, and Jordanians. Each of its constituent groups has the capability to carry out its own independent recruiting and operations.

The groups coordinate through Al-Qaeda's "Shura Council," a kind of board of directors that includes representatives from the many groups. These meet on a regular basis in Afghanistan to review and approve proposed operations. Most of them have maintained close relationships with each other since the end of the war in Afghanistan against the Soviets. They know each other well and work together efficiently.

We learned from the trial that when operations in one place are shut down, the rest of the network soldiers on, virtually unaffected. Even if bin Laden himself were to be killed, this militant Islamic network would survive and continue to expand, sustained by its ideological adhesion. Militant Islam is the glue that keeps these groups together, and fired up.

The court documents also revealed that although bin Laden has had a leading role in formulating and paying for Al-Qaeda, the organization did rely heavily on state sponsorship as well. For example, Sudanese President Omar Bashir himself authorized Al-Qaeda activities in his country and gave it special authority to avoid paying taxes or import duties. More remarkably, he exempted the organization from local law enforcement. Officials of the Iranian government helped arrange advanced weapons and explosives training for Al-Qaeda personnel in Lebanon where they learned, for example, how to destroy large buildings.

Perhaps the most disconcerting revelations from the trial concern Al-Qaeda's entrenchment in the West. For example, its procurement network for such materiel as night vision goggles, construction equipment, cell phones, and satellite telephones was based mostly in the U.S., Britain, France, Germany, Denmark, Bosnia, and Croatia. The chemicals purchased for use in the manufacture of chemical weapons came from the Czech Republic.

In the often-long waits between terrorist attacks, Al-Qaeda's member organizations maintained operational readiness by acting under the cover of front-company businesses and nonprofit, tax-deductible religious charities. These nongovernmental groups, many of them still operating, are based mainly in the U.S. and Britain, as well as in the Middle East. The Qatar Charitable Society, for example, has served as one of bin Laden's de facto banks for raising and transferring funds.

Osama bin Laden also set up a tightly organized system of cells in an array of American cities, including Brooklyn, New York; Orlando, Florida; Dallas, Texas; Santa Clara, California; Columbia, Missouri, and Herndon, Virginia.

Several conclusions follow from this information.

First, we should think of Al-Qaeda not as an organization dominated by one man but as a global militant Islamic "Internet" with gateways and access points around the world.

Second, Al-Qaeda has a worldwide operational reach. Especially noteworthy is its success in the U.S. and Europe, where it recruits primarily (as this trial showed) among Muslim immigrants. The legal implications of this fact are as serious as they are delicate. Clearly, this is a major new area for law enforcement to grapple with.

Finally, this trial shows that trials alone are not enough. In conceptualizing the Al-Qaeda problem only in terms of law enforcement, the U.S. government misses the larger point: Yes, the operatives engage in crimes, but they are better thought of as soldiers, not criminals. To fight Al-Qaeda and other terrorist groups requires an understanding that they (along with some states) have silently declared war on the U.S.; in turn, we must fight them as we would in a war.

Seeing acts of terror as battles, not crimes, improves the U.S. approach to this problem. It means that, as in a conventional war, America's armed forces, not its policemen and lawyers, are primarily deployed to protect Americans. Rather than drag low-level operatives into American courtrooms, the military will defend us overseas. If a perpetrator is not precisely known, then those who are known to harbor terrorists will be punished. This way, governments and organizations that support terrorism will pay the price, not just the individuals who carry it out.

This way, too, Americans will gain a safety that presently eludes them, no matter how many high-profile courtroom victories prosecutors win.

(31 May 2001)

BIN LADEN AND HERNDON, VIRGINIA

Militant Islamic terrorism has afflicted nearly every Western country and is likely to get worse. One reason is the radicals' aggressiveness; another is the feeble Western response. I have just personally experienced both of these problems.

The story begins in early 1998, when John Miller of ABC News sought an interview with Osama bin Laden in Afghanistan. Needing an intermediary, his producers found Tarik Hamdi of Herndon, Virginia, a self-described journalist who helped make contacts and then accompanied the ABC news team to Afghanistan.

Hamdi, it turned out, had his own purposes for traveling to Afghanistan; he was entrusted with bringing bin Laden a replacement battery for his vital link with the outside world, his satellite telephone. From the remoteness of Afghanistan, bin Laden could not simply order a battery himself and have it overnighted to him. He needed someone unsuspected to bring it. So, one of his top aides ordered a replacement battery on May 11, 1998, and arranged for it to be shipped to Hamdi at his home in Herndon. Hamdi took off for Afghanistan with Miller on May 17 and shortly afterward personally delivered the battery.

Just over two months later, two bombs went off nearly simultaneously at the U.S. embassies in Kenya and Tanzania, killing 224 and wounding thousands.

When the U.S. government brought four of the embassy bombers to trial in New York City in 2001, it focused on the phone powered by the battery from Herndon; assistant U.S. attorney Kenneth Karas called it "the phone that Bin Laden and the others will use to carry out their war against the United States." The trial also established Hamdi's centrality to Bin Laden's logistics. After five months, a jury found all four bombers guilty of all 302 charges against them, validating the prosecutor's interpretation of Hamdi's role.

Which is where I come in.

Explaining this guilty verdict in the *Wall Street Journal* on May 31, I co-authored an article with Steven Emerson arguing in favor of this outcome, but pointing out that it did little to protect American lives; defeating Bin Laden and his murderous gang will require the U.S. government to deploy armed forces, not policemen and lawyers.

The article then focused on the huge body of evidence made public in the trial proceedings, noting that Bin Laden had "set up a tightly organized system of cells" in six American cities, including the small town of Herndon—an allusion to Hamdi.

Picking up on this reference, Jeannie Baumann, a reporter at the *Herndon Observer*, contacted us to learn more. Emerson explained to her Hamdi's role and several times referred her to the complete court transcripts available on the Internet. But Baumann spurned his offers, replying that her newspaper is "not equipped to handle such information." Instead of doing research, Baumann turned to Herndon's police chief, Toussaint E. Summers, Jr., for an opinion. He in turn called the FBI, which told him nothing. From this lack of information, Summers blithely concluded that "there appears to be no truth ... at all" to a bin Laden-Herndon connection.

Baumann then cited this opinion to the Council on American-Islamic Relations (CAIR), for a statement. Ibrahim Hooper, the spokesman for this militant Islamic organization (and a sometime bin Laden apologist), pounced on the police chief's statement and declared our *Wall Street Journal* article inaccurate and prejudicial against Muslims. Baumann's article, published on June 15, 2001, then carried the title "Police, Muslims Refute Herndon Link to Terrorism."

This episode clearly demonstrates three problematic Western responses to militant Islamic violence: Law enforcement officials resist the fact that this scourge exists in their jurisdictions. Reporters fail to do the spadework needed to dig out stories in their own backyards. And the most prominent Islamic organizations shamelessly talk away militant Islamic terrorism and smear anyone who points out the realities of this hideous phenomenon.

If bin Laden and his band of killers are to be stopped, it will take more vigilance from law enforcement officers like Summers, better journalism from reporters like Baumann, and the rise of moderate Muslims who will take the microphone out of the hands of extremists like Hooper.

(20 June 2001)

ROLLING BACK THE FORCES OF TERROR

with Steven Emerson

The pizzeria is located on one of the busiest pedestrian intersections in Israel and it was bustling with families when the Palestinian terrorist inconspicuously walked in on August 9, 2001. Deliberately positioning himself among the children and babies, he detonated an explosive pack full of nails and ball bearings, shredding to death himself and sixteen Israelis, as well as mutilating more than 100 others.

Less than two hours later, both the Islamic Jihad and Hamas terrorist groups had claimed credit for the massacre. And later in the day, thousands of Palestinians joyously demonstrated in Ramallah in celebration of the carnage. To prove its sponsorship, Hamas released a photo of the bomber brandishing a Kalashnikov rifle in one hand and a Koran in the other.

That massacre follows about eighty suicide bombings or attempted suicide bombings by Palestinians against Israeli (and American) civilians in the nearly eight years since the signing of the Oslo accords in 1993. The pizzeria killings pushed the total of Israeli deaths by Palestinian terrorists since September 1993 to more than 450.

This violence blatantly contravenes the Oslo accords—in which the Palestinians renounced the use of force and promised to use only political means to achieve their goals. Worse, the Palestinian Authority has sponsored a terrorist infrastructure of frightening proportions, where appeals to suicide bombers are a regular feature on the television programming and an arsenal of automatic weapons, hand grenades, mortars, Katyusha rockets and anti-tank missiles is in place.

Recent months have shown that the PA's own forces (Tanzim, Force 17, and Fatah fighters) are targeting Israeli civilians right alongside such illegal organizations as Hamas, Islamic Jihad, Hezbollah, Osama bin Laden, the Popular Front for the Liberation of Palestine, and the Democratic Front for the Liberation of Palestine.

Despite this surge in violence, most Israelis have continued to hope they could make a deal. Indeed, as recently as May 2001—when the last large-scale suicide bombing took place, killing twenty-one Israeli teenagers—the authorities in Jerusalem did nothing in response, still hoping to reach a settlement. Even the Israeli actions last Friday—closing down some Palestinian buildings in Jerusalem and destroying a completely empty police station—were more symbolic than they were a serious effort to rebuild the country's security.

One has to admire the Israel government's restraint, then and over the past eight years. But one also has to wonder: When is it going to begin more actively to defend its citizens?

The U.S. government, for its part, should stop repeating the old mantra about going back to the bargaining table (as Colin Powell did in response to the Jerusalem suicide bombing). Instead, it should give Israel a green light to protect its citizens, encouraging it to take steps against terrorist savagery.

The time has also come for the U.S. to support Israel in rolling back the forces of terror. The U.S. has other connections to the pizza parlor bombing. It's not just that the restaurant was part of a New York based chain. Nor that at least two victims are American, including a pregnant schoolteacher from Passaic, New Jersey. The American connection goes much deeper: The very existence of both Hamas and Islamic Jihad is largely attributable to organizing and funding from individuals living in the U.S.

This may sound shocking or unbelievable. But here are several aspects of the Islamic Jihad and Hamas American connections:

- *www.qudscall.com.* Like other militant Islamic terror groups, Islamic Jihad has set up Web sites from the safety of the West. Its two primary sites are registered and hosted in Houston, Texas (by an outfit called Web Site Source, Inc.) and Toronto, Canada. The U.S.-based site provides the group's military communiqués, including those taking responsibility for terrorist operations. In addition, www.qudscall.com includes a call to arms: "Our struggle with the sons of Israel in Palestine is on civilization, ideology, history, and existence. Our war with them is long and difficult. Our base is the Koran; our way is the Jihad." Other sections are more explicit, calling for killing Jews and attacking Americans.

  Most brazenly, Islamic Jihad solicits donations on this Web site for its violent jihad (sacred war) against Israel. In user-friendly fashion, it provides three addresses for donations to be sent in towns controlled by the PA —the Charity Association in Gaza, the Charity Association in Jenin, and the Charity Association in Bethlehem. In each case, bank numbers and other details are helpfully provided. A top PA official has testified in an American court that the Charity Association is a front for Islamic Jihad. The Web site explicitly states the purpose of the donation: "Donate money for the military Jihad."

- *www.palestine-info.net.* This is the official Web site of Hamas, maintained and operated from Florida, although officially hosted from Lebanon. It contains claims of credit for terrorist attacks, detailed listings of Hamas's "glorious record" of terrorist attacks, fatwas approving suicide bombings, interviews with Hamas leaders, bios of suicide bombers, and virulent calls to attack Jews.

- *Islamic Association for Palestine*, and the *Holy Land Foundation for Relief and Development*. These two U.S.-based organizations (with offices in Texas, Illinois, and New Jersey) support Hamas politically.

- *Islamic Committee for Palestine*, and the *World and Islam Studies Enterprise*. ICP was one of several U.S.-based "charities" directly connected to Islamic Jihad. (On this basis, it was closed down by the FBI in 1995). A tape made public by the Immigration and Naturalization Service shows Fawwaz Damra, an imam from Cleveland, proudly announcing that ICP "is the active arm of the Islamic Jihad Movement in Palestine." He added that in the U.S., "for security reasons," it is called the Islamic Committee for Palestine. William West of the INS describes the ICP, along with another organization, the World and Islam Studies Enterprise, as "fronts for the purpose of fund-raising activities for the Islamic Jihad and the Hamas terrorist organizations." West also notes that these two organizations have another role: to bring foreigners "into the United States who are leaders and/or operatives of the Islamic Jihad, Hamas and other terrorist organizations." He is referring to the fact that ICP and WISE arranged for entry visas into the U.S. for the entire three-man leadership of Islamic Jihad.

  Of special note is Ramadan Abdullah Shallah, who for several years worked as a professor at the University of South Florida in Tampa, but since 1995 has lived and served in Damascus as none other than the top leader of Islamic Jihad.

  Meanwhile, the person in charge of ICP and WISE was also a tenured professor at the University of South Florida named Sami Al-Arian. Despite what has been known for years about the ICP and WISE, he remains in good standing at his university and has even attended four White House events in the past four years.

It doesn't take a genius to figure out what the U.S. government should do, starting with excluding the leaders of terror front groups from the White House. Once that's done, the federal authorities should use the tools it already has for closing down these websites and organizations. A 1995 executive order signed by the president authorizes them to prohibit any financial transactions in the United States by twelve groups, two of which are Islamic Jihad and Hamas. A 1996 law gives Washington the power to freeze the assets of such groups.

Despite these laws, almost nothing has been done to shut down the front organizations of Hamas and Islamic Jihad. The reason is embarrassingly simple: Both groups are smart enough not to register under their own names. This trivial camouflage works; the U.S. government finds itself stymied and leaves the groups alone.

The time has come to close down terrorist organizations in the United States, even if they don't conveniently carry their full, formal names.

(13 August 2001)

2

AMERICAN RESPONSES POST-9/11

MISTAKES MADE THE CATASTROPHE POSSIBLE

It is likely that more Americans died yesterday, September 11, 2001, due to acts of violence than on any other single day in American history.[*]

Two parties are responsible for this sequence of atrocities. The moral blame falls exclusively on the perpetrators, who as of this writing remain unknown.

The tactical blame falls on the U.S. government, which has grievously failed in its topmost duty to protect American citizens from harm. Specialists on terrorism have been aware for years of this dereliction of duty; now the whole world knows it. Despite a steady beat of major, organized terrorist incidents over eighteen years (since the car bombing of the U.S. embassy in Beirut in 1983), Washington has not taken the issue seriously.

Here are some of its mistakes:

- *Seeing terrorism as a crime.* American officials have consistently held the view that terrorism is a form of criminal activity. Consequently, they have made their goal the arrest and trying of perpetrators who carry out violent acts. That's all fine and good as far as it goes, but it does not go far enough. This legalistic mindset allows the funders, planners, organizers, and commanders of terrorism to continue their work untouched, ready to carry out more attacks. The better approach is to see terrorism as a form of warfare and to target not just those foot soldiers who actually carry out the violence but the organizations and governments who stand behind them.

---

*Initial estimates of fatalities were much higher than what later became known.

- *Relying too much on electronic intelligence.* It's a lot easier to place an oversized ear in the sky than to place agents in the inner circle of a terrorist group, and so the Central Intelligence Agency and other information-gathering agencies have put on their headphones and listened. Clearly, this is not enough. The planning for the events that took place yesterday requires vast preparation over a long period of time involving many people. That the U.S. government did not have a clue points to nearly criminal ignorance. As critics like Reuel Gerecht keep hammering home, American intelligence services must learn foreign languages, become culturally knowledgeable, and befriend the right people.

- *Not understanding the hate-America mentality.* Buildings like the World Trade Center and the Pentagon loom very large as symbols of America's commercial and military presence around the world. The Trade Center was already once before attacked, in a bombing in early 1993. It should have been clear that these buildings would be the priority targets and the authorities should have provided them with special protection.

- *Ignoring the terrorist infrastructure in this country.* Many indications point to the development of a large militant Islamic terror network within the United States, one visible to anyone who cared to see it. Already in early 1997, Steven Emerson told the *Middle East Quarterly* that the threat of terrorism "is greater now than before the World Trade Center bombing [in 1993] as the numbers of these groups and their members expands. In fact, I would say that the infrastructure now exists to carry off twenty simultaneous World Trade Center-type bombings across the United States."

The information was out there but law enforcement and politicians did not want to see it. The time has come to crack down, and hard, on those connected to this terror infrastructure.

If there is any good to come out of yesterday's deaths and trauma, it will be to prompt an urgent and dramatic change of course in U.S. policy, one that looks at the threat to the United States as a military one, that relies on human intelligence, that comprehends the terrorist mentality, and that closes down the domestic network of terror.

An easy assumption pervaded the airwaves yesterday that the morning's horrors will have the effect of waking Americans to the threat in their midst. I am less optimistic, remembering similar assumptions eight years ago in the aftermath of the 1993 bombing of the World Trade Center. But that turned out not to be the wake-up call expected at the time. Perhaps because only six people died then, perhaps because the bombing was not accompanied or followed by other incidents, that episode disappeared down the memory hole. We owe it to yesterday's many victims not to go back to sleep again.

We also owe it to ourselves, for I suspect that yesterday's events are just a foretaste of what the future holds in store. Assuming that the attacks in New York and in the Washington area were only what they seemed to be, they killed and injured only those who were in the buildings under attack or in their immediate vicinity. Future attacks are likely to be biological, spreading germs that potentially could threaten the whole country. When that day comes, this country will truly know what devastation terrorism can cause. Now is the time to prepare for that danger and make sure it never happens.

(12 September 2001)

War, Not Crimes

"Make no mistake: The United States will hunt down and punish those responsible for these cowardly acts." So spoke President Bush in his address to the nation soon after the catastrophic events of September 11.

I agree with the president's sentiments but disagree with two specifics in this statement. First, there was nothing cowardly about the attacks, which were deeds of incredible—albeit perverted—bravery. Second, to "hunt down and punish" the perpetrators is deeply to misunderstand the problem. It implies that we view the plane crashes as criminal deeds rather than what they truly are—acts of war. They are part of a campaign of terrorism that began in a sustained way with the bombing of the U.S. embassy in Beirut in 1983, a campaign that has never since relented. Occurring with almost predictable regularity a few times a year, assaults on Americans have included explosions on airliners, at commercial buildings, and at a variety of U.S. governmental installations. Before 9/11, the total death toll was about 800 American lives.

This sustained record of violence looks awfully much like war, but Washington in its wisdom has insisted otherwise. Official policy has viewed the attacks as a sequence of discrete criminal incidents.

Seeing terrorism primarily as a problem of law enforcement is a mistake, because it means:

- Focusing on the arrest and trial of the dispensable characters who actually carry out violent acts, leaving the funders, planners, organizers, and commanders of terrorism to continue their work unscathed, prepared to carry out more attacks.

- Relying primarily on such defensive measures as metal detectors, security guards, bunkers, police arrests, and prosecutorial eloquence—rather than on such offensive tools as soldiers, aircraft, and ships.

- Misunderstanding the terrorist's motivations as criminal, whereas they are usually based on extremist ideologies.

- Missing the fact that terrorist groups (and the states that support them) have declared war on the United States, sometimes publicly.

- Requiring that the U.S. government have unrealistically high levels of proof before deploying military force. If it lacks evidence that can stand up in a U.S. court of justice, as is usually the case, no action is taken. The legalistic mindset thus ensures that, in the vast majority of cases, Washington does not respond, and killers of Americans pay little or no price.

The time has come for a paradigm shift, toward viewing terrorism as a form of warfare. Such a change will have many implications. It means:

- Targeting not just those foot soldiers who actually carry out the violence but the organizations and governments that stand behind them.

- Relying on the armed forces, not policemen, to protect Americans. It means defense overseas rather than in American courtrooms.

- Making organizations and governments that sponsor terrorism—not just the perpetrators who carry it out—pay a price.

- Dispensing with the unrealistically high expectations of proof so that when reasonable evidence points to a regime's or an organization's having harmed Americans, U.S. military force can be deployed.

- As in conventional war, not having known the names and specific actions of enemy soldiers before fighting them. There are times in war when one strikes first and asks questions later. When an attack takes place, it could be reason to target any of those known to harbor terrorists. If the perpetrator is not precisely known, then punish those who are known to harbor terrorists. Go after the governments and organizations that support terrorism.

• Retaliating every single time terrorism harms an American.

• Using force so that the punishment is disproportionately greater than the attack. The U.S. has a military force far more powerful than any other in the world: Why spend hundreds of billions of dollars a year on it and not deploy it to defend Americans?

I give fair warning: The military approach demands more from Americans than does the legal one. It requires a readiness to spend money and to lose lives. Force works only if it is part of a sustained policy, not a one-time event. Throwing a few bombs (as was done against the Libyan regime in 1986, and against sites in Afghanistan and Sudan in 1998) does not amount to a serious policy. Going the military route requires a long-term commitment that will demand much from Americans over many years.

But it will be worth it, for the safety of Americans depends ultimately not on defense but on offense; on victories not in the courtroom but on the battlefield. The U.S. government needs to establish a newly fearsome reputation, so that anyone who harms Americans knows that retribution will be certain and nasty. No other response can replace the destruction of any organization or government that harms so much as a single American citizen.

To those who say this approach would start a cycle of violence, the answer is obvious: That cycle already exists, as Americans are constantly murdered in acts of terrorism. Further, by baring their teeth, Americans are far more likely to intimidate their enemies than to instigate further violence. Retaliation will reduce violence, not further increase it, providing Americans with a safety they presently do not enjoy.

(1 October 2001)

What Bush Got Right—and Wrong

In his major speech to Congress defining American policy on September 20, 2001, President George W. Bush explained what he meant by declaring "war on terror" and told the American people what it will mean to them. Overall, it was a strong presentation, with some parts exactly right, but it also contains errors that urgently require fixing.

Let's start with five good points:

- *The enemy's goal*: It's "not merely to end lives, but to disrupt and end a way of life." That involves "remaking the world—and imposing its radical beliefs on people everywhere." The president shows no illusions that Al-Qaeda's problem is American freedoms or United States policy in the Middle East, but something far more ambitious—the very existence of the U.S. in its present form. As he put it, "In Afghanistan, we see Al-Qaeda's vision for the world," one which applies no less to New York than to Kabul.

- *The enemy's nature*: It is the heir "of all the murderous ideologies of the twentieth century ... they follow in the path of fascism, and Nazism, and totalitarianism." (What happened to communism, though? Omitted so as not to offend China?)

- *The enemy's method*: Individuals from more than sixty countries are recruited, taken mainly to Afghanistan, trained, then sent to "hide in countries around the world to plot evil and destruction."

- *The enemy's brutality*: Its leadership "commands them to kill Christians and Jews, to kill all Americans, and make no distinction among military and civilians, including women and children."

- *Defining the problem*: The airline hijackings on September 11 constituted an "act of war." They were not crimes, but part of a concerted military effort by Al-Qaeda, "a radical network of terrorists," and the governments supporting it.

But the president also got five matters wrong:

- *The enemy's identity*: He avoids calling America's opponent by its name—militant Islam—preferring euphemisms such as "terrorist group[s] of global reach." There are two problems here: Terrorism is a tactic, not an enemy; and not explicitly defining the enemy leads to confusion and dissension.

- *The enemy's location*: The address dealt only with foreign threats ("drive them from place to place, until there is no refuge or no rest," "pursue nations that provide aid or safe haven to terrorism"), ignoring the more delicate but equally vital U.S. domestic angle. The new "Office of Homeland Security" has not just to protect Americans from foreign attack but to extirpate the enemy within U.S. borders.

- *The enemy's appeal*: The president dismissed Al-Qaeda's version of Islam as a repudiated "fringe form of Islamic extremism." Hardly. Muslims on the streets of many places—Pakistan and Gaza, in particular—are fervently rallying to the defense of Al-Qaeda's vision of Islam. Likewise, the president's calling the terrorists "traitors to their own faith, trying, in effect, to hijack Islam" implies that other Muslims see them as apostates, which is simply wrong. Al-Qaeda enjoys wide popularity; the very best the U.S. government can hope for is a measure of Muslim neutrality and apathy.

- *U.S. goals*: These are inconsistent. "Deliver to United States authorities all the leaders of Al-Qaeda who hide in your land" implies that were the Afghan authorities to hand over a few individuals, the war effort would end, with no further concern about militant Islam. Contrarily, saying that the war effort will continue until "every terrorist group of global reach has been found, stopped and defeated" implies an ambitious effort against the forces of militant Islam. This contradiction contains the seeds of future problems. Bush needs to clarify that the latter is his real goal.

- *U.S. foreign policy*: "From this day forward, any nation that continues to harbor or support terrorism will be regarded by the United States as a hostile regime." This unrealistic bifurcation will not work in the real world of messy and competing interests. Preventing terrorism may seem like the only priority this week but it's not likely to maintain such total paramountcy for long, and making policy on this basis will lead to problems.

In short, while the president showed an excellent understanding of militant Islam—calling it totalitarian was especially important—he shied away from specifying it as the enemy and made unrealistic statements about the nature of the struggle ahead. These mistakes need urgently to be fixed, before they do damage.

(28 May 2002)

STATE'S TERROR UNTRUTHS

Each spring, the State Department issues *Patterns of Global Terrorism*, its major report on the problem it defines as "premeditated, politically motivated violence perpetrated against noncombatant targets by subnational groups or clandestine agents, usually intended to influence an audience."

It has always been a highly politicized document, reflecting the Washington debate and diplomatic imperatives, but in 2002 it has veered into unreliability and even falsehood. It is a dangerous document likely to harm the war on terrorism.

Its problems include:

- *Methodology*: The State Department uses methods that create the misleading impression that the Middle East is marginal to terrorism. It does this by counting damage to property the same as damage to people: So of the 346 terrorist incidents logged in 2001, 178 (slightly over half) involved attacks on a multinational oil pipeline in Colombia, suggesting that South America is the overwhelming source of terrorism. But as the *Middle East Quarterly*'s Martin Kramer puts it, "Obviously, Latin America is not the world's terrorism epicenter, and it is not why you have to take off your shoes at airport departure gates."

  It also logs incidents by location, not perpetrator. Thus, September 11 counts as North American terrorism, not Middle Eastern. By this reckoning, a mere twenty-nine incidents took place in the Middle East, compared to thirty-three in Africa, sixty-eight in Asia, and a whopping 194 in Latin America (remember that pipeline). Of 3,547 deaths last year, a mere sixty lost their lives in the Middle East, compared to ninety in Africa, 180 in Asia, and 3,235 in North America.

- *Denial*: The overwhelmingly most important sources of terrorism are militant Islam and Palestinian nationalism. (It is noteworthy that in addition to the 3,235 people killed on 9/11, all but one of the other eight Americans who lost their lives in terrorist incidents in the course of 2001—one each in the Philippines and Saudi Arabia, five in Israel —were murdered by adherents of militant Islam.) But the report's only allusions to militant Islam are to deny its importance: "The war on terrorism is not a war against Islam." "Adverse mention in this report of individual members of any political, social, ethnic, religious, or national group is not meant to imply that all members of that group are terrorists." And it includes this quote from a Muslim figure: "Our tolerant Islamic religion highly prizes the sanctity of human life." End of discussion.

- *Falsehoods*: It is flatly untrue that "Pakistan sealed its border with Afghanistan to help prevent the escape of fugitives." To the contrary, that border was left basically open. Or this howler: "In the aftermath of 11 September, the United Nations promptly intensified its focus on terrorism, taking steps to provide a mandate for strengthened international engagement in the fight against terrorism." One of those steps, in October 2001, was to elect the Syrian Arab Republic—which the State Department itself considers a terrorist-sponsoring state—to ultra-prestigious membership in the Security Council.

- *Whitewashing Palestinian violence*: Ever intent on enhancing Yasir Arafat's reputation, State hides his responsibility for terrorism. President Bush may have accused Arafat of "enhancing terrorism" but State's bureaucrats suppress every piece of the voluminous evidence pointing to this connection. Worse, State pretends the vast majority of Palestinian terrorist incidents simply did not happen. It defines "significant international terrorist incidents" as ones involving major property damage, abduction or kidnapping, loss of life or serious injury, or the foiled attempt at any of these, and in 2001 it found 123 incidents worldwide that meet this criteria. Of those, a mere eleven concerned violence against Israelis.

  But when the Independent Media Review and Analysis applied State's criteria to anti-Israel violence, its scrupulous research found ninety-seven attacks on Israel that fit this definition. The U.S. government asserts that Palestinian atrocities against Israel made up just 9 percent of the world's serious terrorist incidents in 2001, but in fact they constituted 46 percent of them.

In all, *Patterns of Global Terrorism 2002* reflects a mentality in Washington of reluctance to confront unpleasant realities. The danger is clear: He who fools himself about his enemy in time of war is likely to lose that war.

(28 May 2002)

TERROR AND DENIAL AT LAX

On the 4th of July 2002, an Egyptian immigrant to the United States who believes in wild conspiracy theories about Jews, is known for his great "hate for Israel," and has possible ties to Al-Qaeda, armed himself to the teeth and assaulted the Israeli airline counter at Los Angeles International Airport, killing two.

It is obvious why Hesham Mohamed Ali Hadayet targeted Jews in a highly visible place on so prominent a date: to engage in terrorism against Israel.

But one important institution—the U.S. government—claims not to know Hadayet's goals. An FBI spokesman has said that "there's nothing to indicate terrorism." Another FBI official said of Hadayet: "It appears he went there with the intention of killing people. Why he did that we are still trying to determine." Possible causes named include a work dispute and a hate crime.

Sure, law enforcement should not jump to conclusions, but this head-in-the-clouds approach is ridiculous. It also fits a well-established pattern. Consider three cases of terrorism in the New York City area:

- *Rashid Baz*, a Lebanese cab driver with a known hatred for all things Israeli and Jewish, loaded up with guns in March 1994 and drove around the city looking for a Jewish target. He found his victims—a van full of Hassidic boys—on the Brooklyn Bridge and fired a hail of bullets against them, killing one boy. And how did the FBI classify this crime? As "road rage." Only because the murdered boy's mother relentlessly fought this false description did the bureau in 2000 finally re-classify the murder as "the crimes of a terrorist."

- *Ali Hasan Abu Kamal*, a Palestinian gunman hailing from militant Islamic circles in Florida, took a gun to the top of the Empire State Building in February 1997 and shot a tourist there. His suicide note accused the United States of using Israel as its "instrument" against the Palestinians, but city officials ignored this evidence and instead dismissed Abu Kamal as either "one deranged individual working on his own" (Police Commissioner Howard Safir) or a "man who had many, many enemies in his mind" (Mayor Rudolph Giuliani).

- *Gamil al-Batouti*, an EgyptAir copilot, yelled "I put my faith in God's hands" as he crashed a plane leaving Kennedy Airport in October 1999, killing 217. Under Egyptian pressure, the National Transportation Safety Board report shied away from once mentioning Batouti's possible terrorist motives.

And despite all the "world-has-changed" rhetoric following the horrors of September 2001, Western officialdom continues to pretend terrorism away.

- *Damir Igric*, a Croat immigrant from the former Yugoslavia, used a boxcutter to slash the neck of a Greyhound bus driver in Tennessee last October, causing the bus to roll over, killing six passengers and himself. Although this bus-hijacking scenario echoed similar attacks by Palestinians on Israeli buses, the FBI immediately classified it "an isolated incident" and not an act of terrorism. The media attributed the violence to post-traumatic stress syndrome.

- *Hassan Jandoubi*, an Islamist with possible connections to Al-Qaeda, had started working at the AZF fertilizer factory in suburban Toulouse, France, just days before a massive explosion took place there September 21, 2001. This, the worst catastrophe ever in a French chemical plant, killed Jandoubi and twenty-nine others, injured 2,000, destroyed 600 dwellings, and damaged 10,000 buildings.

The autopsy revealed that Jandoubi was wearing two pairs of trousers and four pairs of underpants, which the coroner compared to what is worn by "Islamic militants going into battle or on suicide missions." Also, the chemical plant was processing ammonium nitrate, a stable chemical that requires a substantial infusion of energy to explode.

Ignoring these signs, the French authorities declared there was "no shred of evidence" of the explosion being a terrorist act and ruled it an accident. They even prosecuted two publications merely for calling Jandoubi a "radical Islamist," making them pay tens of thousands of dollars in fines to Jandoubi's heirs, a mosque and a Muslim organization for their "defamation" of Jandoubi.

Work dispute, hate crime, road rage, derangement, post-traumatic stress, industrial accident...these expressions of denial obstruct effective counterterrorism. The time has come for governments to catch up with the rest of us and call terrorism by its rightful name.

(9 July 2002)

BORDER AGENCIES IN DENIAL

The very first line of defense for the U.S. homeland consists of those who issue visas (the consular division of the State Department) and those who control the borders (the Immigration and Naturalization Service, or INS).** Trouble is, neither of those agencies has understood its security role.

Their disastrous mistakes became painfully evident with two revelations last week. Had the State Department properly applied its own rules, as Joel Mowbray showed in the October 28, 2002, issue of *National Review*, not one of the fifteen September 11 hijackers whose visa forms he inspected could have legally entered the United States. Those applicants failed almost all the tests required for admission (information about addresses, means of support) but nonetheless were allowed in.

As for the INS, Rep. George W. Gekas (R-Pa.), chairman of the Judiciary's Immigration, Border Security and Claims Subcommittee, finally overcame INS stonewalling to learn the disheartening

---

**Subsequently, its duties were assumed by the new Bureau of Citizenship and Immigration Services within the Department of Homeland Security.

saga of how one immigrant terrorist, the Egyptian Hesham Mohamed Ali Hadayet, stayed in the United States.

In an October 2002 hearing of his subcommittee, it came out that Hadayet entered the United States as a tourist in 1992, then applied for asylum claiming discrimination on account of his "religious beliefs." To support this claim, Hadayet told the INS that the Egyptian government had coerced him into signing two documents acknowledging his membership in al-Gama'a al-Islamiyya ("the Islamic Group") and his intentions to overthrow the government of Egypt.

Hadayet denied the validity of these confessions but—given the nature of al-Gama'a al-Islamiyya, a group engaged in terrorism going back to the assassination of Anwar el-Sadat in October 1981— their very existence should have raised red flags. For example, the 1992 edition of *Patterns of Global Terrorism*, the U.S. government's most authoritative source on terrorism, reported that "Most of the attacks [in Egypt] in 1992 were perpetrated by the al-Gama'a al-Islamiyya extremist group.... This group seeks the violent overthrow of the Egyptian Government."

The INS, however, treated Hadayet's case as routine. It did rule against his asylum application in March 1995 (unconvinced by his claims of religious persecution) and formally began the deportation procedures, but like countless other failed applicants, he was allowed to disappear into the vastness of American life. His possible membership in al-Gama'a al-Islamiyya went unremarked and no government agency tried to find him. More appalling yet, the INS authorized Hadayet to work in June 1996, on the same day it issued a deportation memorandum.

In July 1996, Hadayet's wife won a visa from the State Department's annual lottery. Again, the possible connection to terrorism went unheeded, permitting him to take advantage of her luck to become a lawful permanent resident.

Six years later, on July 4, 2002, the full extent of the INS' error became evident when Hadayet launched a shooting spree against the El Al counter at Los Angeles International Airport, killing two before being shot dead himself.

One might think this atrocity would cause the INS to admit its errors. One would be wrong. "The only indication that Mr. Hadayet could pose a threat to others in the United States," it defiantly announced last week, "was his own assertion that he was falsely accused of being a member of an organization that committed terrorist activities."

This cavalier attitude toward Hadayet's possible membership in al-Gama'a al-Islamiyya fits a pattern of unrepentant sloppiness by the INS that has acquired great national significance. To begin the urgent repair work, the INS must take three steps: Own up to its multiple errors with regard to Hesham Mohamed Ali Hadayet; undertake a remedial campaign to go through its archives and arrest or deport all immigrants with ties to terrorism; and hold accountable those employees who behaved with what appears to be criminal negligence.

At a time when Americans are watching corrupt business executives being hauled off in handcuffs, should anything less await an INS staff responsible for allowing into the country the murderers of their fellow citizens?

(16 October 2002)

WHAT'S TRUE ISLAM? NOT FOR U.S. TO SAY

The U.S. government wants you to know that the Taliban, who yet rule part of Afghanistan, are bad Muslims. Instead, it should be showing that they are totalitarian thugs. There is a big difference.

When the Taliban destroyed the ancient Buddhist statues in their country in early 2001, Washington repeatedly decried this demolition as un-Islamic. It contradicts "one of Islam's basic tenets—tolerance for other religions," intoned the State Department spokesman. It is "an act of intolerance, which...has, in our view, nothing to do with Islam," declared one of his colleagues.

The September 11 atrocities prompted Imam George W. Bush to declare that these attacks "violate the fundamental tenets of the Islamic faith." His wife issued a fatwa deeming the repression of women in Afghanistan "not a matter of legitimate religious practice."

More broadly, a State Department Fact Sheet asserts that the Taliban "misuse Islam" to justify their "illegal and dishonorable" policies. American officials even have the nerve to instruct Muslims on how to live their faith. "We accept that Islam is the religion of most Afghans. They can practice it in the way they want," the acting assistant secretary for South Asian Affairs conceded. But, he added, their Islam "should be in a spirit of toleration, in a spirit of acceptance of other faiths and creeds."

Not surprisingly, the Taliban hotly reject these admonishments. Two days after Bill Clinton in 1999 had called their treatment of women "a terrible perversion" of Islam, they replied: "Any criticism regarding Afghanistan's Muslims and women's rights should come from a Muslim. This Clinton is not a Muslim and does not know anything about Islam and Muslims."

Likewise, President Bush's peculiar statements about true Islam being "nonviolent" spurred a Taliban representative to reply: "I am astonished by President Bush when he claims there is nothing in the Koran that justifies jihad or violence in the name of Islam. Is he some kind of Islamic scholar? Has he ever actually read the Koran?"

The Taliban have a point, for it is very strange for U.S. government officials to proclaim what is or is not true Islam. Who are they —neither Muslims nor scholars of Islam but representatives of a secular government—to instruct Muslims about their religion? And, realistically, which Muslims accept spiritual guidance from the White House?

Interestingly, U.S. policy in principle agrees that this hectoring is unacceptable. "Don't presume to lecture Muslims on Islam," reads an internal State Department memo that bore the secretary of state's personal endorsement. The former top State Department official in charge of Afghanistan, Karl Inderfurth, agrees that it is not "appropriate for non-Muslims to presume to give instruction" about Islamic faith and the Koran. Bernard Lewis, the leading American scholar of Islam, puts it less diplomatically: "it is surely presumptuous for those who are not Muslims to say what is orthodox and what is heretical in Islam."

This is good and sensible advice. Rather than initiate a quixotic and unconvincing campaign to delegitimize the Taliban (or any other instances of militant Islam) on religious grounds, Washington should stick to its knitting—politics. The oppression, poverty, violence, and injustice of Taliban rule offer plenty of evidence to indict it, without having also to contest the regime's Islamic credentials.

Life in Afghanistan has been a living hell. Beatings and arbitrary executions are commonplace; for example, eight boys who dared to laugh at Taliban soldiers were shot dead. In 1998, the Taliban massacred 600 Uzbek villagers in the west; in early 2001, they followed with a massacre of 200 civilians in the center. To prevent defections to the Northern Alliance, the Taliban have taken thousands of families of their own soldiers as hostages and some 400 of those soldiers were just massacred to prevent their changing sides.

The United States government has a powerful message for the world, a message of individualism, freedom, secularism, the rule of law, democracy, and private property. But it should have nothing to say about the proper practice of Islam (or any religion).

It's right for President Bush to condemn Taliban rule for the fact that women are "beaten for wearing socks that are too thin. Men are jailed for missing prayer meetings." He just shouldn't give his opinion on whether or not these punishments constitute genuine Islam.

(26 November 2001)

AIM THE WAR ON TERROR AT MILITANT ISLAM

Whom are we fighting? Two main culprits have emerged since September 11: terrorism and Islam. The truth, more subtle, lies between the two—a terroristic version of Islam.

Terrorism. The establishment—politicians, academics, religious leaders, journalists, along with many Muslims—says terrorism is the enemy. It is carried out by "evildoers" who have nothing to do with Islam but adhere to some murky cult of terrorism.

Secretary of State Colin Powell summarized this view by declaring that the acts of September 11 "should not be seen as something done by Arabs or Islamics; it is something that was done by terrorists." Pretending that the enemy is "terrorism" unconnected to Islam is appealing because it finesses some delicate questions about Islam, thereby making it easier to build an international coalition or minimize domestic repercussions.

But it makes no sense at all. The Taliban government, Al-Qaeda, Osama bin Laden, John Walker Lindh, Richard Reid, and Zacarias

Moussaoui—all are self-proclaimed fervent Muslims acting on behalf of their religion. More, they have found wide support across the
Muslim world (remember those huge demonstrations waving pictures of Bin Laden in September 2001?). Terrorists they are, to be
sure, but terrorists with a specific set of beliefs.

Blaming "terrorism" means ignoring those beliefs – at great cost.
If the enemy consists of terrorists "motivated by hate," as President
Bush put it, what can one do other than kill them? Hate lacks an
ideology or intellectual framework that one can refute. The West is
left with nothing but guns to protect itself from the next assault.
There can be no strategy for victory, only tactics to stave off harm.

Islam. The Western "street" prefers to see the problem lying with
the Islamic religion. In this view, Arabs and Muslims have been the
leading enemy of Christians for more than a millennium, remain so
now and will long continue to fill this role.

This enmity stems from the Koran itself and so is permanent, say
spokesmen for this argument, who tend to be political conservatives
or evangelicals. This too does not hold. If Muslims by nature are
hostile, how does one explain Turkey, with its militantly secular culture and abiding good relations with the West? If all Muslims accept
Koranic precepts, how does this account for the tens of thousands of
Algerians who lost their lives resisting Islamic rule?

And if Islam is the problem, then there is no possible strategy for
winning. It implies that the billion or so Muslims—including millions living in the West—are immutable enemies. They can only be
converted from Islam or quarantined, two thoroughly unrealistic programs. Insisting on Islam as the enemy means a permanent clash of
civilizations that cannot be won.

Fingering terrorism or Islam, in short, neither explains the current
problem nor offers a solution.

There is third way of approaching the question, which satisfies
both these requirements.

Islam itself—the centuries-old faith—is not the issue but one extremist variant of it is. Militant Islam derives from Islam but is a
misanthropic, misogynist, triumphalist, millenarian, anti-modern,
anti-Christian, anti-Semitic, terroristic, jihadistic, and suicidal version of it. Fortunately, it appeals to only about 10 percent to 15 percent of Muslims, meaning that a substantial majority would prefer a
more moderate version.

This implies a simple and effective strategy: weaken militant Islam around the world and strengthen the moderate alternatives to it. Fight it militarily, diplomatically, legally, intellectually, and religiously. Fight it in Afghanistan, in Saudi Arabia, in the United States—in fact, everywhere.

Moderate Muslims will be key allies in this fight. Yes, they are weak and intimidated these days, but they are crucial if the Muslim world is to leave its current bout of radicalism. Once the U.S. government helps them, they can emerge as a formidable force. (By analogy, remember how the Northern Alliance seemed hapless before the U.S. invasion of Afghanistan? Subsequently, it has been running Afghanistan.)

Only by focusing on militant Islam can Americans both protect themselves from their most determined enemy and eventually defeat it.

(6 January 2002)

THE WEAKNESS OF AIRPORT SECURITY

Three months into the war on terrorism, how well is the Bush administration doing?

Overall, it deserves high grades, having shown an impressive seriousness of purpose, discipline, and vision. It made winning the war the guiding principle of U.S. foreign policy and almost flawlessly pulled off the military campaign in Afghanistan.

It carefully picked out the next steps (soldiers to the Philippines, pressure on Pakistan and the Palestinian Authority, warning signals to Yemen and Somalia). It correctly made counterterrorism a high priority in American domestic life.

There is just one glaringly weak spot: The Bush team adamantly refuses to acknowledge that there is an ideology that inspires America's enemies, preferring to ascribe its motives to simple "evil." Evil it is, but it follows from the specific set of radical utopian ideas known as militant Islam. Ignoring militant Islam today is like fighting World War II without fighting fascism, or fighting the cold war while wishing away communism.

The consequences of this mistake are practical and far-reaching. For example, airline security is a casualty. U.S. Department of Transportation (DoT) guidelines issued after September 11 forbid airline personnel from relying on "generalized stereotypes or attitudes or beliefs about the propensity of members of any racial, ethnic, religious, or national origin group to engage in unlawful activity."

Appearing to be Middle Eastern, speaking a Middle Eastern language, or having a Middle Eastern accent are inadmissible grounds for paying special attention to a passenger, as are Islamic attributes such as a woman's veil or a man's beard. The government insists on what it calls the "but for" test. "But for this person's perceived race, ethnic heritage or religious orientation," security personnel must ask themselves, "would I have subjected this individual to additional safety or security scrutiny?" If the answer is no, extra scrutiny is not just disapproved of, but illegal. It's like having reports of a tall, bearded mugger but requiring the police to devote equal attention to short females.

Worse, DoT regulations permit additional inspections only if passengers are "properly selected on a truly random basis." Stopping every tenth or twentieth passenger is legal—but not stopping those who are nervous, shifty, or otherwise suspicious to the trained eye. This disallows airline personnel from drawing on their experience or using their common sense, ignoring that many counterterrorism breakthroughs occurred precisely because an inspector followed a hunch. "A lot of it is in the nose," says John Beam, a former head of security for TWA.

Government regulations demand a militant dumbness and a pretense not to know what everyone does know—that the would-be hijackers come overwhelmingly, if not exclusively, from the ranks of militant Islam. They send the unfortunate signal that it is politically easier to send troops to Afghanistan than to confront the fact that the enemy has certain characteristics.

And woe to an airline that has the misfortune of stopping an Arab-American who happens not to be a terrorist but who is politically connected! Rep. Darrell Issa (R-Calif.) "caused quite a scene and ... wasn't very polite" when Air France delayed him a day, according to a company spokesman. A presidential bodyguard named Walied Shater turned "very hostile" and engaged in "confrontational behavior," in the words of the American Airlines captain who denied him transportation.

(They're not terrorists, but both of these two gentlemen do, interestingly, associate with militant Islam. Issa has declared his "tremendous sympathy" for the work of Hezbollah, a group the U.S. government deems to be a terrorist organization. Shater rushed with his case of alleged bias to the Council on American-Islamic Relations, a Washington-based group with ties to another designated terrorist organization, Hamas. The extra attention given them turns out not to be entirely undeserved.)

The time has come for the Bush administration to find the courage to acknowledge that the enemy is not made up of random and featureless "terrorists" but is specifically staffed by the cadres of militant Islam. The sooner it does so, the more efficiently the country will be able to protect itself by clamping down on the forces of militant Islam. The more the government delays, the more likely that attacks will continue.

The question boils down to this: How many more lives must be unnecessarily lost before American leaders have the courage to stand up to political correctness?

(21 January 2002)

A WAR AGAINST WHAT?

Militant Islam keeps on killing, but politicians and journalists still avert their eyes.

One terrible example comes from Pakistan, where a sequence of assaults on Christians, both local and foreign, has taken place:

- October 28, 2001: an attack on St. Dominic's Church in Behawalpur kills sixteen.

- March 17, 2002: an attack on the Protestant International Church in Islamabad kills five (including two Americans).

- May 22, 2002: an attack on the executive secretary of Karachi Diocese of Church Pakistan, who was tied to a chair and injected with poison.

- August 5, 2002: an attack on the Murree Christian School kills six.

- August 9, 2002: an attack on the Christian Hospital in Taxila kills four.

- September 25, 2002: an attack on the Institute for Peace and Justice, a Christian charity in Karachi, kills seven.

- Plus many more non-lethal assaults on churches and church services.

There is no doubt about the motives of the perpetrators: militant Islamic groups brazenly speak their minds, declaring their goal is "to kill Christians" and afterwards bragging of having "killed the nonbelievers."

Victims know full well why they are targeted "just for being Christians," as one person put it. A local Christian leader states "that the terrorist attack was an act by Al-Qaeda or some pro-Taliban organizations." A survivor of that slaughter recounts that the murderers separated Christians from Muslims by requiring each hostage to recite a verse from the Koran. Those who could not were seated at a table in the library, bound to chairs, gagged, and shot in the head (except for one person who was shot in a bathroom).

Pakistani law enforcement also recognizes who engages in this violence and why. "We are investigating whether there is an anti-Christian gang operating in Karachi, made up of jihadis," the city's chief investigator explains. A provincial police chief comments about the September 25 carnage: "Unlike the usual terrorists, the killers [on that occasion] showed no haste. They took a good 15 minutes in segregating the Christians and making sure that each one of their targets gets the most horrific death."

Politicians and journalists, however, pretend not to recognize the problem.

Pakistan's President Pervez Musharraf reacted to the September 25 butchery with seeming bewilderment: "I could not say who [was behind the killings]. It could be Al-Qaeda, it could be any sectarian extremists within, or foreign elements of RAW." (RAW is the Research and Analysis Wing, India's intelligence agency.) Pakistan's interior minister likewise emphasizes that RAW's role "cannot be ruled out."

The media is almost as bad: Paul Marshall of Freedom House shows that American and European reporting on these many massacres in Pakistan overlooks the militant Islamic dimension, instead presenting the atrocities as vaguely anti-Western in purpose.

This pattern of reluctance and euphemism in the case of Pakistan fits into a more general context. President Bush declared war not on militant Islam but on a faceless enemy he has variously called "terrorists," "a radical network of terrorists," "terrorists in this world who can't stand the thought of peace," "terrorism with a global reach," "evildoers," "a dangerous group of people," "a bunch of cold-blooded killers," and even "people without a country."

The establishment media has been complicit. With the notable exception of CNN's Lou Dobbs, who talks about "the war against radical Islamists," it unthinkingly echoes the government's line that the conflict has nothing to do with religious motives. It's as though Franklin D. Roosevelt, after Pearl Harbor, declared war on surprise attacks rather than on the Japanese empire.

This evasion has consequences, for an enemy who cannot be named cannot be defeated. Only when "war on terrorism" becomes "war on militant Islam" can the war actually be won. Fortunately, the president has on occasion hinted at this, as in May 2002, when he called the enemy those "defined by their hatreds: they hate…Jews and Christians and all Muslims who disagree with them."

It is not a war on terrorism, nor a war on Islam. It is a war on a terroristic version of Islam. Authorities in the United States, Pakistan and elsewhere need to face this unpleasant fact. Not to do so will mean the unnecessary loss of lives.

(1 October 2002)

THE ISLAMIST ENEMY WITHIN

The day after 9/11, Texas police arrested two Indian Muslim men riding a train and carrying about $5,000 in cash, black hair dye and boxcutters like those used to hijack four planes just one day earlier.

The police held the pair initially on immigration charges (their U.S. visas had expired); when further inquiry turned up credit card fraud this then justified keeping them longer in detention. But law enforcement's real interest, of course, had to do with their possible connections to Al-Qaeda.

To investigate this matter—and here our information comes from one of the two prisoners, Ayub Ali Khan, after he was released and back in India—the authorities put them through some pretty rough treatment. Khan says the interrogation "terrorized" him. He recounts how "Five to six men would pull me in different directions very roughly as they asked rapid-fire questions. . . . Then suddenly they would brutally throw me against the wall." They also asked him political questions: had he, for example, "ever discussed the situation in Palestine with friends?"

Eventually exonerated of connections to terrorism and freed from jail, Khan is—not surprisingly—bitter about his experience, saying that he and his traveling partner were singled out on the basis of profiling. This is self-evidently correct: Had Khan not been a Muslim, the police would have had little interest in him and his boxcutters.

Khan's tribulation brings to attention the single most delicate and agonizing issue in prosecuting the war on terror. Does singling out Muslims for additional scrutiny serve a purpose? And if so, is it legally and morally acceptable?

In reply to the first question—yes, enhanced scrutiny of Muslims makes good sense, for several reasons:

- In the course of their assaults on Americans, Islamists —the supporters of militant Islam—have killed nearly 4,000 people since 1979. No other enemy has remotely the same record.

- Islamists are plotting to kill many more Americans, as shown by the more than one-group-a-month arrests of them since 9/11.

- While most Muslims are not Islamists and most Islamists are not terrorists, all Islamist terrorists are Muslims.

- Islamist terrorists do not appear spontaneously, but emerge from a milieu of religious sanction, intellectual justification, financial support and organizational planning.

These circumstances—and this is the unpleasant part—point to the imperative of focusing on Muslims. There is no escaping the unfortunate fact that Muslim government employees in law enforcement, the military, and the diplomatic corps need to be watched for connections to terrorism, as do Muslim chaplains in prisons and the armed forces. Muslim visitors and immigrants must undergo additional background checks. Mosques require a scrutiny beyond that applied to churches and temples.

Singling out a class of persons by their religion feels wrong, if not downright un-American, prompting the question: Even if useful, should such scrutiny be permitted? If Americans want to protect themselves from Islamist terrorism, they must temporarily give higher priority to security concerns than to civil libertarian sensitivities. Preventing Islamists from inflicting further damage implies the regrettable step of focusing on Muslims. Not to do so is an invitation to further terrorism.

This solemn reality suggests four thoughts:

First, as Khan's experience shows, Muslims are already subjected to added scrutiny; the time has come for politicians to catch up to reality and formally acknowledge what are now quasi-clandestine practices. Doing so places these issues in the public arena, where they can openly be debated.

Second, because having to focus heightened attention on Muslims is inherently so unpleasant, it needs to be conducted with utmost care and tact, remembering, above all, that seven out of eight Muslims are not Islamists, and fewer still are connected to terrorism.

Third, this is an emergency measure that should end with the war on terror's end.

Finally, innocent Muslims who must endure added surveillance can console themselves with the knowledge that their security, too, is enhanced by these steps.

(24 January 2003)

3

MILITANT ISLAM POST-9/11

A MIDDLE EAST PARTY

In Stockholm, people stood outside the gates of the U.S. embassy with long burning candles to express their sorrow on 9/11. In Berlin, they placed flowers at the embassy. Austria's parliament flew a black flag. "We are all Americans!" editorialized the not-usually pro-American newspaper *Le Monde*. A Kenyan newspaper recalled Osama bin Laden's bombing in that country three years ago and stated that "Few nations will understand America's grief as deeply as the Kenyan nation." "I feel that my heart is breaking when I see it on television," said a Chinese.

And so it was around the world, as news was received of the catastrophic events in the eastern United States three days ago. Peoples and governments in most places responded with the grief and humanity one would hope for at such a moment.

There was, however, one major and conspicuous exception to this solemnity, and that was in the Middle East, where the day's events prompted a giant party.

"We're ecstatic," said a Lebanese. "Bull's-eye," commented Egyptian taxi drivers as they watched a rerun of the World Trade Center collapse. "It's payback time," said a Cairene. Other Egyptians expressed a wish for George W. Bush to have been buried in the buildings or exulted that this was their happiest moment since the war against Israel in 1973.

And so it went around the region. In Lebanon and the West Bank, Palestinians shot guns into the air, a common way of showing delight. In Jordan, Palestinians handed out sweets in another expression of joy.

55

Even outside the Middle East, a good many Muslims said the United States got what it deserved. Nigerian papers reported that the Islamic Youth Organisation in Zamfara province organized an event to celebrate the attacks. "Whatever destruction America is facing, as a Muslim I am happy," came a typical quote from Afghanistan. A Pakistani leader said that Washington is paying for its policies against Palestinian, Iraqi, Bosnian, and other Muslims, then warned that the "worst is still to come."

To be sure, most governments were on best behavior, decrying this and bemoaning that. But even here, there were cracks. In Syria, the restrained message of condolence came from an anonymous "official information source" rather than (as is normally the case) from President Bashar al-Assad. In Iran, the milder of the newspaper analyses portrayed the airplane crashes as America "Paying the price for its blind support of the Zionist regime." The worse of them actually accused Israel of organizing the attacks, in a supposed effort to deflect world opinion from its own conflict with the Palestinians.

And then there is Iraq, where the state-controlled media cheered on the violence, commenting with satisfaction that the "the American cowboys are reaping the fruit of their crimes against humanity." It also announced, with unabashed delight, that the "myth of America was destroyed along with the World Trade Center."

Why this unvarnished rage against the West, and against the United States in particular? Because two extremist ideologies maintain a grip on much of the Middle East and even beyond.

- *Palestinian nationalism.* Often portrayed as having the relatively benign goal of creating a Palestinian state alongside of Israel, it actually has the far more virulent one of destroying Israel and replacing it with a Palestinian state that stretches "from the river to the sea." The sheer strength of Israel had long tamped down the hold of this ideology over Palestinians and other Arabic speakers. It arose with new vigor thanks to the Oslo process, which made Israel appear weakened and demoralized. As a result, even the mild American approbation of Israeli policies toward Palestinian violence over the past year has engendered a rare fury against the United States government, the American people, and all their works. Delight in American deaths is the natural result.

- *Militant Islam.* This is the body of ideas that takes the religion of Islam and makes it the basis of a radical utopian ideology along the lines of fascism and Marxism-Leninism. It has ambitions to replace capitalism and liberalism as the reigning world system. Militant Islam accounts for the anti-American hatred coming out of places remote from the Arab-Israeli conflict, like Nigeria and Afghanistan.

Adherents of this outlook are not, as one might expect, self-consciously aggressive but see themselves surrounded and besieged by the West. Around the world, Islamists feel, they are stymied by an arrogant and imperialist West. In the words of an Egyptian, the Americans "have us by the throat."

Islamists discern a long list of countries—Algeria, Turkey, Egypt, and Malaysia are prominent examples—where they believe local Muslim rulers are doing the West's dirty business in suppressing their movement. They also have another list—Kashmir, Afghanistan, and Sudan rank high here—where they see the West actively suppressing the best militant Islamic efforts to establish a just society. Whenever Muslims move towards the emergence of an Islamic State, one Islamist explains, the "treacherous hands of the secular West are always there in the Muslim world to bring about the defeat of the Islamic forces." The solution lies in fundamentally changing the nature of the United States, so that it becomes sympathetic to such militant Islamic efforts.

It bears noting that while Palestinian nationalists and Islamists share a hatred of all things American, their goals are different: the former merely aspire to a change in the country's foreign policy, whereas the latter seek to change the very nature of the country. In the meantime, however, both take indecent pleasure from American suffering.

That Palestinian nationalists and Islamists have so crudely revealed their enmity to the United States gives clear proof of their attitudes and intentions. This has an obvious policy significance for Westerners: it means that we know who some of our most devoted enemies are. Western governments had for years fooled themselves into thinking that they could appease these extremist movements or maybe simply ignore them. At least now, after thousands of lost lives, we know what a bitter falsehood that is.

(14 September 2001)

MUSLIMS ♥ BIN LADEN

What do Muslims think of Osama bin Laden?

Ask Westerners and you'll hear how marginal he is. President Bush says bin Laden's outlook is "rejected by Muslim scholars and the vast majority of Muslim clerics." Western specialists on Islam agree. "Osama bin Laden is to Islam like Timothy McVeigh is to Christianity," says Mark Juergensmeyer of the University of California. Karen Armstrong, author of a best-selling book about Islam, reports that the "vast majority of Muslims...are horrified by the atrocity of September 11."

Well, that "vast majority" is well hidden and awfully quiet, if it exists. With the exception of one government-staged anti-bin Laden demonstration in Pakistan and very few prominent Islamic scholars, hardly anyone publicly denounces him. The only Islamic scholar in Egypt who unreservedly condemns the September 11 suicide operations admits he is completely isolated. American officials are still waiting for Muslim politicians to speak up. "It'd be nice if some leaders came out and said that the idea the United States is targeting Islam is absurd," notes one U.S. diplomat.

They don't because the Muslim world is bursting with adulation for the Saudi militant.

- "Long live bin Laden" shout 5,000 demonstrators in the southern Philippines.

- In Pakistan, bin Laden's face sells merchandise and massive street rallies have left two persons dead. Ten thousand march in the capitals of Bangladesh and Indonesia.

- In northern Nigeria, bin Laden has (according to Reuters) "achieved iconic status" and his partisans set off religious riots leading to 200 deaths.

- Pro-bin Laden demonstrations took place even in Mecca, where overt political activism is unheard of.

Everywhere, the *Washington Post* reports, Muslims cheer bin Laden on "with almost a single voice." The Internet buzzes with odes to him as a man "of solid faith and power of will." A Saudi explains that "Osama is a very, very, very, very good Muslim." A Kenyan adds: "Every Muslim is Osama bin Laden." "Osama is not an individual, but a name of a holy war," reads a banner in Kashmir. In perhaps the most extravagant statement, one Pakistani declared that "Bin Laden is Islam. He represents Islam." In France, Muslim youths chant bin Laden's name as they throw rocks at non-Muslims.

Palestinians are especially enamored. According to Hussam Khadir, a member of Arafat's Fatah party, "Bin Laden today is the most popular figure in the West Bank and Gaza, second only to Arafat." A ten-year-old girl announces that she loves him like a father. Nor is she alone. "Everybody loves Osama bin Laden at this time. He is the most righteous man in the whole world," declares a Palestinian woman. A Palestinian Authority policeman calls him "the greatest man in the world and our Messiah" even as he (reluctantly) disperses students who march in solidarity with the Saudi.

Survey research helps us understand these sentiments. In the Palestinian Authority, a Bir Zeit poll found that 26 percent of Palestinians consider the September 11 attacks consistent with Islamic law. In Pakistan, a Gallup found a nearly identical 24 percent reaching this conclusion.

Even those who consider the attacks an act of terrorism (64 percent of both Palestinians and Pakistanis) show respect for these as acts of political defiance and technical prowess. "Of course we're upset that so many died in New York. But at the same time, we're in awe of what happened," said a young Cairene woman.

An online survey of Indonesians found 50 percent seeing bin Laden as a "justice fighter" and 35 percent a terrorist. More broadly, I estimate that bin Laden enjoys the emotional support of half the Muslim world.

That America's politicians and experts on Islam insist on seeing bin Laden as an isolated McVeigh-like figure is worrisome; they miss the danger that bin Laden's militant Islam poses to existing governments—perhaps their greatest challenge of recent times. Their fear of him goes far to explain why the authorities so heavily discourage pro-bin Laden sentiments (forbidding posters of him, arresting militant Islamic leaders, blocking street gatherings, closing schools and universities, patrolling streets with loaded machine guns, and even shooting demonstrators).

The wide and deep Muslim enthusiasm for bin Laden is an extremely important development that needs to be understood, not ignored.

(22 October 2001)

11/9 vs. 9/11

Early on November 9, 2001, the Taliban regime ruled almost 95 percent of Afghanistan. Ten days later, it controlled just 15 percent of the country. Key to this quick disintegration was the fact that, awed by American air power, many Taliban soldiers switched sides to the U.S.-backed Northern Alliance. According to one analyst, "Defections, even in mid-battle, are proving key to the rapid collapse across Afghanistan of the formerly ruling Taliban militia."

This development fits into a larger pattern; thanks to American muscle, Afghans now look at militant Islam as a losing proposition. Nor are they alone; Muslims around the world sense the same shift. If militant Islam achieved its greatest victory ever on September 11, by November 9 (when the Taliban lost their first major city) the demise of this murderous movement may have begun.

"Pakistani holy warriors are deserting Taliban ranks and streaming home in large numbers," reported the Associated Press on Friday. In the streets of Peshawar, we learn, "portraits of Osama bin Laden go unsold. Here where it counts, just across the Khyber Pass from the heartland of Afghanistan, the Taliban mystique is waning."

Before 11/9, large crowds of militant Islamic men filled Peshawar's narrow streets, especially on Fridays, listening to vitriolic attacks on the United States and Israel, burning effigies of President Bush, and perhaps clashing with the riot police. On the Friday after 11/9, however, things went very differently in Peshawar. Much smaller and quieter crowds heard more sober speeches. No effigy was set on fire and one observer described the few policemen as looking like "a bunch of old friends on an afternoon stroll."

The Arabic-speaking countries show a similar trend. Martin Indyk, former U.S. ambassador to Israel, notes that in the first week after the U.S. air strikes began on October 7, nine anti-American demonstrations took place. The second week saw three of them, the third week one, the fourth week, two. "Then—nothing," observes Indyk. "The Arab street is quiet."

And so too in the further reaches of the Muslim world—Indonesia, India, Nigeria—where the supercharged protests of September are distant memories.

American military success has also encouraged the authorities to crack down. The effective ruler of Saudi Arabia admonished religious leaders to be careful and responsible in their statements ("weigh each word before saying it") after he saw that Washington meant business. Likewise, the Egyptian government has moved more aggressively against its militant Islamic elements. Similarly in China, the government prohibited the selling of badges celebrating Osama bin Laden ("I am bin Laden. Who should I fear?") only after the U.S. victories began.

This change in mood results from the change in American behavior. For two decades after Ayatollah Khomeini reached power in Iran in 1979 spouting "Death to America," U.S. embassies, planes, ships, and barracks were assaulted, leading to hundreds of American deaths. In the face of this, Washington hardly responded.

As Muslims watched militant Islam inflict one defeat after another on the far more powerful United States, they reasonably concluded that America, for all its resources, was tired and soft. They watched with awe as the audacity of militant Islam increased, culminating with Osama bin Laden's declaration of jihad against the entire Western world and the Taliban leader calling for nothing less than the "extinction of America."

The September 11 attacks were expected to take a major step toward extinguishing America by demoralizing the population and leading to civil unrest, perhaps starting a sequence of events that would lead to the U.S. government's collapse. Instead, the 3,000 deaths served as a rousing call to arms. Just two months later, the deployment of U.S. might has reduced the prospects of militant Islam.

The pattern is clear: So long as Americans submitted passively to murderous attacks by militant Islam, this movement gained support among Muslims. When Americans finally fought militant Islam, its appeal quickly diminished. Victory on the battlefield, in other words, has not only the obvious advantage of protecting the United States but also the important side effect of lancing the anti-American boil that spawned those attacks in the first place.

The implication is clear: There is no substitute for victory. The U.S. government must continue the war on terror by weakening militant Islam everywhere it exists, from Afghanistan to Atlanta.

(19 November 2001)

ARABIA'S CIVIL WAR

The four bombings in Saudi Arabia in mid-May 2003, which killed thirty-four, including eight Americans, are symptomatic of a deep fissure in that country. The argument is over religion, politics, and foreigners—and it goes back a long way. The West must react by helping the Saudi family win this dispute, while putting pressure on it to reform.

Saudi Arabia's origins lie in the mid-eighteenth century, when a tribal leader named Muhammad Al Saud joined forces with a religious leader named Muhammad bin Abd al-Wahhab. The first gave his name to the kingdom that (with the exception of two interim periods) still exists; the second gave his name to the version of Islam that still serves as the kingdom's ideology.

On first appearance, the Wahhabi version of Islam was seen as wildly extreme and was widely repudiated. Its fanatical enmity toward other Muslims and its rejection of long-standing Muslim customs made it anathema, for example, to the Ottoman rulers who dominated the Middle East. The Saudi kingdom disappeared twice because its military and religious aggressiveness made it so loathsome to its neighbors.

The current iteration of the Saudi kingdom came into being in 1902 when a Saudi leader captured Riyadh. Ten years later, there emerged a Wahhabi armed force known as the Ikhwan (Arabic for "Brethren")* which in its personal practices and its hostility toward non-Wahhabis represented the most militant dimension of this already militant movement. One war cry of theirs went: "The winds of Paradise are blowing. Where are you who hanker after Paradise?"

The Ikhwan served the Saudi family well, bringing it one military victory after another. A key turning point came in 1924, when the father of today's Saudi king captured Mecca from the great-great-grandfather of today's Jordanian king. This victory had two major implications. It vanquished the last remaining rival of the Saudis and established the family as the leading force on the Arabian peninsula. And it brought under Saudi control not just another town but the holiest city of Islam and a cosmopolitan urban area that hosted divergent interpretations of Islam.

These changes turned the Saudi insurgency into a state and brought a desert movement to the city. This meant the Saudi monarch could no longer give the Ikhwan and the traditional Wahhabi interpreta-

---

*Not to be confused with the *Ikhwan al-Muslimin* ("Muslim Brethren"), an organization that emerged separately in the late 1920s in Egypt.

tion of Islam free rein, but had to control it. The result was a civil war in the late 1920s that ended in the monarchy's victory over the Ikhwan in 1930.

In other words, the less fanatical version of Wahhabism triumphed over the more fanatical. The Saudi monarchs presided over a kingdom extreme by comparison with other Muslim countries but tame by Wahhabi standards.

Yes, the Saudi state deems the Koran to be its constitution, forbids the practice of any religion but Islam on its territory, employs an intolerant religious police, and imposes gender apartheid. But it also enacts non-Koranic regulations, employs large numbers of non-Muslims, constrains the religious police, and allows women to attend school and work.

The Ikhwan may have lost the fight in 1930, but its way of thinking lived on, representing the main opposition to an ever-more grandiose and corrupt Saudi state. The potency of this alternative became startlingly evident in 1979, when an Ikhwan-inspired group violently seized the Grand Mosque in Mecca. On a larger scale, the Ikhwan spirit dominated jihad efforts against the Soviet Union in Afghanistan during the 1980s. And the Taliban regime that ruled Afghanistan in the period 1996-2001 embodied the Ikhwan in power.

Osama bin Laden, a Saudi who spent formative years in Afghanistan, is the leading representative of the Ikhwan movement today. He wants to depose the corrupt and hypocritical Saudi monarchy, install a Taliban-like government, evict non-Muslim foreigners, and return women to the harem. His vision has real appeal in Saudi Arabia; it's widely reported that in a fair election, he would handily defeat the current ruler, King Fahd.

Thus, the recent violence in Riyadh ultimately reflects not just a hatred of Americans but a titanic clash of visions and a struggle for power; in this, it recapitulates the civil war of the 1920s. Is Saudi Arabia to remain a monarchy that at least partially accommodates modernity and the outside world? Or is it to become the Islamic Emirate of Arabia, a reincarnation of the Taliban's completely regressive rule in Afghanistan?

For the outside world, the choice is clear; however unattractive, the Saudi monarchy is preferable to the yet worse Ikhwan alternative. This implies a two-step approach: help the monarchy defeat its Ikhwan-inspired enemy and put serious pressure on the kingdom to reform everything from its school system to its sponsorship of Wahhabi organizations abroad.

(14 May 2003)

MILITANT ISLAM'S NEW STRONGHOLDS

with Jonathan Schanzer

The October 13, 2002, bombing of a nightclub in Bali, Indonesia, killing almost 202 and injuring many more, fits into a larger pattern. Militant Islam used to be mostly confined to Middle Easterners, but in recent years it has spread to Muslims in other parts of the world.

This can be seen especially in the cases of Indonesia, Bangladesh, and Nigeria, three countries with a combined population of about 494 million inhabitants. Their Muslim population of some 378 million constitutes about a third of the global Muslim community.

Indonesia: This Southeast Asian country, 88 percent Muslim, hosts Islamist efforts to impose Islamic law (Shari'a) through both legal and violent means.

In the province of Aceh alone, more than 6,000 lives have been lost in fighting between government forces and the Islamist "Free Aceh Movement" (which some intelligence sources believe may be an Al-Qaeda affiliate). The goal of these and other radicals, CNS News reports, is "to turn the world's most populous Muslim country into an extremist Islamic state by 2003." Muslim-Christian tensions have led to a full-blown religious war on other islands.

In Sulawesi, Islamists have deployed roadblocks, armored bulldozers, and rocket launchers, thereby isolating the indigenous Christian community. They have also systematically targeted Christians, forcing them to convert, circumcising their children, burning churches and other buildings.

In all, Muslim-Christian clashes in Indonesia have killed more than 19,000 since 1999 and left over 600,000 displaced from their homes.

Bangladesh: Islamists in this 83 percent Muslim country of South Asia aspire to establish an "Islamic Republic of Bangladesh" with a constitution based on the Shari'a. The goal, says the head of one group, is to "pursue a slow but steady policy towards Islamization of the country"—much like Afghanistan under the Taliban.

Not surprisingly, Al-Qaeda has tentacles in Bangladesh. "Harakat ul-Jihad Islami, Bangladesh" was reportedly established with direct aid from Osama bin Laden in 1992 and calls itself the "Bangladeshi Taliban." The group claimed responsibility for attacking U.S. government offices in Calcutta, killing five policemen in January 2002.

Since September 11, thousands of Al-Qaeda supporters have taken to the streets of Dhaka after Friday prayers, touting posters that read: "Osama is our Hero," while burning effigies of George W. Bush.

Meanwhile, members of minority religions have suffered from ghastly violence, including collective terror. The *Nation* reports that some Buddhists and Christians were blinded, had fingers cut off or had hands amputated, while "others had iron rods nailed through their legs or abdomen." Women and children have "been gang-raped, often in front of their fathers or husbands." In addition, hundreds of temples were desecrated and statues destroyed; thousands of homes and businesses looted or burned.

As for Hindus, the human rights organization Freedom House reports they have been subject to "rape, torture and killing and the destruction of their cultural and religious identity at the hands of Muslims." In one indicative step, Islamists sometimes force Hindu women to dress in the Islamist fashion.

Nigeria: Disregarding both the Nigerian constitution (which stipulates a separation of church and state) and demographic realities (only 50 percent of the population is Muslim), Islamists of this West African country have adopted or announced plans to adopt some version of Islamic law in twelve of its thirty-six states since 1999.

Implementing Islamic law means forbidding such practices as the construction of churches, music performances, the wearing of pants, drinking alcohol, and riding in mixed-gender taxis. Forced conversions to Islam are reported, as well as coerced divorces of Muslim women from Christian men.

Vigilantes enforce Islamic law via punishments that include stoning, flogging, and the chopping off of hands. Solidarity visits from Sudanese, Pakistani, Saudi, Palestinian, and Syrian Islamists tie Nigeria to the wider forces of militant Islam. Freedom House concludes that Nigeria is undergoing a process of "Talibanization."

That militant Islam and its companion violence have spread from the Middle Eastern core to the periphery of the Muslim world is of great concern. It means that the enemies of the United States, moderate Islam, and of civilization itself are far more numerous and entrenched than previously thought. This implies that the current war will likely be longer, bloodier and more demanding than most people imagine.

TERRORIST PROFS

"It was quiet in [Cooper Hall] 464 Thursday night," noted the University of South Florida student newspaper, "where [Sameeh] Hammoudeh's 6 P.M. Arabic IV class was scheduled to meet. Two students who hadn't heard of his arrest came to class, and a substitute was assigned to teach in Hammoudeh's place."

Hammoudeh missed teaching his Arabic class that day, February 20, 2003, due to a slight inconvenience: He had just been charged with racketeering and conspiracy to murder. In fact, he was one of eight men indicted at a U.S. District Court in Florida as "material supporters of a foreign terrorist organization," that organization being Palestinian Islamic Jihad (PIJ).

It is striking that three of those eight are academic specialists on Middle Eastern and Islamic subjects. Their arrests reveal to what extent Middle East studies is a field that serves as an extension of the region's radicalism. (Other defendants teach computer engineering, manage a medical clinic, own a small business and serve as imam in a mosque.)

The three instructors on Middle East topics all have establishment credentials:

- *Ramadan Abdullah Shallah*, forty-five. Born in the Gaza Strip, he earned a doctorate in economics from the University of Durham in the United Kingdom. He arrived in Tampa, Florida., in 1991, taught Middle East studies as an adjunct professor at the University of South Florida (USF) and headed the World and Islam Studies Enterprise (WISE), a think tank dealing with Middle East issues that was affiliated with USF during the period 1992-95. He left USF in 1995 and later that year turned up in Damascus, where he is now secretary-general of PIJ.

- *Bashir Musa Mohammed Nafi*, fifty. Born in Egypt, Nafi has two Ph.D.s and was a researcher at WISE. He was deported for visa violations in 1996 and went to England where, as an Irish citizen he lives in Oxfordshire. He teaches at two London institutions, Birkbeck College of the University of London ("Social and Political Issues in Islam") and the Muslim College ("State and Society in Islamic History"). Nafi is also associated with the Institute of Contemporary Islamic Thought (which in 2000 published his analysis, "The Rise and Decline of the Arab-Islamic Reform Movement"). He has written for the Virginia-based *Middle East Affairs Journal* and a book of his appeared in Arabic in 1999, "Imperialism and Zionism: The Palestinian Case." (He uses a pseudonym, Ahmad Sadiq, when writing for militant Islamic journals.)

- *Sameeh Hammoudeh*, forty-two. Born in the West Bank, he worked at the Arab Studies Society in Jerusalem before reaching America in 1992. He began teaching at USF in 1995. At the time of his arrest, he lived in the Tampa area, taught Arabic at USF and was working toward a master's degree in religious studies at that university.

All three alleged terrorists succeeded in talking the academic talk, fooling nearly everyone. Shallah wrote in 1993, in his capacity as director of WISE, that the organization's long-term goal is "to contribute to the understanding of the revivalist Islamist trends, misleadingly labeled 'fundamentalist' in Western and American academic circles." Almost any North American academic specialist on Islam could have written those same sneering and duplicitous words. Many do.

The three passed for genuine scholars. Carrie Wickham, a specialist on Egyptian Islam at Emory University, said she "felt deceived" on learning who Shallah really was and expressed surprise that "a serious intellectual counterpart" like him could also be a terrorist. Even after the indictment, Arthur Lowrie, formerly vice chairman of USF's Committee for Middle Eastern Studies, praises Shallah for his "good scholarly work." And Gwen Griffith-Dickson, director of Islamic studies at Birkbeck, describes Nafi as "highly respected," lauding him for his efforts "with energy and commitment, to encourage critical thinking about religious issues and academic balance in his students, and thus to encourage social responsibility."

That three accused terrorists passed without suspicion as genuine Middle East studies scholars points to the crisis in this academic discipline. This academic field is already criticized for providing refuge to what might be called intellectual terrorists—scholars known for their extremism, intolerance, and dishonesty. Now we learn it apparently has been harboring the real thing.

Conclusion: This field must be scrutinized very closely, especially by the U.S. Congress, which provides vital subsidies to Middle East studies programs.

(24 February 2003)

AL-QAEDA'S LIMITS

A day after suicide bombers killed twenty-nine people in Morocco in mid-May 2003, that country's interior minister noted that the five nearly simultaneous attacks "bear the hallmarks of international terrorism." More strongly, the Moroccan justice minister asserted a "connection to international terrorism" and the prime minister spoke of a "foreign hand" behind the violence.

Westerners were more specific about the source: "Al-Qaeda is back with a vengeance," declared Sen. Robert Byrd (D-W.Va.), referring to this attack and one a few days earlier in Saudi Arabia. "Al-Qaeda is back on the rampage," agreed the BBC and many others.

But they were caught out when the police investigation found every last one of the fourteen suicide bombers in Casablanca, as well as all of their accomplices, to be Moroccan nationals. Local groups such as Assirat Al-Moustaqim and Salafia Jihadia apparently carried out the operation. As *Newsweek* summarizes the situation, "While financed by Al-Qaeda, the Moroccan terrorists were an offshoot group."

This incident points to a routine overemphasis on shadowy international networks, Al-Qaeda in particular, to the neglect of local groups. Legal documentation, which provides our main window onto Al-Qaeda, points to its limited role in most instances. Consider information from two cases:

- *East African embassies*: In a 2001 New York trial that convicted four Islamists of plotting the 1998 bombing of U.S. embassies in Kenya and Tanzania, testimony established that Al-Qaeda serves as an umbrella organization for such groups as Islamic Jihad, al-Gama'a al-Islamiya and the Armed Islamic Group, each of which does its own recruitment and operations. Their leaders met periodically in Afghanistan and coordinated actions via Al-Qaeda. The trial transcripts showed how this network could survive the loss of any part of it, even the Afghanistan headquarters.

- *Strait of Gibraltar warships*: A 2002 Moroccan indictment of three Saudi Islamists for planning suicide attacks against U.S. and British warships in the Strait of Gibraltar offers insight into Al-Qaeda's inner workings. Jason Burke of London's *Observer* reports how the group's leader, Zuher Hilal Mohamed Al Tbaiti, traveled in 1999 to Afghanistan to request Al-Qaeda funding for a "martyrdom mission" but was rebuffed and told he had to develop a detailed plan before receiving financial support. So Tbaiti went to Morocco, recruited suicide bombers, and then returned to Afghanistan armed with a specific plan. Satisfied this time, Al-Qaeda granted him funds for an operation.

When the Taliban regime fell in December 2001, Al-Qaeda lost most of its training, communications, and funding capabilities. Some Al-Qaeda personnel moved to northern Iraq—until coalition forces took over there; others remain active in Iran. Elsewhere, the organization lacks a secure base, leading some informed observers to conclude it no longer operates effectively; one U.S. intelligence official calls it "a wounded animal." Burke of the *Observer* goes further: "Al-Qaeda, conceived of as a traditional terrorist group with cadres and a capability everywhere, simply does not exist."

Looking back, Al-Qaeda's role seems to divide into two: Some attacks (Somalia, East African embassies, the *USS Cole*, 9/11, perhaps the recent Riyadh bombings) it ran with its own staff, while depending on others for the key ingredients—energy, commitment, and self-sacrifice. In most operations (the Millennium plot, Strait of Gibraltar, London ricin, perhaps the recent Casablanca bombings), Al-Qaeda provided some direction, funding and training, but left the execution to others. In *Newsweek*'s colorful formulation, it "has always been more of a pirate federation than a Stalinist top-down organization."

The ultimate worry is not Al-Qaeda but a diffuse, global, militant Islamic ideology that predates Al-Qaeda's creation, is locally organized and constantly recruits new volunteers. Even the usually maladroit Syrian president, Bashar al-Assad, understands this: "We blame everything on Al-Qaeda, but what happened is more dangerous than bin Laden or Al-Qaeda. . . . The issue is ideology, it's not an issue of organizations." Bin Laden concurs, noting that his own presence is unnecessary for mounting new acts of violence. "Regardless if Osama is killed or survives," he said of himself, "the awakening has started."

Burke proposes replacing the concept of a structured, hierarchical Al-Qaeda organization with a more amorphous "Al-Qaeda movement." When law enforcement and intelligence agencies adopt this more flexible understanding, they can better do battle against militant Islamic terrorism.

(28 May 2003)

PART 2
ISLAM AND MUSLIMS

4

WRIT LARGE

THE EVIL ISN'T ISLAM

"ISLAM IS EVIL." That was the message a U.S. Secret Service agent illicitly left on an Islamic prayer calendar on July 18, 2002, as he took part raiding a suspected Al-Qaeda operative in Dearborn, Michigan. The agent's crude graffito sums up a point of view increasingly heard since 9/11 in the United States. It's also one that is troubling and wrong.

Here is the rub: It is a mistake to blame Islam (a religion fourteen centuries old) for the evil that should be ascribed to militant Islam (a totalitarian ideology less than a century old). The terrorism of Al-Qaeda, Hamas, the Iranian government, and other Islamists results from the ideas of such contemporary radicals as Osama bin Laden and Ayatollah Khomeini, not from the Koran.

To which you might respond: But bin Laden and Khomeini get their ideas from the Koran. And they are only continuing a pattern of Muslim aggression that is centuries old.

Not exactly. Let's look closer at both points:

- *Aggressive Islam*: The Koran and other authoritative Islamic scriptures do contain incitements against non-Muslims. The eminent historian Paul Johnson, for example, cites two Koranic verses: "Strongest among men in enmity to the Believers will you find the Jews and Pagans" (Sura 5, verse 85) and "Then fight and slay the pagans wherever you find them. And seize them, beleaguer them and lie in wait for them." (9:5).

- *Aggressive Muslims*: Fourteen centuries of Islam have witnessed a long history of Muslims engaged in jihad to expand the area under Islamic rule, from the early conquests of the caliphs to what Samuel Huntington terms Islam's "bloody borders" today.

Yes, these points are accurate. But they are one side of the story.

- *Mild Islam*: Like other sacred writings, the Koran can be mined for quotes to support opposing arguments. In this case, Karen Armstrong, a bestselling apologist for Islam, quotes two gentler passages from the Koran: "There must be no coercion in matters of faith!" (2:256) and "O people! We have formed you into nations and tribes so that you may know one another." (49:13).

- *Mild Muslims*: There have been occasions of Muslim moderation and tolerance, such as those in long-ago Sicily and Spain. And in one telling example, Mark R. Cohen notes that "The Jews of Islam, especially during the formative and classical centuries (up to the 13th century), experienced much less persecution than did the Jews of Christendom."

In other words, Islam's scriptures and history show variation.

At present, admittedly, it is hard to recall the positive side, at a moment when backwardness, resentment, extremism, and violence prevail in so much of the Muslim world. But the present is not typical of Islam's long history; indeed, it may be the worst era in that entire history.

Things can get better. But it will not be easy. That requires that Muslims tackle the huge challenge of adapting their faith to the realities of modern life.

What does that mean in practical terms? Here are some examples: Five hundred years ago, Jews, Christians, and Muslims agreed that owning slaves was in principle acceptable but paying interest on money was not. After bitter, protracted debates, Jews and Christians changed their minds. Today, no Jewish or Christian body endorses slavery or has religious qualms about paying reasonable interest.

Muslims, in contrast, still think the old way. Slavery yet exists in a host of majority-Muslim countries (especially Sudan and Mauritania, also Saudi Arabia and Pakistan) and it is a taboo subject. To enable pious Muslims to avoid interest, an Islamic financial industry worth an estimated $150 billion has developed.

The challenge ahead is clear: Muslims must emulate their fellow monotheists by modernizing their religion with regard to slavery, interest, and much else. No more fighting jihad to impose Muslim rule. No more endorsement of suicide terrorism. No more second-class citizenship for non-Muslims. No more death penalty for adultery or "honor" killings of women. No more death sentences for blasphemy or apostasy.

Rather than rail on about Islam's alleged "evil," it behooves everyone—Muslim and non-Muslim alike—to help modernize this civilization. That is the ultimate message of 9/11. It is much deeper and more ambitious than Western governments presently seem to realize.

(30 July 2002)

Islam's Future

"I am surprised at your lack of courage, Mr. Pipes," one reader scolded me. "Your point of view is for people who believe in the tooth fairy and Santa Claus," opined another. "You really dropped the ball on this one!" "I hope you are not beginning to lose your nerve." "Totally wrong." Or, more charitably: "Maybe your hope is overshadowing your understanding of the truth."

Those are a sampling of the many negative responses (found on the comments section of my website) to my column "The Evil Isn't Islam." Rather than rail on about Islam's alleged "evil," I wrote, we all need to pitch in and "help modernize this civilization." By about a 5-to-1 margin, my readers disagree. Three main points emerge from their letters.

- *Militant Islam is Islam.* They insist that the evils I attribute to a modern, radical utopian ideology inheres to the faith at large. What I call militant Islam, they say, "should properly be called, 'real Islam.'" One writer asks, "what exactly is it that the Wahhabis and other Islamic extremists are doing that is not in accord with Muhammad's doctrine?" He then replies: "The answer is they are behaving very true to Muhammad's doctrine!"

- *Mild Koranic verses were abrogated.* The readers argue that the Koran contains contradictory passages that Muslim scholars handled by deciding that chronologically latter verses superseded earlier ones. Specifically, the conciliatory verses I quoted ("There must be no coercion in matters of faith!" and "O people! We have formed you into nations and tribes so that you may know one another,") were voided by one of the aggressive ones I cited ("Then fight and slay the pagans wherever you find them. And seize them, beleaguer them and lie in wait for them").

- *Islam has always been on the warpath.* "The violent conquest against the infidel was present at [Islam's] inception," writes one respondent.

It "is based on war, conquest and forced conversion," asserts another. "The war, declared by Muhammad in [the year] 600 . . ., continues to this day," notes a third.

My response, however, is that no matter what Islam is now or was in the past, it will be something different in the future. The religion must adapt to modern mores.

This can be done. One recent example: In May 2002, the Turkish religious authorities ruled—completely contrary to Islamic custom —to permit women to pray next to men and to attend mosque services while menstruating. The High Religious Affairs Board decided this on the (distinctly modern) basis that men and women are "equal and complementary beings." In September 2002, this same board will take up the extremely delicate topic of permitting Muslim women to marry non-Muslim men, when it will perhaps again rule against centuries of practice.

If Turkish theologians can execute such changes, why not theologians in other countries, too? And if practices concerning women can be changed, why not those concerning jihad or the role of Islamic law as a whole? Islam can adjust to modernity no less than have other faiths.

Conversely, if one sees Islam as irredeemably evil, what comes next? This approach turns all Muslims—even moderates fleeing the horrors of militant Islam—into eternal enemies. And it leaves one with zero policy options. My approach has the benefit of offering a realistic policy to deal with a major global problem.

In conclusion, a reflection: Americans have acquired an impressive knowledge of Islam. Contrary to the incessant bleating by apologists for militant Islam about American ignorance of this topic, my readers know what they are talking about. Their critiques are sometimes erudite (for example, on the subject of Koranic abrogations), sometimes eloquent ("The next time you watch a film clip of the miniscule and microscopic body parts of Israeli citizens being scraped from the streets, sidewalks and buildings, just think about what is truly evil").

These readers, surely, are not typical of American opinion, but their informed antagonism to Islam bears remarking. It is likely to have a larger political role as Islam becomes an ever-more central topic of discussion in the West.

(13 August 2002)

ISLAMISTS—NOT WHO THEY SAY THEY ARE

Islamists often appear to outsiders to be the most authentic adherents of their faith. They refer constantly to God and conspicuously pray in public. Men sport full beards and women wear veils. They urge Muslim solidarity and demonstrate a suspicion of non-Muslims.

A closer look, however, finds that Islamists are hardly model Muslims.

Preoccupied with gaining power (and succeeding in several countries—such as Iran, Sudan, and Afghanistan under the Taliban), they often show more talent at politics than at living by Islam's precepts. In fact, Islamists, for all their ostentatious piety, tend to be severely deficient as believers.

Financial probity, for example, is a recurring challenge for them. On the grand scale, the Bank of Credit and Commerce International (BCCI) was the militant Islamic bank par excellence; when it failed in 1991, spawning perhaps the largest and most complex banking scandal in history, its seemingly devout owners had embezzled billions of dollars from 1.3 million mostly Muslim depositors in over seventy countries.

On a slightly lesser scale, the "Islamic capital-investment companies" that flourished in Egypt in the 1980s also collapsed from corruption, as did similar institutions in Turkey. And a 1998 University of Texas study found that "Islamic banks in Iran and Sudan are avenues for corruption and embezzlement."

Nor are Islamists above petty theft. As the two men who carried out the suicide attack on the *USS Cole* in October 2000 prepared for their operation, they knew they would not be returning to their rented living quarters, so they cheated their Yemeni landlord out of the last month's rent. "I was angry," commented their landlord, adding almost unnecessarily: "There was nothing Islamic in that."

But it is Islam's strict code of sexual modesty that Islamists most often transgress. Militant Islamic terrorists kill in the name of Islam, but frequently are hardly models of Islamic probity. The man who directed the World Trade Center bombing, Ramzi Yousef, once lived in the Philippines where, his biographer Simon Reeve recounts, he was seen "gallivanting around Manila's bars, strip-joints and karaoke clubs, flirting with women." Rashid Baz, convicted of killing a

Hassidic boy on the Brooklyn Bridge, was described by his father as someone who "never went to a mosque in his life. He likes girls and cars and sports."

Drawn to pornography like moths to light, Islamists integrate dirty pictures even into their terrorism. In one case, U.S. law-enforcement officials found that a wide variety of militant Islamic organizations—Osama bin Laden's Al-Qaeda, Hamas, Hezbollah, and others—had placed encrypted information such as maps, photographs, and instructions within the X-rated pictures on pornographic websites.

In offices, Islamists are known to be sexual harassers. Thus did a female employee at the Saudi mission to the United Nations in New York publicly complain in September 2000 about enduring years of sexual harassment from "male fundamentalist members" of the Saudi mission. When in authority, Islamists exploit women. The Iranian government recently arrested the head of an Islamic revolutionary court on charges of running a prostitution ring involving runaway underage girls.

Perhaps the most appalling instance of militant Islamic sexual degeneracy takes place in the course of hostage taking, when rape is common. In the Philippines, for example, Islamists violated at least one of the Western women whom they held hostage on Jolo Island in late 2000. "It was without doubt the worst thing that happened there," a fellow hostage commented afterwards, adding that the sexual molestation "was particularly surprising" because otherwise the hostages were relatively well treated.

This pattern of misbehavior is important because it reveals the Islamists' true profile: these are ruthless, power-hungry operatives who cannot rightly claim the aura of piety they strenuously assert. They are less observant Muslims than they are political extremists.

Their record of stealing and fornicating has another implication: as the analyst Khalid Durán notes, Islamist demands for power are based not on worldly experience, technical accomplishments, or policy sophistication, but on their allegedly higher moral standards. The sort of flagrant misconduct documented here completely undercuts such claims to authority.

For true Islamic ethics, one needs to turn to those many traditional Muslims who live according to the precepts of a faith as it organically developed over fourteen centuries. Not radical, not inclined to force their vision on others via violence, these are pious Muslims who deserve respect.

(9 May 2001)

WHERE DOES RELIGIOUS FREEDOM EXIST?

The U.S. Department of State fulfilled a Congressional requirement in September 1999 and released its first *Annual Report on International Religious Freedom*, a gigantic work, covering 194 countries in over one thousand pages that called on the labor of hundreds of individuals over a period of eighteen months.

Read the report and one thing stands out: the twenty-one states of the Middle East (plus the Palestinian Authority)—have no rival internationally when it comes to telling people how to pray and live.

Let's start right at the bottom of the heap: this region boasts the only state in the world—Saudi Arabia—that the report flat-out describes as a place where "Freedom of Religion does not exist." The report explains why: "Islam is the official religion, and all citizens must be Muslims.... The Government prohibits the public practice of other religions." Does it! In late 1990, as hundreds of thousands of U.S. troops were in Saudi Arabia to protect it against Iraq, President Bush visited the soldiers to celebrate the American holiday of Thanksgiving with them. But: he planned to say grace before sitting down to a feast, so he had to eat that meal on a ship off the Saudi coast. A few weeks later, American troops could not attend Christmas services on Saudi soil but only "C-word morale services" held in unmarked tents or mess halls.

The Saudi authorities also insist on exactly the kind of Islam. They persecute their Shi'i population and permit only a certain form of Sunni Islam. The report delicately, but also ominously explains: "Islamic practice generally is limited to that of the Wahhabi order," the most narrow-minded in existence, and "Practices contrary to this interpretation...are discouraged."

The next worst countries are Sudan, Iraq, and Afghanistan, all described as places where the authorities "severely" restrict religious rights. Afghanistan under the Taliban is where a top military man says that some two-thousand-year-old Buddhist statues must be destroyed because they "are not Islamic." In Iraq, it is the usual story of Stalinist repression: "the one-party Government controlled by Saddam Hussein has for decades conducted a brutal campaign of murder, summary execution, and protracted arbitrary detention against the religious leaders and adherents of the Shi'a Muslim population." Sudan is waging a horrendous war against its non-Muslim population, creating what is perhaps the worst humanitarian disaster anywhere in the world today.

One level less awful are Iran and Libya where the government merely "restricts" religious rights. In Iran, the main victims are the estimated third of a million Baha'is, with Sunni Muslims and others also feeling the brunt of the regime's wrath. In Libya, a more homogeneous country, beware to anyone who disagrees with Mu'ammar al-Qadhdhafi's eccentric ideas about religious devotion: "Islamic groups whose beliefs and practices are at variance with the state-approved teaching of Islam are banned."

Then follow the great bulk of states in the Middle East, characterized by two features: Islam as the official religion of state and a nominal freedom of religion. Egypt is typical in this regard: "religious practices that conflict with Islamic law are prohibited." Roughly the same situation obtains also in Algeria, Jordan, and Kuwait. In these and another ten states, Islam is privileged while other religions exist on sufferance.

Finally, the State Department's few words of praise go to an unlikely quintet: Tunisia, Israel, Syria, Turkey, and the United Arab Emirates, where the governments are said "generally" to respect religious rights.

Odder yet, only one polity gets a full endorsement, the Palestinian Authority, which "respects" religious rights without qualification. "There was no pattern of PA discrimination against and harassment of Christians," the report claims, thereby overlooking a vast pattern of discrimination and intimidation against the dwindling Christian minority, as well as such outrages as a Muslim attempt to take two rooms from the holiest church in Christendom to convert them into toilets.

These results prompt three conclusions. First, the whole concept of religious freedom remains alien to most Middle Eastern governments. Second, the State Department needs further to refine its methodology, for any report that finds Syria in the same category as Israel needs some very basic rethinking. Third, its listing the PA as the finest practitioner of religious freedoms in the whole region shows again that no distortion of truth is too great in the effort to promote Arab-Israeli negotiations.

(23 September 1999)

WHAT IS JIHAD?

What does the Arabic word *jihad* mean?

One answer came in late December 2002, when Saddam Hussein had his Islamic leaders appeal to Muslims worldwide to join his jihad to defeat the "wicked Americans" should they attack Iraq; then he himself threatened the United States with jihad.

As this suggests, jihad is "holy war." Or, more precisely: It means the legal, compulsory, communal effort to expand the territories ruled by Muslims at the expense of territories ruled by non-Muslims.

The purpose of jihad, in other words, is not directly to spread the Islamic faith but to extend sovereign Muslim power (faith, of course, often follows the flag). Jihad is thus unabashedly offensive in nature, with the eventual goal of achieving Muslim dominion over the entire globe.

Jihad did have two variant meanings through the centuries, one more radical, one less so. The first holds that Muslims who interpret their faith differently are infidels and therefore legitimate targets of jihad. (This is why Algerians, Egyptians, and Afghans have found themselves, like Americans and Israelis, so often the victims of jihadist aggression.) The second meaning, associated with mystics, rejects the legal definition of jihad as armed conflict and tells Muslims to withdraw from the worldly concerns to achieve spiritual depth.

Jihad in the sense of territorial expansion has always been a central aspect of Muslim life. That's how Muslims came to rule much of the Arabian Peninsula by the time of the Prophet Muhammad's death in 632. It's how, a century later, Muslims had conquered a region from Afghanistan to Spain. Subsequently, jihad spurred and justified Muslim conquests of such territories as India, Sudan, Anatolia, and the Balkans.

Today, jihad is the world's foremost source of terrorism, inspiring a worldwide campaign of violence by self-proclaimed jihadist groups:

- *The International Islamic Front for the Jihad Against Jews and Crusaders*: Osama bin Laden's organization;

- *Laskar Jihad*: responsible for the murder of more than 10,000 Christians in Indonesia;

- *Harakat ul-Jihad-i-Islami*: a leading cause of violence in Kashmir;

- *Palestinian Islamic Jihad*: the most vicious anti-Israel terrorist group of them all;

- *Egyptian Islamic Jihad*: killed Anwar El-Sadat in 1981, many others since, and

- *Yemeni Islamic Jihad*: killed three American missionaries in December 2002.

But jihad's most ghastly present reality is in Sudan, where until recently the ruling party bore the slogan "Jihad, Victory, and Martyrdom." For two decades, under government auspices, jihadists there have physically attacked non-Muslims, looted their belongings, and killed their males.

Jihadists then enslaved tens of thousands of females and children, forced them to convert to Islam, sent them on forced marches, beat them, and set them to hard labor. The women and older girls also suffered ritual gang rape, genital mutilation, and a life of sexual servitude.

Sudan's state-sponsored jihad has caused about two million deaths and the displacement of another 4 million—making it the greatest humanitarian catastrophe of our era.

Despite jihad's record as a leading source of conflict for fourteen centuries, causing untold human suffering, academic and Islamic apologists claim it permits only defensive fighting, or even that it is entirely non-violent. Three American professors of Islamic studies colorfully make the latter point, explaining jihad as:

- An "effort against evil in the self and every manifestation of evil in society" (Ibrahim Abu-Rabi, Hartford Seminary);

- "Resisting apartheid or working for women's rights" (Farid Eseck, Auburn Seminary), and

- "Being a better student, a better colleague, a better business partner. Above all, to control one's anger" (Bruce Lawrence, Duke University).

It would be wonderful were jihad to evolve into nothing more aggressive than controlling one's anger, but that will not happen simply by wishing away a gruesome reality. To the contrary, the pretense of a benign jihad obstructs serious efforts at self-criticism and reinterpretation.

The path away from terrorism, conquest, and enslavement lies in Muslims forthrightly acknowledging jihad's historic role, followed by apologies to jihad's victims, developing an Islamic basis for non-violent jihad and (the hardest part) actually ceasing to wage violent jihad.

Unfortunately, such a process of redemption is not now under way; violent jihad will probably continue until it is crushed by a superior military force (Defense Secretary Donald Rumsfeld, please take note). Only when jihad is defeated will moderate Muslims finally find their voice and truly begin the hard work of modernizing Islam.

(31 December 2002)

THE SUICIDE JIHAD MENACE

Soon after an EgyptAir plane crashed into the Atlantic shortly after takeoff from New York in October 1999, killing 217, the plane's copilot came under suspicion of intentionally bringing down the aircraft. To which the Egyptian reaction was adamant: no way – Egyptians don't engage in suicide. "Committing suicide is not a trait that Egyptians and Muslims are known for," commented the head of the pilots' association.

Militant Islamic leaders in the United States emphasized that, being a religiously observant Muslim, the copilot would never commit suicide. "Suicide is a major sin in Islam," Maher Hathout, imam of the Islamic Center in Los Angeles, explained. Ibrahim Hooper of the Council on American-Islamic Relations pronounced that suicide "would not be in accord with Islamic beliefs and practices."

Well, sort of. the Koran does tell Muslims, "Do not kill yourselves" and warns that those who disobey will be "cast into the fire." The Prophet Muhammad is reported to have said that a suicide cannot go to paradise. Islamic laws oppose the practice. This religious prohibition has had the intended effect. According to Franz Rosenthal, a scholar of the subject, "suicide was of comparatively rare occurrence" in traditional Muslim society. In contemporary Egypt, statistics bear out that suicide is exceedingly rare.

But this is not the whole story, for Islamists consider suicide as not just legitimate but highly commendable when undertaken for reasons of jihad. Going into war knowing with certainty that one will die, they argue, is not suicide (*intihar*) but martyrdom (*istishhad*), a much-praised form of self-sacrifice in the path of God, a way to win the eternal affection of the doe-eyed houris in paradise.

A leading Islamist authority, Sheikh Yusuf al-Qaradawi, recently explained the distinction this way: attacks on enemies are not suicide operations but "heroic martyrdom operations" in which the kamikazes act not "out of hopelessness and despair but are driven by an overwhelming desire to cast terror and fear into the hearts of the oppressors."

In other words, Islamists find suicide for personal reasons abominable, suicide for jihad admirable. If the EgyptAir copilot brought the plane down because he was depressed about his daughter's illness, he will burn forever in hell. If he did it to kill Americans in suburban Long Island, they might endorse his act.

Jihad suicide has been around for a millennium. The Assassins, a fanatical religious sect that flourished in the twelfth century developed jihad suicide into a powerful tool of war that succeeded in killing dozens of leaders and cast a long shadow over the region's politics for decades. The Assassins' suicide soldiers' mission, as explained by the historian Bernard Lewis, had a distinctly familiar flavor: "by striking down oppressors and usurpers, they gave the ultimate proof of their faith and loyalty, and earned immediate and eternal bliss."

In recent times, the revival of jihad suicide began as an Iranian project, starting with the 1981 blowing up of the Iraqi embassy in Beirut, killing twenty-seven, and followed by a long sequence of attacks on U.S. installations around the Middle East, killing as many as nineteen, sixty-three, and 241. During its eight-year war with Iraq, Tehran dispatched young soldiers to detonate land mines, then commemorated their deaths as martyrs.

The Iranians also sponsored a suicide campaign against Israeli troops in southern Lebanon during 1983-85 that did much to push those troops nearly out of Lebanon. Tehran persisted afterwards too. Islamic Jihad, its main Palestinian anti-Israel ally, already complained in 1995 that it had just one problem: "We have too many candidates for martyrdom and not enough resources to prepare them all."

The Palestinian Authority (PA) eventually noticed the effectiveness of this Iranian war instrument and recently adopted it, urging everyone from schoolboys to hardened criminals to hurl their lives against Israel, with many takers. Their actions have appalled Israelis while spurring impassioned support across the Middle East for the Palestinians.

The danger here is considerable: Yasir Arafat's PA has successfully adopted what had been the unique tool of Khomeini's militant Islamic regime, suggesting that suicide jihad is a flexible method potentially available to a wide array of non-militant Islamic rogue Muslim states (such as Iraq, Syria, and Libya) and maybe even to some terrorist organizations.

It's yet another danger from the Middle East for everyone to worry about.

(27 July 2001)

"I Wish I Had Done It Myself": A Father's Pride

Hours after the killing of fifteen Israelis in a Jerusalem restaurant in August 2001, the brother of the twenty-three-year-old suicide bomber delightedly announced that "this is a unique operation for its quality and success... Palestinians everywhere can now hold up their heads." Likewise, after a twenty-two-year-old suicide bomber two months earlier killed twenty-one Israelis at a Tel Aviv discotheque, his father announced: "I am very happy and proud of what my son did and, frankly, am a bit jealous... I wish I had done it myself."

And so it has been with nearly all Palestinian suicide operations—family members rejoicing at the "martyrdom" of their brothers and children. Some fathers even publicly announce a hope that their children will kill Israelis in suicide operations.

Puzzled by this apparent denial of the primal human urge to protect one's young, George W. Bush has commented, "I just can't understand this." He is hardly alone.

Two main factors account for this bizarre behavior. The first concerns the Palestinian Authority drumming into impressionable youth the glory of suicidal death while killing Israelis. PA television harps constantly on this message. On the Children's Club (a Sesame Street-like children's program), a young boy sings: "When I wander into Jerusalem, I will become a suicide bomber." A repeatedly shown television clip calls on children to "Drop your toys. Pick up rocks." In another, the words to a children's song go: "How pleasant is the smell of martyrs, how pleasant the smell of land, the land enriched by the blood, the blood pouring out of a fresh body."

Ikrima Sabri, the PA's ranking religious leader, says, "The younger the martyr, the greater and the more I respect him," while praising mothers who "willingly sacrifice their offspring for the sake of freedom." PA schools indoctrinate pupils on the virtues and joys of martyrdom, then honor and celebrate suicide killers. Four summer camps are currently training eight- to twelve-year-olds for suicide bombings. Organizations like Hamas promise to look after the killers' families' financial needs. In all, notes Meyrav Wurmser, a Hudson Institute specialist on the indoctrination of pupils, the PA has developed "a state-run ideology that pushes [children] to their death."

Why does this indoctrination work and why do Palestinian families enthusiastically send their children to die? What pressure could overcome the human instinct to protect one's loved ones? That pressure is not hard to locate, for it pervades Middle Eastern life. It is an unrelenting, compulsive preoccupation with family honor. The power of this obligation goes far beyond anything Westerners encounter. The fixation on family honor takes two main forms.

The negative one, called 'ird in Arabic, concerns the sexual purity of women and it accounts for the Middle Eastern custom of murdering female relatives for perceived offenses to the family. Such honor killings are intended to purge the family of its shame; thus do brothers kill sisters, cousins kill cousins, fathers kill daughters, and even sons kill mothers. These men do so not because they want to—almost nothing could be more horrifying in the context of the tight-knit Middle Eastern family—but because they feel obliged to. Allowing a dishonored woman to remain alive brings ridicule and disdain on the entire family. In such circumstances, mere love for a daughter or sister dwindles into insignificance; she must be killed.

Thus, after an Egyptian father strangled his unmarried but pregnant daughter, cut her corpse into eight parts, and threw those down the toilet, he explained his reasons: "Shame kept following me [before the murder] wherever I went. The village's people had no mercy on me. They were making jokes and mocking me. I couldn't bear it and decided to put an end to this."

The positive form of honor (*sharaf* in Arabic) involves efforts to enhance the family's status by taking steps to win it praise and renown; and nothing can win a family as much glory as its willing sacrifice of a family member for a noble cause. Thanks to PA propaganda, suicide bombing has become a highly honored act. Thus, the Tel Aviv bomber's father crowed about his son, "He has become a hero! Tell me, what more could a father ask?"

Combined, the monstrous social environment created by the PA and the families' preoccupation with social status goes far to explain why Palestinians glory in the destruction of their youth.

(15 August 2001)

ARAFAT'S SUICIDE FACTORY

In declaring his own war on terrorism in December 2001, Israel's Prime Minister Ariel Sharon made a surprising claim. He said that Yasir Arafat, the Palestinian leader, "is responsible for everything that is happening here," a reference to the onslaught of four suicide operations that had just left twenty-six Israelis dead and some 200 wounded.

To which one might reasonably ask: Why blame Arafat? No one blames President Bush for the catastrophe on September 11 or other politicians for the terrorism that occurs on their watch. Why should it be different with Arafat? Isn't Sharon unfair?

Let's look at the evidence.

Every inquiry into Palestinian suicide attacks, and especially Nasra Hassan's remarkable report in a November 2001 issue of the *New Yorker*, finds that these do not just happen spontaneously but result from a large and sophisticated infrastructure.

This infrastructure exists for one reason: to make normal men want to die. Because Islamic law prohibits suicide, a suicidal person cannot be recruited to go on a mission. Rather, it is (perversely) necessary to dispatch only those who are not suicidal.

Islamic Jihad, which along with Hamas trains the suicide killers, explains: "We do not take depressed people. If there were a one-in-a-thousand chance that a person was suicidal, we would not allow him to martyr himself. In order to be a martyr bomber, you have to want to live." The same strange logic applies for Hamas, which rejects anyone "who commits suicide because he hates the world."

Convincing healthy individuals to blow themselves up is obviously not easy, but requires ideas and institutions. The process begins with the Palestinian Authority inculcating two things into its population, starting with the children: a hatred of Jews and a love of death. School curricula, camp activities, TV programming, and religious indoctrination all portray Israelis in a Nazi-style way, as subhuman being worthy of killing; and then deprecate the instinct for self-preservation, telling impressionable young people that sacrificing their lives is the most noble of all goals.

The system works: Hassan reports that "hordes of young men" clamor to be sent to their own obliteration. Hamas and Islamic Jihad have established a process of selection based in the mosques, where "a notably zealous youth" ready for martyrdom gets noted by clerics who recommend him for selection.

Those who make the cut enter a protracted, highly supervised, and disciplined regimen of spiritual studies and military-like training. These adepts are taught to see suicide operations as a way to "open the door to Paradise" for themselves and their families. "I love martyrdom," says one such "living martyr."

Just before setting off on an attack, the men engage in exquisitely pious preparations (ablutions, clean clothing, a communal prayer service). Their deaths are celebrated by Hamas or Islamic Jihad by orchestrating a festive funeral celebration ("as if it were a wedding," Hassan observes) and distributing video cassettes with a statement from beyond the grave. The sponsoring organizations then make sure that the family receives both social kudos and financial rewards.

These facts tell us three things: Militant Islamic suicide killers are not born; they are manufactured. Like the four simultaneous suicide hijackings on September 11, the four nearly simultaneous suicide attacks in Israel in December 2001 resulted from long-term planning by sophisticated organizations. They cannot operate clandes-tinely, but require the permission of a ruling authority, either the Taliban or the PA.

All of which leads to the conclusion that Sharon was right to hold Arafat responsible for the onslaught of suicide attacks on Israelis.

(9 December 2001)

5

IN THE WEST

HOW MANY AMERICAN MUSLIMS?

How many Muslims live in the United States?

For years, basically, no one had any idea. By law, the U.S. Census cannot ask questions about religion. There are also plenty of other difficulties in coming up with a number, starting with the problem of defining who is a Muslim: Does one include non-standard believers like Louis Farrakhan and the Druze?

Uncertainty has generated some wildly divergent numbers. A large 1990 demographic survey counted 1.3 million Muslims. In 1998, a Pakistani newspaper put the number at 12 million. Even the usually authoritative *Yearbook of American and Canadian Churches* found 527,000 American Muslims in 1996 and six times as many (3.3 million) in 1998.

Needing some kind of consensus figure, Muslim organizations came up with a self-acknowledged "guestimation" of 6 million, which this year they decided to raise to 7 million. These numbers were so widely adopted (even by this writer) that they acquired a sheen of authority. But repetition does not transform a guess into a fact. The problem is a generic one; religious organizations commonly inflate their membership to enhance their voice in the public square.

Fortunately, the smog of imprecision finally lifted in October 2001, with the appearance of two authoritative studies by highly regarded demographers. (Each study relied on respondents' religious self-identification.) Interestingly, they agreed on a very similar number, one much smaller than the old guestimate.

The American Religious Identification Survey 2001 carried out by the Graduate Center of the City University of New York polled more than 50,000 people and found the total American Muslim population to be 1.8 million. Meanwhile, the University of Chicago's Tom Smith reviewed prior national surveys and (in a study sponsored by the American Jewish Committee) found that the best estimate puts the Muslim population in 2000 at 1,886,000. (With a nod toward figures supplied by Islamic organizations, he allowed that this number could be as high as 2,814,000 Muslims.)

In other words, two authoritative studies carried out by scholars found that American Muslims number under 2 million—less than a third of the hitherto-consensus number.*

To this, the militant Islamic groups in Washington—widely but erroneously seen as representative of American Muslims—responded with predictable hyperbole. The Council on American-Islamic Relations (CAIR) furiously accused Smith's report of working "to block Muslim political participation." The American Muslim Council (AMC) charged Smith with nothing less than trying to "deny the existence of 41/2 million American Muslims" and blamed him for "tearing at the very heart of America."

The AMC also amusingly claimed that its own estimate of "more than 7 million" Muslims came from the 2000 Census figures—erroneously thinking that the census asks about religion. Oh, and that's the same AMC which in 1992 pressured a researcher named Fareed Nu'man to find 6 million Muslims in the country; Nu'man later testified that he counted just 3 million and was fired by the AMC when he refused to inflate his number above 5 million.

Why does the militant Islamic lobby insist on the 6-7 million figures? Because a larger number, even if phony, offers it enhanced access and clout. Convincing the Republican Party that Muslims number 8 million, for example, led to urgent calls from its chairman for "meeting with [Muslim] leaders," something which becomes less of a priority when the Muslim population turns out to be much smaller.

Knowing the real number of Muslims will, most immediately, likely impede two militant Islamic efforts now underway: one (pushed by the *Minaret* magazine) to get Americans to acknowledge that their own misdeeds partially caused the atrocities of September 11; and

---

The World Almanac and Book of Facts subsequently took these calculations into account: its 1997 edition (p. 644) says there are 5.1 million Muslims in the United States; the 2003 edition (p. 635) found only 2.8 million.

another (led by CAIR) to halt the U.S. military campaign in Afghanistan. The longer-range implications will be yet more significant.]

(29 October 2001)

It Matters What Kind of Islam Prevails

American Muslims—immigrants and native-born converts alike —look at the United States in one of two predominant ways.

Members of one group, the moderates, have no problem being simultaneously patriotic Americans and committed Muslims. Symbolic of this positive outlook on the United States, the Islamic Supreme Council of America displays an American flag on the home page of its website.

These moderates find that the West's norms—neighborly relations, diligence on the job, honesty—are essentially what Islam teaches. Conversely, they present Islam as the fulfillment of American values and see Muslims as a very positive force to improve America. As one moderate put it, to be a good Muslim, you have to be a good American and vice versa. Or, as the American black leader W. Deen Mohammed put it, "Islam can offer something to the West, rather than represent a threat to the West." Moderates accept that the United States will never become a Muslim country and are reconciled to living within a non-Islamic framework; they call for Muslims to immerse themselves in public life to make themselves both useful and influential.

In contrast, Islamists aspire to make the United States a Muslim country, perhaps along the Iranian or Sudanese models. Believing Islamic civilization superior to anything American, they promote Islam as the solution to all of the country's ills. In the words of their leading theorist, Ismail Al-Faruqi, "Nothing could be greater than this youthful, vigorous and rich continent [of North America] turning away from its past evil and marching forward under the banner of Allahu Akbar [God is great]." Or, in the words of a teacher at the Al-Ghazly Islamic School in Jersey City, New Jersey, "Our short-term goal is to introduce Islam. In the long term, we must save American society. Allah will ask why I did not speak about Islam, because this piece of land is Allah's property."

Some Islamists even talk about overthrowing the U.S. government and replacing it with an Islamic one. Although it sounds bizarre, this attitude attracts serious and widespread support among Muslims, some of whom debate whether peaceful means are sufficient or whether violence is a necessary option. (Omar Abdel Rahman, the blind sheikh who inspired the 1993 World Trade Center bombing, clearly belongs among those who believe violence is necessary.)

In short, moderates are delighted to live in a democratic country where the rule of law prevails, whereas Islamists wish to import the customs of the Middle East and South Asia. If one group accepts the concept of an Americanized Islam as no less valid than an Egyptian or Pakistani Islam, the other finds very little attractive in American life.

Which of these two elements prevails has great significant for the United States and for the world of Islam. If the great majority of American Muslims adopt a moderate approach, the Muslim community should fit well into the fabric of American life. There is also the added benefit that the well-educated, affluent, and ambitious community of American Muslims will spread their version of a modern and tolerant Islam to the Middle East, South Asia, and elsewhere.

But if the Islamists are numerous and (as today) run most of the Muslim institutions in the United States, the consequences could be bitter indeed. Take the March 1996 incident when Mahmoud Abdul-Rauf, a black twenty-seven-year-old convert Islam then playing in the National Basketball Association, decided to sit down as the American national anthem was played before each game. As a Muslim, he said, he could not pay such respect to the American flag, which he considered a "symbol of oppression, of tyranny." The disaffection of this wealthy and successful Muslim has dire implications if it becomes widespread.

There's a role here for everyone—Muslim, non-Muslim, business executive, Hollywood producer, journalist, teacher, religious leader —to explain what it means to be an American and to argue against militant Islam. One might think it obvious that life in this country is immeasurably preferable to that in Iran or Sudan, but that's clearly not obvious to everyone. Those of us who understand this simple truth must explain it to our fellow citizens.

WHY I AM NOT A MUSLIM

In March 1989, shortly after Ayatollah Khomeini issued his decree sentencing Salman Rushdie to death for his novel *The Satanic Verses*, London's *Observer* newspaper published an anonymous letter from Pakistan. In it, the writer, a Muslim who did not give his name, stated that "Salman Rushdie speaks for me." He then explained:

> mine is a voice that has not yet found expression in newspaper columns. It is the voice of those who are born Muslims but wish to recant in adulthood, yet are not permitted to on pain of death.
>
> Someone who does not live in an Islamic society cannot imagine the sanctions, both self-imposed and external, that militate against expressing religious disbelief. "I don't believe in God" is an impossible public utterance even among family and friends .... So we hold our tongues, those of us who doubt.

"Ibn Warraq," the pseudonym of a lapsed Muslim, has decided no longer to hold his tongue. Identified only as a man who grew up in a country now called an Islamic republic, presently living and teaching in Ohio, the Khomeini decree so outraged him that he wrote *Why I Am Not a Muslim* (Amherst, N.Y.: Prometheus, 1995), a book that surpasses *The Satanic Verses* in terms of sacrilege. Where Rushdie offered elusive critique in an airy tale of magical realism, Ibn Warraq brings a scholarly sledgehammer to the task of demolishing Islam. Writing a polemic against Islam, especially for an author of Muslim birth, is an act so incendiary that he must write under a pseudonym; not to do so could be an act of suicide.

And what does Ibn Warraq have to show for this act of unheard-of defiance? A well-researched and quite brilliant, if somewhat disorganized, indictment of one of the world's great religions. While the author disclaims any pretence to originality, he has read widely enough to write an essay that offers a startlingly novel rendering of the faith he left.

To begin with, Ibn Warraq draws on current Western scholarship to make the astonishing claim that Muhammad never existed, or if he did, he had nothing to do with the Koran. Rather, that holy book was fabricated a century or two later in Palestine, then "projected back onto an invented Arabian point of origin." If the Koran is a fraud, it's not surprising to learn that the author finds little authentic in other parts of the Islamic tradition. For example, he dispatches "the whole of Islamic law" as "a fantastic creation founded on forgeries and pious fictions." The entirety of Islam, in short, he portrays as a concoction of lies.

Having thus dispensed with religion, Ibn Warraq takes up history and culture. Turning political correctness exactly on its head, he condemns the early Islamic conquests and condones European colonialism. "Bowing toward Arabia five times a day," he writes, referring to the Islamic prayer toward Mecca, "must surely be the ultimate symbol of...cultural imperialism" In contrast, European rule, "with all its shortcomings, ultimately benefited the ruled as much as the rulers. Despite certain infamous incidents, the European powers conducted themselves, on the whole, very humanely."

To the conventional argument that the achievements of Islamic civilization in the medieval period shows the greatness of Islam, Ibn Warraq revives the Victorian argument that Islamic civilization came into existence not because of the Koran and Islamic law but despite it. The stimulus in science and the arts came from outside the Muslim world; where Islam reigned, these accomplishments took place only where the dead hand of Islamic authority could be avoided. Crediting Islam for the medieval cultural glories, he believes, would be like crediting the Inquisition for Galileo's discoveries.

Turning to the present, Ibn Warraq argues that Muslims have experienced great travails trying to modernize because Islam stands foursquare in their way. Its regressive orientation makes change difficult: "All innovations are discouraged in Islam—every problem is seen as a religious problem rather than a social or economic one." This religion would seem to have nothing functional to offer. "Islam, in particular political Islam, has totally failed to cope with the modern world and all its attendant problems-social, economic, and philosophical." Nor does the author hold out hope for improvement. Take the matter of protecting individuals from the state: "The major obstacle in Islam to any move toward international human rights is God, or to put it more precisely...the reverence for the sources, the Koran and the Sunna."

In a chapter of particular delicacy, given that he himself is a Muslim living in the West, Ibn Warraq discusses Muslim emigration to Europe and North America. He worries about the importation of Islamic ways and advises the British not to make concessions to immigrant demands but to stick firmly by their traditional principles.

"Unless great vigilance is exercised, we are all likely to find British society greatly impoverished morally" by Muslim influence. At the same time, as befits a liberal and Western-oriented Muslim, Ibn Warraq argues that the key dividing line is one of personal philosophy and not (as Samuel Huntington would have it) religious adherence. "[T]he final battle will not necessarily be between Islam and the West, but between those who value freedom and those who do not." This argument in fact offers hope, implying as it does that peoples of divergent faiths can find common ground.

As a whole, Ibn Warraq's assessment of Islam is exceptionally severe: the religion is based on deception; it succeeded through aggression and intimidation; it holds back progress; and it is a "form of totalitarianism." Surveying nearly fourteen centuries of history, he concludes, "the effects of the teachings of the Koran have been a disaster for human reason and social, intellectual, and moral progress."

As if this were not enough, Ibn Warraq tops off his blasphemy with an assault on what he calls "monotheistic arrogance" and even religion as such. He asks some interesting questions, the sort that we in the West seem not to ask each other any more. "If there is a natural evolution from polytheism to monotheism, then is there not a natural development from monotheism to atheism?" Instead of God appearing in obscure places and murky circumstances, "Why can He not reveal Himself to the masses in a football stadium during the final of the World Cup"? In 1917, rather than a miracle in Fatima, Portugal, why did He not end the carnage on the Western Front?

This discussion points out just how much these issues are no longer discussed in mainstream American intellectual life. Believers and atheists go their separate ways, criticizing the other without engaging in debate. For this reason, many of Ibn Warraq's anti-religious statements have a surprisingly fresh quality.

It is hard for a non-Muslim fully to appreciate the offense Ibn Warraq has committed, for his book of deep protest and astonishing provocation goes beyond anything imaginable in our rough-and-tumble culture. We have no pieties remotely comparable to Islam's. In the religious realm, for example, Joseph Heller turned several Biblical stories into pornographic fare in his 1984 novel *God Knows*, and no one even noticed. For his portrayal of Jesus' sexual longings in the 1988 film *The Last Temptation of Christ*, Martin Scorsese faced a few pickets but certainly no threats to his life. Rushdie himself has recently raised hackles in India by making fun of Bal Thackeray, a fundamentalist Hindu leader—yet no threats have come from that quarter. In the political arena, Charles Murray and Dinesh D'Souza published books on the very most delicate American topic, the issue of differing racial abilities, and neither had to go into hiding as a result.

In contrast, blasphemy against Islam leads to murder—and not just threats against Salman Rushdie or in places like Egypt and Bangladesh. At least one such execution has taken place on American soil. Rashad Khalifa, an Egyptian biochemist living in Tucson, Arizona, analyzed the Koran by computer and concluded from some rather complex numerology that the final two verses of the ninth chapter do not belong in the holy book. This insight eventually prompted him to declare himself a prophet, a very serious offense in Islam (which holds Muhammad to be the last of the prophets). Some months later, on January 31, 1990, Muslims angered by his teachings stabbed Khalifa to death. The incident sent a clear and chilling message: even in the United States, deviancy leads to death.

Writers deemed unfriendly to Islam are murdered all the time. Dozens of journalists have lost their lives in Algeria as well as prominent writers in Egypt and Turkey. Taslima Nasrin had to flee her native Bangladesh for this reason. A terrible silence has descended on the Muslim world, so that a book of this sort can only be published in the West.

In this context, Ibn Warraq's claim of the right to disagree with Islamic tenets is a shock. And all the more so when he claims even the Westerner's right to do so disrespectfully! "This book is first and foremost an assertion of my right to criticize everything and anything in Islam-even to blaspheme, to make errors, to satirize, and mock." *Why I Am Not a Muslim* does have a mocking quality, to be sure, but it is also a serious and thought-provoking book. It calls not for a wall of silence, much less a Rushdie-like fatwa on the author's life, but for an equally compelling response from a believing Muslim.

(22 January 1996)

AN AMERICAN RUSHDIE?

In an eerie echo of the Rushdie affair, an Islamist leader living in the Middle East has called for the death of a freethinking Muslim living in Bethesda, Maryland in response to a book he has written.

Khalid Durán, sixty-one, is an accomplished scholar and original thinker. Born of a Spanish mother and a Moroccan father, he speaks five languages and was educated in Spain, Germany, Bosnia, and Pakistan. A German citizen, he has lived in the United States since 1986, teaching and writing mostly about Islam at leading universities and think tanks. Durán has published six books and is an important analyst of Islam and politics, an authority on the current wave of militant Islam and an expert with an excellent record of predictions.

Durán is also an activist on behalf of causes like the revival of Afghan culture and the promotion of dialogue between the three major monotheistic religions ("trialogue"). He heads the IbnKhaldun Society, a cultural association of moderate Muslims opposed to militant Islam. His is a rare and welcome voice of Muslim liberalism at a time when radicals dominate the mosques, the media, and the counsels of state.

Given this background, it was natural that when the American Jewish Committee (AJC) sponsored a book called *Children of Abraham: An Introduction to Islam for Jews* (New York, 2001), it sought Durán out to write the volume, and that he accomplished this task with distinction. Fourteen scholars of Islam approved the manuscript prior to publication; in addition, it won glowing reviews from such authoritative figures as Cardinal William Keeler of Baltimore, the eminent church historian Martin Marty, and Prince Hassan of Jordan.

Then, just as the book was being readied for release in spring 2001, the Council on American-Islamic Relations (CAIR) weighed in. This fringe militant Islamic organization promotes a Khomeini-like agenda but has the smarts to hide its extremism. It issued two press releases in which it insulted Durán personally and demanded that *Children of Abraham* be withheld until a group of CAIR-appointed academics review the book to correct what it assumed (without having read the manuscript) would be "stereotypical or inaccurate content."

CAIR being part of an international network of Islamists, like-minded publications in the United States, Europe, and the Middle East quickly picked up its message. With the retelling. naturally, the story grew. Thus, Cairo's *Al-Wafd* announced that Durán's book "spreads anti-Muslim propaganda" through its "distortions of Islamic concepts."

The campaign of vilification culminated in early June 2001, when a weekly in Jordan reported that 'Abd al-Mun'im Abu Zant, one of that country's most powerful militant Islamic leaders, had declared that Durán "should be regarded as an apostate" and on this basis called for an Islamic ruling that "religiously condones Durán's death."

Days later, Durán's car was broken into, with a dead squirrel and excrement thrown inside. And CAIR, far from apologizing for the evil results of its handiwork, had the gall to accuse the AJC of fabricating the death edict as a "cheap publicity stunt to boost book sales."

Abu Zant was applying the "Rushdie rules" that Ayatollah Khomeini had established back in 1989, whereby anyone critical of Islam or militant Islam is liable to be fined, jailed, or perhaps threatened with death. Already applied in most Muslim countries and many Western ones (Canada, Holland, France, Israel), these rules now threaten to be extended to the United States.

Actually, they already have been applied: in 1990, not long after the Council of Religious Scholars in Mecca called Rashad Khalifa an infidel, thereby marking him as someone to be eliminated, this Egyptian immigrant living in Tucson, Arizona, was murdered by members of an extremist Islamic group. CAIR, it bears noting, has never denounced that assassination.

The threat against Durán requires that all of us, whatever our politics or religions, stand together as one and with a loud, clear voice condemn Abu Zant's threat and reaffirm the sanctity of free speech. In this case, if Americans truly do join forces, they can stop those who would instill the Middle East's violent religious habits in the United States.

Khalid Durán has noted how, given that "some two dozen" of his good friends have been killed in recent decades, his even being alive is a miracle. His security is now a trust that all Americans must safeguard.

(4 July 2001)

CRISIS OF ILLEGAL IMMIGRATION

Something unprecedented and possibly highly significant happened in August 2001, when the Australian government resorted to military force to keep out 434 would-be refugees, nearly all of them from Afghanistan, along with some Pakistanis and Sri Lankans.

The story began on August 24, when the 434 left western Indonesia aboard the Palapa 1, an unseaworthy wooden ferry that was supposed to land them illegally in Australia, making them eligible for asylum. But a day later, while still close to Indonesia, the ferry began to sink and sent out an alarm. The Norwegian freighter *Tampa*, one of the largest roll-on roll-off vessels in the world, replied to its emergency appeal and on August 26 rescued the passengers and crew of four even as the ferry was actually breaking apart.

The *Tampa* then set sail for the closest port, in Indonesia. A few hours into the trip, however, a delegation of Afghans said to be acting in an "aggressive and highly excited manner," threatened the *Tampa*'s tiny twenty-seven-man crew if the ship did not reverse course and take them to Australia. Fearful, the captain complied with their demands. When the Australians realized the *Tampa* was coming their way on August 27, Prime Minister John Howard forbade it from entering the country's territory, saying that Australia cannot be seen "as a country of easy destination." The captain obeyed, stopping just nine kilometers outside Australian waters.

But two days later, citing health problems among the Afghans, he moved the *Tampa* into Australian waters, heading toward land. In response, saying he must "draw a line on what is increasingly becoming an uncontrollable number of illegal arrivals" Howard sent crack Australian troops to board the ship and prevent it from reaching land.

An impasse followed as the giant 44,000-ton ship loomed over a tiny Australian island. What to do with its passengers turned into a minor international crisis until, on August 31, New Zealand announced a willingness to take 150 of the asylum seekers and Nauru (a tiny, impoverished island state in the Pacific Ocean) accepted the remainder in return for an infusion of cold Australian cash. Pending the decision of an Australian court, this strange outcome resolved the issue.

The *Tampa* episode marks the first time in recent history that a Western government used military force to prevent a group of peoples at its doorstep from requesting asylum.

Predictably, the government's action was massively criticized by foreign leaders ("destroying its reputation"), international agencies ("unacceptable"), and excoriated by elite opinion in Australia, both media ("farcical") and academic ("we are heading in the direction of a pariah state"). Just as predictably, polls showed that a resounding 78 percent of Australians backed Howard's "resolve," and his party gained five percentage points in popularity. This broad support reflected two public worries.

The first is a sizable growth of illegal immigration, mostly of Afghans, Iraqis, and Iranians. The eleven days before the *Tampa*'s arrival saw more than 1,500 illegals landing in Australia on small boats, and reports were circulating of another 5,000 would-be immigrants readying to set sail from Indonesia. Many Australians felt under siege.

Second, recent police reports of Lebanese men gang-raping non-Muslim women specifically to humiliate them (one victim quoted her attacker, "You deserve it because you're an Australian") aroused anger. According to Agence France-Presse, "much of the support for the government stand was driven by anti-Muslim sentiment rather than anti-boatpeople attitudes."

A similar divergence of views is emerging throughout the West (most notably, in Austria), with the establishment basically welcoming nearly anyone knocking at the door while the population deeply resents the influx of peoples with alien customs and outlooks.

Howard's action in calling out the military to close his country's borders to illegal immigrants may have been a fluke. More likely, however, it has set a precedent that will be oft imitated as uncontrolled immigration becomes an ever-more central issue for Western societies. Four main factors are fueling this trend.

- The growing disparity between the terrible conditions in so many failed states and the good life in the West (which includes such countries as Japan, Singapore, and Israel).

- An increasing awareness by people in failed states about the West.

- The declining costs of transportation from failed states to the West.

- The West's favorable treatment of those who reach its territories, even if illegally.

Watch to see whether the "Howard solution" is a one-time eccentricity or the start of a trend. I bet on the latter.

(5 September 2001)

SOMETHING ROTTEN IN DENMARK?

with Lars Hedegaard

A Muslim group in Denmark announced in August 2002 ago that a $30,000 bounty would be paid for the murder of several prominent Danish Jews, a threat that garnered wide international notice. Less well known is that this is just one problem associated with Denmark's approximately 200,000 Muslim immigrants. The key issue is that many of them show little desire to fit into their adopted country.

For years, Danes lauded multiculturalism and insisted they had no problem with Muslim customs —until one day they found that they did. Some major issues:

- *Living on the dole*: Third-world immigrants—most of them Muslims from countries such as Turkey, Somalia, Pakistan, Lebanon and Iraq—constitute 5 percent of the population but consume upwards of 40 percent of the welfare spending.

- *Engaging in crime*: Muslims are only 4 percent of Denmark's 5.4 million people but make up a majority of the country's convicted rapists, an especially combustible issue given that practically all the female victims are non-Muslim. Similar, if lesser, disproportions are found in other crimes.

- *Self-imposed isolation*: Over time, as Muslim immigrants increase in numbers, they wish less to mix with the indigenous population. A recent survey finds that only 5 percent of young Muslim immigrants would readily marry a Dane.

- *Importing unacceptable customs*: Forced marriages—promising a newborn daughter in Denmark to a male cousin in the home country, then compelling her to marry him, sometimes on pain of death—is one problem. Another is threats to kill Muslims who convert out of Islam. One Kurdish convert to Christianity, who went public to explain why she had changed religion, felt the need to hide her face and conceal her identity, fearing for her life.

- *Fomenting anti-Semitism*: Muslim violence threatens Denmark's approximately 6,000 Jews, who increasingly depend on police protection. Jewish parents were told by one school principal that she could not guarantee their children's safety and were advised to attend another institution. Anti-Israel marches have turned into anti-Jewish riots. One organization, Hizb-ut-Tahrir, openly calls on Muslims to "kill all Jews ... wherever you find them."

- *Seeking Islamic law*: Muslim leaders openly declare their goal of introducing Islamic law once Denmark's Muslim population grows large enough—a not-that-remote prospect. If present trends persist, one sociologist estimates, every third inhabitant of Denmark in forty years will be Muslim.

Other Europeans (such as the late Pim Fortuyn in Holland) have also grown alarmed about these issues, but Danes were the first to make them the basis for a change in government. In a momentous election in November 2001, a center-right coalition came to power that—for the first time since 1929—excluded the socialists. The right broke its seventy-two-year losing streak and won a solid parliamentary majority by promising to handle immigration issues, the electorate's first concern, differently from the socialists.

The next nine months did witness some fine-tuning of procedures: Immigrants now must live seven years in Denmark (rather than three years) to become permanent residents. Most non-refugees no longer can collect welfare checks immediately on entering the country. No one can bring into the country an intended spouse under the age of twenty-four. And the state prosecutor is considering a ban on Hizb-ut-Tahrir for its death threats against Jews.

These minor adjustments prompted howls internationally—with European and U.N. reports condemning Denmark for racism and "Islamophobia," the *Washington Post* reporting that Muslim immigrants "face habitual discrimination," and a London *Guardian* headline announcing that "Copenhagen Flirts with Fascism."

In reality, however, the new government has barely addressed the existing problems. Nor did it prevent new ones, such as the death threats against Jews or a recent Islamic edict calling on Muslims to drive Danes out of the Nørrebro quarter of Copenhagen.

The authorities remain indulgent. The military mulls permitting Muslim soldiers in Denmark's volunteer International Brigade to opt out of actions they don't agree with—a privilege granted to members of no other faith. Mohammed Omar Bakri, the self-proclaimed

London-based "eyes, ears and mouth" of Osama bin Laden, won permission to set up a Danish branch of his organization, Al-Muhajiroun.

Contrary to media reports, the real news from Denmark is not a flirtation with fascism but a government getting mired in inertia. Leaders elected specifically to deal with a set of problems has made minimal headway. Their reluctance has potentially profound implications for the West as a whole.

(27 August 2002)

6

PRESENTING AND REPRESENTING ISLAM IN AMERICA

THINK LIKE A MUSLIM

Could it be that an important textbook is proselytizing American twelve-year-olds to convert to Islam?

The book in question is *Across the Centuries* (Boston: Houghton Mifflin, second edition, 1999), a 558-page history that covers the millennium and a half between the fall of Rome and the French Revolution. In the multicultural spirit, about half of its eight sections are devoted to the West, and the other four deal with Islam, Africa, Asian empires, and pre-Columbian America.

Across the Centuries is a handsome artifact, well written, packed with original graphics, and generally achieving the publisher's goal that "students learn best when they are fascinated by what they are learning."

At the same time, there is much in it one can argue with, such as its idiosyncratic coverage of subjects (sub-Saharan Africa gets four times more space than India?). But the really serious problem concerns the covert propagation of Islam, which takes four forms:

- *Apologetics*: Everything Islamic is praised; every problem is swept under the rug. Students learn about Islam's "great cultural flowering," but nothing about the later centuries of stasis and decline. They read repeatedly about the Muslims' broadmindedness (they "were extremely tolerant of those they conquered") but not a word about their violence (such as the massacres carried out by Muhammad's troops against the Jews of Banu Qurayza).

- *Distortion*: Jihad, which means "sacred war," turns into a struggle mainly "to do one's best to resist temptation and overcome evil." Islam gives women "clear rights" not available in some other societies, such as the right to an education. This ignores the self-evident fact that Muslim women enjoy fewer rights than perhaps any other in the world. (*Across the Centuries* implicitly acknowledges this reality by blaming "oppressive local traditions" for their circumstances.)

- *Identification as Muslims*: Homework assignments repeatedly involve mock-Muslim exercises. "Form small groups of students to build a miniature mosque." Or: "You leave your home in Alexandria for the pilgrimage to Mecca.... write a letter describing your route, the landscapes and peoples you see as you travel and any incidents that happen along the way. Describe what you see in Mecca." And then there is this shocker: "Assume you are a Muslim soldier on your way to conquer Syria in the year A.D. 635. Write three journal entries that reveal your thoughts about Islam, fighting in battle, or life in the desert."

- *Piety*: The textbook endorses key articles of Islamic faith. It informs students as a historical fact that Ramadan is holy "because in this month Muhammad received his first message from Allah." It asserts that "the very first word the angel Gabriel spoke to Muhammad was 'Recite.'" It explains that Arabic lettering "was used to write down God's words as they had been given to Muhammad." And it declares that the architecture of a mosque in Spain allows Muslims "to feel Allah's invisible presence." Similarly, the founder of Islam is called "the prophet Muhammad," implying acceptance of his mission. (School textbooks scrupulously avoid the term Jesus Christ in favor of Jesus of Nazareth.)

Learning about Islam is a wonderful thing; I personally have spent more than thirty years studying this rich subject. But students, especially in public schools, should approach Islam in a critical fashion —learning the bad as well as the good, the archaic as well as the modern. They should approach it from the outside, not as believers, precisely as they do with every other religion.

Some parents have woken up to the textbook's problems. Jennifer Schroeder of San Luis Obispo, California, publicly protested its "distinct bias toward Islam." But when she tried to remove her son Eric from the classroom using this book, the school refused her permission and she filed suit in protest a few weeks ago (with help from the Pacific Justice Institute).

Across the Centuries involves a larger issue as well—the privileging of Islam in the United States. Is Islam to be treated like every other religion or does it enjoy a special status? The stakes go well beyond seventh-grade textbooks.*

(11 February 2002)

"BECOME A MUSLIM WARRIOR"

"Become a Muslim warrior during the crusades or during an ancient jihad." Thus read the instructions for seventh graders in *Islam: A Simulation of Islamic History and Culture, 610-1100* (Carlsbad, CA: Interaction Publishers, Inc., undated), a three-week curriculum. In classrooms across the United States, students who follow its directions find themselves fighting mock battles of jihad against "Christian crusaders" and other assorted "infidels." Upon gaining victory, our mock-Muslim warriors "Praise Allah."

Is this a legal activity in American public schools? Interaction says it merely urges students to "respect Islamic culture" through identification with Islam. But the Thomas More Law Center, a public-interest law firm based in Michigan, disagrees and last week filed a federal lawsuit to prohibit one school district, in Byron, California, from further using the Interaction materials on Islam.

The Interaction unit contains many other controversial elements. It has students adopt a Muslim name ("Abdallah," "Karima," etc.). It has them wear Islamic clothing: for girls this means a long-sleeved dress and the head covered by a scarf. Students unwilling to wear Islamic clothes must sit mutely in the back of the class, seemingly punished for remaining Westerners.

Interaction calls for many Islamic activities: taking off shoes, washing hands, sitting on prayer rugs, and practicing Arabic calligraphy. Students study the Koran, recite from it, design a title page for it, and write verses of it on a banner. They act out Islam's Five Pillars of Faith, including giving *zakat* (Islamic alms) and going on the pilgrimage to Mecca. They also build a replica of the "sacred Kaaba" in Mecca or another holy building.

---

*Houghton Mifflin responded the day after this article was first published with a press release attacking me by name and defending *Across the Centuries*, then softened this press release. For the original press release, see http://www.danielpipes.org/118.php; for the later, softened version, see http://www.hmco.com/news/release_021202.html.

It goes on. Seventh graders adopt the speech of pious believers, greeting each other with "assalam aleikoom, fellow Muslims" and using phrases such as "God willing" and "Allah has power over all things." They pronounce the militant Islamic war-cry, *Allahu akbar* ("God is great.") They must even adopt Muslim mannerisms: "Try a typical Muslim gesture where the right hand moves solemnly...across the heart to express sincerity."

In the same pious spirit, the curriculum presents matters of Islamic faith as historical fact. The Kaaba, "originally built by Adam," it announces, "was later rebuilt by Abraham and his son Ismail." Really? That is Islamic belief, not verifiable history. In the year 610, Interaction goes on, "while Prophet Muhammad meditated in a cave ...the angel Gabriel visited him" and revealed to him God's Message" (yes, that's Message with a capital "M.") The curriculum sometimes lapses into referring to "we" Muslims and even prompts students to ask if they should "worship Prophet Muhammad, God, or both."

The Thomas More Law Center is absolutely correct: This simulation blatantly contradicts Supreme Court rulings which permit public schools to teach about religion on condition that they do not promote it. Interaction openly promotes the Islamic faith, contrary to what a public school should do. As Richard Thompson of the center notes, the Byron school district "crossed way over the constitutional line when it coerced impressionable 12-year-olds to engage in particular religious rituals and worship, simulated or not."

Islam: A Simulation serves as a recruitment tool for Islam; having children adopt a Muslim persona over several weeks amounts to an invitation to them to convert to Islam. (One can't but wonder: did John Walker Lindh take this course?) The educational establishment permits this infraction due to an impulse to privilege non-Western cultures over Western ones. It never, for example, would permit Christianity to be promoted in like fashion ("Become a Christian warrior during the crusades," for example.)

Militant Islamic lobbying groups want Islam taught as the true religion, not as an academic subject. They take advantage of this indulgence, exerting pressure on school systems and on textbook writers. Not surprisingly, Interaction Publishers thanks two militant Islamic organizations by name (the Islamic Education and Information Center and the Council on Islamic Education) for their "many suggestions."

Americans and other Westerners face a choice: They can insist that Islam, like other religions, be taught in schools objectively. Or, as is increasingly the case, they can permit true believers to design instruction materials about Islam that serve as a mechanism for proselytizing. The answer will substantially affect the future course of militant Islam in the West.

(3 July 2002)

PBS, Recruiting for Islam

What would be the best way to convert lots of Americans to Islam?

Forget print, go to film. Put together a handsome documentary with an original musical score that presents Islam's prophet Muhammad in the most glowing manner, indeed, as a model of perfection. Round up Muslim and non-Muslim enthusiasts to endorse the nobility and truth of his message. Splice in vignettes of winsome American Muslims testifying to the justice and beauty of their Islamic faith. Then get the U.S. taxpayer to help pay for it.

Show it at prime time on the most high-minded TV network. Oh, and screen it at least once during the holidays, when anyone out of synch with Christmas might be especially susceptible to another religion's appeal.

This is precisely what the producers of "Muhammad: Legacy of a Prophet" have done. In a documentary the *Washington Post* calls "absorbing,...enjoyable and informative," exotic images of the desert and medieval miniatures mix with scenes of New York City and the American flag. Born- and convert-American Muslims speak affectingly about their personal bond to their prophet.

The Public Broadcasting Service (PBS) premieres this two-hour documentary across the nation on December 18, 2002, then repeats the broadcast in most areas. The film's largest tranche of funding comes from the Corporation for Public Broadcasting, a private, non-profit corporation created by Congress that in fiscal 2002 received $350 million in taxpayers' funds.

The heart of the film consists of nine talking heads competing with each other to praise Muhammad the most extravagantly. Not one of them criticizes him.

Some of their efforts are laughable, as when one commentator denies allegations about Muhammad contracting a marriage of convenience with a rich, older woman named Khadija: "He deeply, deeply loved Khadija." Oh, and his many marriages were "an act of faith, not of lust." How could anyone know this?

Other apologetics are more consequential. What Muhammad did for women, viewers learn, was "amazing"—his condemning female infanticide, giving legal rights to wives, permitting divorce and protecting their inheritance rights. But no commentator is so impolite as to note that however admirable this was in the seventh century, Muslim women today suffer widely from genital mutilation, forced marriages, purdah, illiteracy, sexual apartheid, polygamy, and honor killings.

The film treats religious beliefs—such as Muhammad's "Night Journey," when the Koran says he went to heaven and entered the divine presence—as historical fact. It presents Muslim wars as only defensive and reluctant, which is simply false. All this smacks of a film shown by missionaries.

Move to the present and the political correctness is stifling. Hostility is said to be "hurled" at American Muslims since 9/11—but there's no mention about the prior and vastly greater (foreign) Muslim hostility "hurled" at Americans, killing several thousand. The narrator exaggerates the number of American Muslims, overestimates their rate of growth and wrongly terms them the country's "most diverse" religious community.

But these are details. "Muhammad: Legacy of a Prophet" is an outrage on two main counts.

- PBS has betrayed its viewers by presenting an airbrushed and uncritical documentary of a topic that has both world historical and contemporary significance. Its patronizing film might be fine for an Islamic Sunday school class, but not for a national audience. For example, PBS ignores an ongoing scholarly reassessment of Muhammad's life that disputes every detail – down to the century and region Muhammad lived in—of its film. This is especially odd when contrasted with the 1998 PBS documentary, *From Jesus to Christ*, which focuses almost exclusively on the work of cutting-edge scholars and presents the latest in critical thinking on Jesus.

- The U.S. government should never fund a documentary whose obvious intent is to glorify a religion and proselytize for it. Doing so flies in the face of American tradition and law. On behalf of taxpayers, a public-interest law firm should bring suit against the Corporation for Public Broadcasting, both to address this week's travesty and to win an injunction against any possible repetitions.

(17 December 2002)

HARVARD ♥ JIHAD

Imagine it's June 1942—just a few months after Adolf Hitler declared war on the United States. At Harvard University, a faculty committee has chosen a German-American to give one of three student orations at the festive commencement ceremony. He titles it "American Kampf," purposefully echoing the title of Hitler's book, *Mein Kampf* ("My Struggle") in order to showcase the positive side of "Kampf."

When this title prompts protests, a Harvard dean defends it as a "thoughtful oration" that defines the concept of Kampf as a personal struggle "to promote justice and understanding in ourselves and in our society." The dean promises, "The audience will find his oration, as did all the Harvard judges, a light of hope and reason in a world often darkened by distrust and conflict."

Then the student turns out to be past president of the Harvard German Society, a group with a pro-Nazi taint—but the administration still isn't bothered. Nor is it perturbed that he praised a Nazi front group for its "incredible work" as well as its "professionalism, compassion and dedication to helping people in dire need," then raised money for it.

Far-fetched? Sure. But exactly this scenario unfolded last week at Harvard. Just replace "German," "Nazi," and "Kampf" with "Islamic," "militant Islamic" and "jihad."

Faculty members chose Zayed Yasin, twenty-two and the past president of the Harvard Islamic Society, to deliver a commencement address. He had earlier sung the praises of and raised money for the Holy Land Foundation for Relief and Development, a militant Islamic group since closed down by President Bush.

Yasin titled his talk "American Jihad," echoing Osama bin Laden's jihad against the United States. He declared an intention to convince his audience of 32,000 that "Jihad is not something that should make someone feel uncomfortable."

Hmm. The authoritative *Encyclopaedia of Islam* (second edition.) defines jihad as "military action with the object of the expansion of Islam," and finds that it "has principally an offensive character." The scholar Bat Ye'or explains for non-Muslims through history this has meant "war, dispossession, dhimmitude, slavery and death." That does indeed sound like "something that should make someone feel uncomfortable."

Sadly, this episode is no aberration, but indicative of two important developments.

- *Apologizing for militant Islam*: Hiding jihad's awful legacy is standard operating procedure at Harvard. A professor of Islamic history portrays jihad as "a struggle without arms." The Harvard Islamic Society's faculty adviser defines true jihad as no more fearsome than "to do good in society." All this is part of a pattern of pretending Islam had nothing to do with 9/11.

- *Neutrality in wartime.* Harvard appears neutral in the current war, as Harvard Business School student Pat Collins pointed out in a scathing *Washington Times* op-ed. Take the example of Hamas: While President Bush has called it "one of the deadliest terrorist organizations in the world today," a Harvard spokesman replies "no comment" when asked if it is a terrorist organization and the university has allowed fund-raising on its premises on behalf of Hamas. Even today, militant Islamic groups have full access to university facilities and the right to advertise their activities. In contrast, the Reserve Officers Training Corps (ROTC), a training program for the U.S. armed forces, is the only student group at Harvard to be denied access to university facilities and disallowed from advertising its activities.

Unfortunately, Harvard's stance is typical of nearly all North America universities. Almost every Middle East specialist hides the truth about jihad and (as shown by a chilling report from the American Council of Trustees and Alumni, *Defending Civilization*) almost every campus drips contempt for the U.S. war effort (typical statement: "The best way to begin a war on terrorism might be to look in the mirror").

"You are with us, or you are against us": Harvard and other universities need to look hard into their soul and decide on which side they stand.

(11 June 2002)

AMERICAN MUSLIMS FOR JERUSALEM BEHIND CLOSED DOORS

The 9/11 terror attacks could not have taken place without a sophisticated infrastructure of agents operating inside the United States that gathered information, planned, and then executed the four hijackings. That infrastructure, in turn, could operate thanks in large part to the protection provided by America's militant Islamic lobby.

The militant Islamic lobby impeded law enforcement's ability to devote special attention to Middle Eastern passengers, a procedure that surely would have caught the four suicide teams. The lobby also forestalled the closing down of websites and the expulsion of foreigners associated with terrorist organizations like Osama bin Laden's. Which raises a question: How could a lobby protecting violent extremists acquire such influence? By very carefully covering its tracks—saying one thing in private and another in public.

To see how this duality works, consider the case of American Muslims for Jerusalem. This certainly appears to be a moderate organization. Founded in May 1999 and located near Capitol Hill, AMJ portrays itself as an innocent "association dedicated to providing a Muslim perspective on the issue of Jerusalem" and it movingly appeals for "a Jerusalem that symbolizes religious tolerance and dialogue." AMJ notes "the profound attachment Muslims have to Jerusalem" and reasonably calls for free access by all to the city's religious sites. Only somewhat more assertively does it repeat standard Palestinian rhetoric about the inadmissibility of sovereignty gained through force, the imperative to stop the building of housing for Jews, and the right of return for Palestinian refugees. So tame is AMJ's public stance that it does not repeat the usual Palestinian claim to Jerusalem being the capital of Palestine, much less does it deny Jewish ties to Jerusalem.

Unfortunately, this public moderation hides a totally different private discourse.

At its closed events, AMJ reveals its true colors, purveying precisely the kind of hate that might inspire a suicide hijacker. The pattern was set at AMJ's first major event, a fundraising dinner in November 1999, which one participant has described as "crudely anti-Jewish." Speakers like Nihad Awad and Abdurahman Alamoudi vied with one another in verbally assaulting the State of Israel and American Jews. In particular, they spun an elaborate conspiracy theory about Jewish control of the United States and Zionist brainwashing of American Christians.

Those Christians, AMJ speakers insisted, are now ready to rebel against this alleged Jewish domination—except that they fear going public out of fright of their Jewish "masters." Here Muslims have a crucial role in encouraging Christians to rise up to end their subjugation. Only a united Muslim-Christian front, led by Muslims, can break the supposed Zionist lock on America.

The dinner's keynote speaker, Issa Nakhleh of the Arab Supreme Council for Palestine (and himself a Christian), proposed a specific scheme for achieving this goal. By his (fanciful) calculations, the Israel lobby spends $20 million a year to buy members of Congress and have them impose the "Jewish" message on Christians. Arabs and Muslims can easily do better, Nakhleh suggested, by sending fundraising delegations to Saudi Arabia and the United Arab Emirates. "I am sure you will get $10 million from these two, and Iran will give you $10 million," thereby surpassing the supposed pro-Israel funding. (Never mind that it is illegal to lobby Congress with money that comes from abroad).

The evening's excess of inaccuracy, misunderstanding, conspiracy theorizing, fanaticism, and illegality is all the more noteworthy, because American Muslims for Jerusalem is no fringe outfit but a joint effort sponsored by six of the most powerful American Islamic institutions (the American Muslim Alliance, American Muslim Council, Council on American-Islamic Relations, Islamic Circle of North America, Islamic Society of North America, and the Ministry of Imam W.D. Mohammed), including those most often invited to the White House and cited by the media. AMJ itself has won signal victories lobbying such American corporations as Burger King and Disney.

The covert radicalism of American Muslim organizations has two implications. First, AMJ and its six sponsoring organizations must all be systematically excluded and marginalized. Government and corporate policymakers should not meet with them. The media should not quote them as authorities. Immigration officials should study closely whom they invite from abroad. Tax authorities should scour their books for illegal transactions. Religious leaders should exclude them from ecumenical events.

Second, moderate Muslim Americans need to organize themselves and repudiate organizations like AMJ and its ilk. This task will likely become even more urgent as those organizations' role in easing the way for terrorism is more fully revealed.

(20 September 2001)

CAIR: "MODERATE" FRIENDS OF TERROR

The Washington-based Council on American-Islamic Relations presents itself as just another civil rights group. "We are similar to a Muslim NAACP," says spokesman Ibrahim Hooper. Its public language—about promoting "interest and understanding among the general public with regards to Islam and Muslims in North America" —certainly boosts an image of moderation. That reputation has permitted CAIR to prosper since its founding in 1994, garnering sizeable donations, invitations to the White House, respectful media citations and a serious hearing by corporations.

In reality, CAIR is something quite different.

For starters, it's on the wrong side in the war on terrorism. One indication came in October 1998, when the group demanded the removal of a Los Angeles billboard describing Osama bin Laden as "the sworn enemy," finding this depiction "offensive to Muslims." The same year, CAIR denied bin Laden's responsibility for the twin East African embassy bombings. As Hooper saw it, those explosions resulted from some vague "misunderstandings of both sides." (A New York court, however, blamed bin Laden's side alone for the embassy blasts.) In 2001, CAIR denied his culpability for the September 11 massacre, saying only that "if [note the "if"] Osama bin Laden was behind it, we condemn him by name." (Only in December was CAIR finally embarrassed into acknowledging his role.)

CAIR consistently defends other militant Islamic terrorists too. The conviction of the perpetrators of the 1993 World Trade Center bombing it deemed "a travesty of justice." The conviction of Omar Abdel Rahman, the blind sheikh who planned to blow up New York City landmarks, it called a "hate crime." The extradition order for suspected Hamas terrorist Mousa Abu Marook it labeled "anti-Islamic" and "anti-American."

Not surprisingly, CAIR also backs those who finance terrorism. When President Bush closed the Holy Land Foundation in December for collecting money he said was "used to support the Hamas terror organization," CAIR decried his action as "unjust" and "disturbing."

CAIR even includes at least one person associated with terrorism in its own ranks. On February 2, 1995, U.S. Attorney Mary Jo White named Siraj Wahhaj as one of the "unindicted persons who may be alleged as co-conspirators" in the attempt to blow up New York City monuments. Yet CAIR deems him "one of the most respected Muslim leaders in America" and includes him on its advisory board.

For these and other reasons, the FBI's former chief of counterterrorism, Steven Pomerantz, concludes that "CAIR, its leaders and its activities effectively give aid to international terrorist groups."

Nor is terrorism the only disturbing aspect of CAIR's record. Other problems include:

- *Intimidating moderate Muslims.* In at least two cases (Hisham Kabbani and Khalid Durán), CAIR has defamed moderate Muslims who reject its extremist agenda, leading to death threats against them.

- *Embracing murderers.* CAIR responded to the arrest and conviction of Jamil Al-Amin (the former H. Rap Brown) by praising him, raising funds for him and then denying his guilt after his conviction for the murder of an Atlanta policeman. Likewise with Ahmad Adnan Chaudhry of San Bernardino, Calif.: disregarding his conviction for attempting murder, CAIR declared him "innocent" and set up a defense fund for him.

- *Promoting anti-Semitism.* The head of CAIR's Los Angeles office, Hussam Ayloush, uses the term "zionazi" when referring to Israelis. CAIR co-hosted an event in May 1998 at which an Egyptian militant Islamic leader, Wagdi Ghunaym, called Jews the "descendants of the apes."

- *Aggressive ambitions.* As reported by the *San Ramon Valley Herald*, CAIR Chairman Omar M. Ahmad told a crowd of California Muslims in July 1998, "Islam isn't in America to be equal to any other faith, but to become dominant. The Koran…should be the highest authority in America, and Islam the only accepted religion on earth."

CAIR's real record is one of extremism. North American Muslims themselves are beginning to discover—and the government, leading media, churches, and businesses should follow—that CAIR represents not the noble civilization of Islam but an aggressive and radical strain similar to that which led to the suicide hijackings last September. CAIR must be shunned as a fringe group by responsible institutions and individuals throughout North America.

(22 April 2002)

AMC: "MAINSTREAM" MUSLIMS?

FBI directors don't make a habit of breaking bread with organizations their agents may soon be investigating, perhaps even closing. Robert S. Mueller III, however, is about to make precisely this blunder: On June 28, 2002, he is scheduled to deliver a lunch talk to the American Muslim Council.

Mueller accepted this invitation, his spokesman Bill Carter explains, because the FBI regards the AMC as "the most mainstream Muslim group in the United States."

The AMC does indeed seek to convey a message of moderation. Its event this month, for example, is reassuringly titled "American Muslims: Part of America." AMC also boasts of having initiated "many of the historic events marking the entrance of Muslims into mainstream American culture and life."

Public relations, however, is not reality. The FBI may have missed the AMC's true nature because until just days before the planned talk, its guidelines prohibited it from collecting general information on an organization of this sort. To help it catch up, then, here are five compelling reasons why Director Mueller should break his lunch date:

- *Apologetics for terrorism*: The U.S. government years ago formally certified Hamas and Hezbollah to be terrorist groups; AMC sings their praises. In 2000, Abdurahman Alamoudi, the group's longtime executive director, exhorted a rally outside the White House with "We are ALL supporters of Hamas. Allahu Akhbar! … I am also a supporter of Hezbollah." The American Muslim Council also has ties to other terrorists. For example, Jamal Barzinji, whose Virginia house and business were raided by federal authorities in an anti-terrorism investigation in March 2002, is on the AMC board and will be on the podium at the forthcoming AMC conference. Alamoudi has vehemently defended Omar Abdel Rahman, the blind sheikh now imprisoned for his role in New York-area terrorism. And AMC has both held press conferences supporting Sudan's National Islamic Front (a Department of State-designated terrorist group) and, in 1992, hosted the NIS's leader on a visit to the United States. Also, AMC's Dallas chapter gave an award to Ghassan Dahduli in December 2000. Eleven months later, he was deported from the United States on account of his connections to Al-Qaeda and Hamas.

- *Helping fund-raise for terrorism*: The Holy Land Foundation is one of the main American conduits of money to Hamas; not surprisingly, AMC has lavished praise on it, bestowing an award on it for a "strong global vision." When President Bush closed Holy Land after 9/11 for collecting money "used to support the Hamas terror organization," AMC responded by condemning the president's act as "particularly disturbing...unjust and counterproductive."

- *Run-ins with the law*: AMC leaders have a long and colorful history of legal problems. Jamil Abdullah Al-Amin (the former H. Rap Brown), a one-time president of AMC's executive board, has the nearly unique distinction of having been listed not just once but twice as one of the FBI's Ten Most Wanted Fugitives. Oh, and today he is sitting out a life sentence without parole for murdering a policeman. Other employees have less horrible but still troubled resumes. For example, AMC's current director, Eric Vickers, has been admonished, sanctioned or suspended by courts over a ten-year period due to his faulty practice of law.

- *Hostility to law enforcement*: Even after 9/11, AMC's Web site linked to a document, "Know Your Rights" that advises "Don't Talk to the FBI." Indeed, AMC has fervently opposed successive administrations' efforts to stave off terrorism. And Vickers personally has, to put it delicately, a strained relationship with law enforcement. In his youth, he admits, he was "against the cops." He remains hostile but expresses himself more elegantly today, for example, accusing Attorney General John Ashcroft of "using national security as a pretext" to engage in a pattern of ethnic and religious discrimination.

- *Hostility to the United States*: Its apparent patriotism aside, AMC harbors an intense anti-Americanism. "Let us damn America," Sami Al-Arian, a featured speaker at recent AMC events, has declaimed. Alamoudi, the longtime executive director, has dilated on the agony of living in a country he loathes: "I think if we are outside this country, we can say oh, Allah, destroy America, but once we are here, our mission in this country is to change it. There is no way for Muslims to be violent in America, no way. We have other means to do it. You can be violent anywhere else but in America." In January 2002, Alamoudi participated—alongside leaders of Hamas, Hezbollah, Islamic Jihad, and Al-Qaeda—in a Beirut conference whose communiqué called for a boycott of American products.

Far from being "the most mainstream Muslim group in the United States," the AMC is among their most extreme. That explains why George W. Bush in 2000 returned a $1,000 donation from Alamoudi to his campaign.

Rather than endorse AMC by his presence, Robert Mueller should find other lunch companions next Friday. Then he should put the organization under surveillance, ascertain its funding sources, look over its books, and check its staff's visa status.

(18 June 2002)

HUSSEIN IBISH: U.S. ARABS' FIREBRAND

He sports the modest title of communications director of the American-Arab Anti-Discrimination Committee, a lobby group, but Hussein Ibish is a fast-rising star who appears frequently on top-rated television talk shows, in leading newspapers, at think tanks and in the corridors of power.

Ibish has been appearing with increasing frequency in places like the *Los Angeles Times* and on *The O'Reilly Factor*, *Nightline*, BBC, *The Early Show with Bryant Gumble*, CNN, MSNBC, *All Things Considered*, *The Evening News with Dan Rather* and *The Nightly News with Tom Brokaw*. He's appeared at the Woodrow Wilson Center, and his group is often at the White House. Indeed, few people with views as extremist as his have been given as much recognition.

Unlike most of today's prominent Muslim spokesmen, the thirty-eight-year-old Ibish does not advocate militant Islam. Instead, he pushes a set of far left-wing views.

These start, not surprisingly, with a deep antagonism to the U.S. government. An immigrant from Lebanon, he believes Washington has imperial ambitions in the Middle East. To achieve these, he says, Washington relies extensively on terrorism. First, it has stitched together a system of puppet rulers who "terrorize the region." Second, it "has the ability to murder and rampage at will" and sometimes does just that—as during its "terrorist" 1986 air strike against Libya. It gets worse. Ibish has described former Secretary of State Madeline Albright as "vermin." He has compared comments by Colin Powell about Iraqi civilian deaths during the 1991 war to those by Timothy McVeigh about the children he murdered in Oklahoma City.

Ibith may be tough on American diplomats, but for the second-worst mass murderer of the twentieth century, China's Mao Zedong, Ibish shows a touching affection ("The achievements of Mao can hardly be overstated"). Ibish apologizes for many groups the U.S. government deems terrorist, starting with Osama bin Laden. "I'm skeptical," was his reaction after a federal grand jury indicted bin Laden for bombing two U.S. embassies in East Africa. Ibish dismisses bin Laden as a blowhard who gives "blood-curdling interviews," a guy who "lives in a cave in Afghanistan" and someone seen by Arabs as "a crank and a dangerous fanatic."

The list of apologetics goes on. President Bush calls Hamas "one of the deadliest terrorist organizations in the world today" but our lobbyist friend touts its accomplishments "running hospitals and schools and orphanages."

Ibish's words prompt other comments, too:

- He plays with facts—at will doubling U.S. governmental aid to Israel or tripling the number of Iraqis killed by the sanctions regime. One exasperated columnist characterizes his writings as "systematic deceit."

- Anyone he dislikes is liable to be compared to Nazis. Officers of the Massachusetts Alcoholic Beverages Control Commission are "stormtroopers." A mild newspaper article about Islam is "genocidal" and "reminiscent of the most bizarre passages of Adolf Hitler's Mein Kampf." U.S. sanctions on Iraq are "genocidal."

- He bandies about accusations of espionage for Israel. American journalists he disagrees with are "transparently operating in concert and at the direction of the Israeli government." The Anti-Defamation League is an arm of Israeli intelligence.

- As co-editor, Ibish turned the *Graduate Voice* at the University of Massachusetts into what one writer calls "such an anti-Semitic rag" that the university chancellor had to establish an anti-Semitism task force to respond to his activities.

- In a bizarre twist, Ibish takes pride in his own immoral lifestyle, advocating "redemption through intoxication." He contends that "Those of us who smoke, drink, speak freely and have unauthorized sex occupy both the intellectually sound position and the moral high ground" compared to the "neo-puritans" who frown on such activities.

- In 1997, while a teaching assistant at the University of Massachusetts, he railed against a university regulation prohibiting sex between employees (like himself) and students, calling this an "all-out assault on

fucking." He especially decried the impact this would have on homo-
sexuals, furious at the exposure this could bring if "you are gay and
don't feel comfortable in announcing that fact to a homophobic world."

Anti-American, anti-Semitic, inaccurate and immoral; Hussein
Ibish makes for a peculiar choice to serve as the public face of Arab-
Americans.

More broadly, the media, think tanks and politicians should consider Ibish's record and close their doors to someone so far removed
from the mainstream of the American debate.

(25 March 2002)

PART 3
THE ARAB-ISRAELI
AND OTHER CONFLICTS

7

THE OSLO DIPLOMACY

A PALESTINIAN STATE: A NIGHTMARE FOR ARABS*

An independent Palestinian state would pose well-known dangers to Israel and the United States, but a close look shows that if such a state ever came into existence the biggest losers would be the Arabs. The citizens of this state would suffer human rights abuses, and Arab states in the neighborhood would be threatened by a whole range of new dangers.

We must assume that a Palestinian state would be run by the Palestine Liberation Organization, for no other Palestinian group now or in the near future can compete with it. In addition to the PLO's symbolic power, it controls a network of well-established institutions and funds estimated in the billions of dollars, enjoys wide international recognition—and it has the guns. Together, these make it the only serious Palestinian claimant to power.

We have a very good idea what rule by the Palestine Liberation Organization would mean, for the record since its founding in 1964 has consistently been one of an avaricious, self-serving leadership living by a non-democratic ethos. Ignore for the moment the many atrocities against Israelis and the citizens of other countries, including the United States. Just recall the contempt that the PLO has shown for the lives of non-PLO Palestinians in Jordan, the West Bank, and elsewhere.

---

*Alongside this April 1988 article, the *New York Times* ran another one, by Ibrahim Abu-Lughod favoring a Palestinian state. His prediction? "Under a Palestinian state in the West Bank and Gaza, which surely will be democratic and secular, Palestinian Arabs and Israeli Jews will be bonded in a political order not yet experienced in the Middle East."

The closest the PLO has come to a state was in southern Lebanon between 1975 and 1982. There it enjoyed nearly sovereign authority. For seven years, PLO members ran amok, grabbing possessions and women as they wished, dealing in drugs and operating protection rackets. Their insolence was so great that many Palestinians, not to speak of terrorized Lebanese, actually welcomed the PLO's removal by Israeli troops. Given the PLO's long record of indifference and brutality, there is no reason to expect this pattern of behavior to change were Yasir Arafat to achieve power in a Palestinian state.

As for its impact on Middle Eastern countries, the creation of a PLO polity would foment instability for years to come, for those with trouble on their minds would flock to it. President Hafez al-Assad of Syria could be counted on to goad the new state against Israel as a way to keep his hand in the Arab-Israeli conflict and assure his position at home. Col. Muammar el-Qaddafi of Libya would try to make the new state an instrument of his power. And would the Ayatollah Ruhollah Khomeini, who has just founded his own Palestinian group, be far behind?

Imagine, if the PLO wielded the powers of a state, how much more effectively it would extort money and favors from the rich but weak countries of the Persian Gulf. But it would be the frail monarchy of Jordan that, as ever, would be most exposed to this new menace. In 1970, when the PLO was only an irredentist movement, it almost overturned King Hussein. It would threaten him even more once it controlled real territory and real resources.

Behind closed doors, Arab leaders recognize these dangers, and they worry. As President Jimmy Carter so indiscreetly revealed in 1979, "I have never met an Arab leader that in private professed the desire for an independent Palestinian state."

Even if a PLO state poses fewer dangers for Israel than for the Arab countries, it offers Israel no advantages. Through seventy years of Arab-Zionist conflict, the Palestinian leadership has consistently taken the most extreme, violent stands, preventing a resolution of that conflict.

Empowering the PLO simply would boost the worst Palestinian elements and create new obstacles to peace. Certainly, no one should expect a Palestinian state on the West Bank and Gaza to end the Arab-Israeli conflict: it would merely move it to a new stage.

Finally, a PLO state would harm United States interests, for it would offer Moscow a new outpost of influence strategically wedged between two important friends of America. Recognizing its value, Moscow would surely pour agents and arms into the new state. For the Kremlin, a PLO state between Israel and Jordan would offer almost as many opportunities as moving East Germany to the English Channel.

The Palestinian Liberation Organization embodies many ironies. It is, for example, a weak institution with a worldwide presence as well as a terrorist organization whose only success lies in diplomacy. But the greatest irony of all is that its rise to statehood would hurt Arabs far more than Israelis.

(25 April 1988)

DIM PROSPECTS FOR PALESTINIAN STATE

The Palestine Liberation Organization's declaration of an independent Palestinian state last month [November 1998] and the U.S. decision to open a dialogue with the PLO have inspired many Americans to hope that finally an unhappy people may be on the route to peace and prosperity. If only the Palestinians can enjoy the benefits of a sovereign state, Middle East problems will recede, leaving all of us better off. This argument holds a compelling appeal for Americans, for it is we who, since Woodrow Wilson's time, have most of all championed the right to national self-determination.

But the stirring words of the Palestinian spokesmen are empty; anyone who would believe that national independence is the route to happiness ignores some of the most powerful lessons derived from recent decades. Whatever one's views on the Israeli occupation, it would be a profound mistake to expect much of an independent Palestinian state. Indeed, should it come to exist, there is every reason to anticipate new misery for Palestinians and others.

Nationalist calls for liberation and independence have had an extraordinary worldwide appeal over the course of the past 200 years. They took on special force in the non-Western world during the middle third of the twentieth century, as colonial empires crumbled and disappeared. In part they had such wide resonance because the cry for national independence included other promises too. Self-determination was not an end in itself, but the path to a great range of benefits, including social justice, educational reform, cultural renaissance and individual dignity. Independence would bring far more than just a change in ruler: it would right ancient wrongs and guarantee a brighter future.

Thus, the Congress Party of India foresaw a prosperous and powerful country after the British left. The Chinese Communist Party overturned the old order in pursuit of a renewed civilization. Ho Chi Minh rallied the Vietnamese troops by evoking images of the just society. Elsewhere around the world—Indonesia, Algeria. Tanzania —similar aspirations moved large numbers to fight and die for independence and the expected benefits.

Of course, the nationalists got what they wanted. With the one exception of the Russians (who long held on to their colonies by renaming them "socialist republics"), Europeans ceded power almost everywhere. On taking the colonialists' place, nationalist leaders wasted no time in setting about to translate their long-held dreams into reality.

And the result? It is painful, after a generation or two of nationalist rule, to recall the bright hopes once attached to national independence. Hardly a single government achieved its goals. Warfare and communal violence became endemic in many countries. As repression increased, jails filled with political prisoners. States that boasted ample financial surpluses at independence—Ghana and Egypt come to mind—quickly became debtors. Illiteracy remained high almost everywhere, while obtuse political interference caused a decline in cultural standards. Income levels stayed low, yet disparities of wealth usually increased. Social justice was an illusory hope, rarely fulfilled. Full democracy became endangered in large regions of the globe. The noble goal of self-determination turned out to mean nothing more than replacing a foreign dictator by a local one.

Comparing yesterday's hopes with today's reality is not a happy undertaking, for virtually every aspiration of years past now is dead. Comparing Third World conditions today with those of a half-century ago is a still more dismal exercise, for few governments even managed to match the record of their colonial predecessors in economic, political, or basic administrative terms.

Middle Eastern states fit this pattern—and have additional woes of their own, for this region suffers from a special curse of violence and political volatility. Military rulers dominate, the threat of terrorism hangs over every airplane and government building, and the region has become the international testing ground for new weapons. The region today simultaneously hosts no less than three major conflicts (Arab-Israeli, Iraq-Iran, Afghanistan) and five minor ones (Western Sahara, Chad, Cyprus, Lebanon, and the Kurds). Oh yes, the oil-exporting countries have enjoyed spectacular economic growth, but theirs was a freakish wealth that cannot last or produce real, sustainable well-being.

This bleak record must affect the outlook for a Palestinian state. It is simply too late for the old, naïve hopes. By now, we have a good idea of the choices facing a new Middle East government. Will it resemble Iran in adopting the militant Islamic model of religious extremism? Or the Iraqi model under Saddam Hussein—civil war and near-total repression? Or the Syrian model, where the government calls out the air force to destroy one of its own largest cities and kill many thousands of unarmed inhabitants? The Lebanese model of anarchy and carnage? The Jordanian model of a mild police state in a cultural desert? The Saudi model of archaic monarchy and no individual rights? Or the Egyptian model of military rule, political disenfranchisement, and sinking poverty?

These choices are the realistic alternatives facing the potential citizens of a Palestinian state. And should it be the PLO that runs that new state, we then have an even better idea of what lies in store for them. The PLO's record since its founding in 1964 has been an unhappy one of an arrogant leadership ruling with an iron fist and disregarding the interests of non-PLO Palestinians. There is no reason to expect this well-established behavior to change if the organization ever comes to power.

As Sidney Zion has put it: "Suppose there was a Palestinian state in Gaza and the West Bank? Does anyone believe the Arabs would be free? There's not a free Arab state in the world."

These dismal prospects suggest the need for caution in considering the attractive visions sketched out by Palestinian spokesmen. We have to remember that visions no less sweet have been proposed many times in the past, only to create oppressive regimes and impoverished societies when actually applied. Smooth-talking proponents of Palestinian nationalism are hawking the political equivalent of snake oil. The seductive charms of nationalism usually turn out to be a prelude to rape: it serves no one—not Palestinians, Israelis, or Americans—to fall for this romantic myth.

(26 December 1988)

THE OSLO ACCORDS? NO "NEW EPOCH"

President Clinton described the signing of an agreement by Israel and the Palestine Liberation Organization (PLO) nine days ago as a "great occasion of history." Yasir Arafat called it an "historic event, inaugurating a new epoch," while Israel's Foreign Minister Shimon Peres called it no less than "a revolution." As though to confirm this extravagant view, American newspapers devoted as many as seven full pages to the White House ceremony while television offered hours of uninterrupted programming.

But a nagging question remains. Was it really such a major event? Probably not, and for two reasons. Arabs have for the most part repudiated Arafat's act of compromise; and Palestinians are not—despite the enormous attention paid them—the key actors on the Arab side of this drama.

To begin with, many Palestinians and Arab rulers have denounced the Rabin-Arafat accord, few have supported it. Palestinian opponents divide into several types: Islamists, who predominate in Gaza; radical leftist organizations based in Damascus; and rebellious elements within Arafat's own group, Al-Fatah.

The militant Islamic groups—Hamas and Islamic Jihad—absolutely and vehemently reject the accord; while they have reached an apparent agreement with Arafat not to wage an internecine war, they have also done their best to undermine the accord through a series of terrorist acts against Israelis. And that's just the start. Similarly, all ten PLO groups in Syria reject the accord. These include George Habash's Popular Front for the Liberation of Palestine (PFLP), Ahmad Jibril's Popular Front for the Liberation of Palestine-General Command (PFLP-GC); Na'if Hawatma's Democratic Front for the Liberation of Palestine (DFLP); Abu Nidal's Fatah Revolutionary Council; and Abu Musa's group.

Even within Fatah, Arafat's own organization, the accord inspires profound unease. Many of Fatah's leading figures have denounced it, including the organization's number-two man, Faruq Qaddumi;

its representative in Lebanon, Shafiq al-Hut; and the poet Mahmud Darwish. Basically, only Arafat and his aides support the pact; and they cannot impose their will on the many Palestinian leaders who do not. This explains why only eight of the eighteen members in the PLO's Executive Committee voted in favor of the accord. It also recalls Shimon Peres' choice observation back in 1988 (when he spoke more candidly about these matters): "There is nothing more fake than the PLO; there is no eel slicker than Arafat. He has no control over the PLO, Na'if Hawatma, or George Habash."

What about the Palestinian masses? Despite the parades and flag-waving in recent days, there's not much reason to be hopeful. Palestinian political life has long had a self-acknowledged radical quality verging on the anti-rational. A Palestinian activist explained this in 1991 when attempting to explain his confidence in Saddam Hussein beating the U.S.-led coalition: "When you believe in what you are doing, you don't think about the consequences." As'ad 'Abd ar-Rahman, a member of the Palestine National Council, put the matter even more explicitly: "We [Palestinians] are desperate. We are not in the mood for rational discussion."

So much for the bad old days. Does the future look brighter? Prime Minister Yitzhak Rabin counts on the PLO-controlled area turning into an economically vibrant and politically stable state, hoping that once Palestinians become prosperous and bourgeois, they will lose their taste for radical ideologies and violence. Maybe; but the Middle East boasts plenty of rich and conservative societies ruled by extremely bellicose regimes (think of Libya, Iraq, and Iran). In this part of the world, leaders count much more than followers, and most Palestinian leaders remain unreconstructed.

Turning to the Middle Eastern states, two middleweights support the accord, Egypt and Saudi Arabia and two heavyweights oppose it, Iran and Syria. The Iranian regime has ferociously denounced the accord and vowed to oppose it with its violent legions among the Palestinians and in Lebanon, Jordan, and Egypt. President Hafez al-Assad of Syria also wants to undo the accord, but he plays a more coy game, announcing he will neither fight the accord himself nor restrain those who do want to oppose it. This subtle policy permits him to deploy the PLO factions in Damascus without antagonizing the U.S. government. He's a smart one, Assad.

Such powerful opposition is likely to limit the importance of the Rabin-Arafat compromise. In this context, it's worth remembering that Anwar al-Sadat also hailed the Egypt-Israel peace treaty in 1979 as "an historic turning point." But it was less that than a change of lanes. Because Palestinians and Arab leaders did not follow Sadat in making peace with Israel, that treaty did not end the Arab-Israeli confrontation; it merely altered the terms. For example, just as Egypt retreated from the conflict, the brand-new revolutionary regime in Iran jumped in and effectively took Egypt's place as one of the states most dangerous to Israel's security. The new accord is likely to be similarly limited.

The fact that Islamist and radical leftist Palestinians reject Arafat's turn toward peace points to a larger issue; Palestinian leaders are not masters of their own destiny, but rely to a great extent on the states of the Middle East. They do not make the ultimate decisions of war and peace; states do this. They control neither the fighter planes in Syria nor the missiles in Iran nor even the knives of the Islamist Palestinians. If Iran and Syria decide to continue the conflict against Israel, it goes on.

In April 1990, I conjured up in print a fantasy: suppose Arafat and the Israelis reach complete agreement on Palestinian self-government, what would change? "Not much. Syrian missiles and Jordanian soldiers would remain in place, as would the cold peace with Egypt, while anti-Arafat elements of the PLO would continue to engage in terrorism. The intifada would probably go on, even if weakened." I'd change some words now, but the basic point remains valid: states are the key actor in the conflict with Israel.

On the other hand, what if Hafez al-Assad signed a peace treaty with the Israelis? "In that case, the inter-state war would come to a virtually end because Amman would immediately follow Damascus's example. Some of the Syrian-backed Palestinian groups would come to terms with Israel, as would Arafat. Even though Palestinian extremists would continue to riot, the conflict would become much less dangerous."

Because Yasir Arafat cannot impose his will either on Gaza or on a single state, he is ultimately more a media figure than a power broker. If he and his lonely band are left out on a limb, as appears to be the case, his accord with Israel will probably wither. If it does succeed, it will not be a solution to the Arab-Israeli conflict but an interim agreement with yet many hurdles to overcome.

(22 September 1993)

THE OSLO ACCORD'S IMPLICATIONS

The controversial accord signed by Prime Minister Yitzhak Rabin of Israel Yasir Arafat of the Palestine Liberation Organization (PLO) has the capacity both to exacerbate the conflict and to induce peace. It all depends, basically, on whether or not it signals a willingness by Middle Easterners to coexist with Israel. Let's consider three negative possibilities and three positive ones.

If things go badly, the accord:

- *Gives the bad old PLO a lease on life.* On paper, at least, the PLO has capitulated. It accepts the permanent existence of Israel, renounces the goal of destroying Israel, forswears terrorism (yet again) as well as "armed struggle," and gives up the dream of returning refugees to their homes. Does this mean the PLO has in fact disavowed its heritage? Shimon Peres, Israel's Foreign Minister, has no doubts: "I think the PLO has changed its character." But there's plenty of reason to wonder: it appears that Arafat has merely adopted a flexible approach to fit adverse circumstances, saying whatever needed to be said to survive. The PLO had not a change of heart—merely a change of policy.

    Along these lines, it's worth noting that Arafat still harbors dreams of Israel falling apart from within. In March 1993 he observed that "the Soviet Union, for all its formidable power, collapsed. This could happen to Israel." Assuming he really believes this, the deal with Israel represents a lease on life for the PLO so that it can stay in business until Israel falters, when it can deal it a death blow.

- *Turns Gaza into another Lebanon.* The real danger lies not in the powerful PLO state that Israel's Likud Party fears, but in anarchy. When the Israeli military administration abandons Gaza, will Arafat be able to take control of it? Or will the widespread animosity toward the PLO's secular, compromising approach lead to civil war? Should Gaza spin out of control, it could become a source of great danger to Israel and PLO-affiliated Palestinians. It could export terrorists to the West as Lebanon once did. More ominous yet, it might become a place of refuge for Egyptian Islamists trying to overthrow the Mubarak government.

- *Enhances militant Islamic power.* Arab nationalists once led the effort to destroy Israel; this accord ends that era and gives Islamists the chance to lead. Both Hamas and Islamic Jihad categorically refuse to recognize the State of Israel; they now inherit the PLO's old mantle as leader of the anti-Zionist opposition. These organizations hate Israel with a passion that's hard to summarize. For a taste, here's what Sheikh As'ad at-Tamimi, spiritual guide to Islamic Jihad, had to say some years ago on the possibility of a PLO compromise with Israel:

> All the proposed solutions will fail because it is the destiny of the Jews to reject them until the final solution comes, when the stones and the trees will speak, saying: "O Muslim, servant of God, behold there is a Jew behind me. Come and kill him." O sons of the blessed land of Palestine, burn everything that you can touch-burn vehicles, shops, and factories and take of their money what you want. There is no sanctity for a Jew's money or blood. Kill them where you find them and expel them from where they have expelled you.

Nothing coming out of the tired leftist organizations headquartered in Damascus sounds like this. The accord may actually widen the appeal of the Islamist organizations. If they win the elections that the agreement says must be held by mid-1994, the Rabin-Arafat accord would be defunct.

But if all goes well, the accord:

- *Puts Palestinians on the winning side.* Palestinians have an astonishing record for picking the wrong allies. They aligned with the Central Powers in World War I, the Nazis in World War II, the USSR in the Cold War, and Saddam Hussein in the Kuwait War. Not coincidentally, they always picked the side that happened to be the aggressor and the enemy of the United States. Staying true to form, Palestinians would now side with today's most aggressive and the most fervid anti-American power in the Middle East—the Islamic Republic of Iran. Arafat's deal with Rabin offers a way out of this old rut.

- *Reduces Israel's role in Arab mythology.* For decades, Arab leaders portrayed Zionism as a cosmic threat. Already in 1905, the Lebanese Christian Négib Azoury predicted that Arab nationalists and Zionists, "are destined to fight each other continually until one of them wins. The fate of the entire world will depend on the final result of this struggle between these two peoples representing two contrary principles." More recently, Syria's foreign minister, Faruq ash-Shar' made the astonishing declaration in 1991 that "Had there been no Israeli occupation [of the West Bank and Gaza] for the last twenty-four years …perhaps there would have been no Iraqi invasion of Kuwait." If Palestinians are ready to make peace with Israel, Arab leaders will have to give Israel up as their universal alibi. No more will we hear King Fahd spouting nonsense about tiny Israel being "the root cause of instability and turmoil" in the Arab countries. And Middle Easterners might actually deal with real problems.

- *Ends Israel's pariah status.* Throughout its short history, the Jewish state has had a multitude of enemies—Muslims, Marxist-Leninists, anti-Semites, oil company executives, Arabists. Symbolic of this hostility, Israel suffered far more lop-sided votes at the United Nations than any other country. If Yasir Arafat, the international symbol of anti-Zionism, really does business with Jerusalem, Israel wins protection from most criticism. Those who obsessively wish to harm Israel find themselves pushed to the margins. Whole warehouses full of U.N. documents are rendered obsolete. Israel becomes a nearly ordinary country.

In short, the Rabin-Arafat accord opens up many new possibilities. If they go badly, the accord could bring anarchy to Gaza and help Islamists overthrow the government in Egypt. If things go well, it reduces the emotional quality of the Arab-Israeli conflict and helps bring further diplomatic agreements (most notably between Syria and Israel).

(24 September 1993)

THE END OF THE REIGN OF OPTIMISM

The massacre carried out by Baruch Goldstein in Hebron in March 1994 probably marked the end of an era. With it, the optimists' three-year reign over the Arab-Israeli conflict concludes; starting now, more of us will realize that an Arab-Israeli peace is an elusive, highly fragile undertaking, and that it might well fail.

Optimism became policy in the heady aftermath of Saddam Hussein's defeat. Because the George H.W. Bush administration believed the Arab-Israeli conflict was ripe for solution, the Madrid conference of late 1991 dealt with the Arab-Israeli conflict and not—as you might expect—the Persian Gulf. Rather than use its new prestige and influence to confront the intractable problems of Iraq and Iran (where should their borders run? how do we prevent future acts of aggression?), the U.S. government shifted its gaze one thousand miles to the West (what are Israel's terms for withdrawing from the Golan Heights? who should represent the Palestinians?). In March 1991, President Bush boldly asserted that "the time has come to put an end to Arab-Israeli conflict." The Clinton administration adopted the same approach and displayed, if possible, even more hope in the Arab-Israeli peace process.

In Israel, the Labor Party's electoral victory in June 1992 brought a sunny disposition to the negotiations. Yitzhak Rabin and Shimon Peres fundamentally changed the conduct of Israel's foreign relations. They dropped the old style of confrontation and stalemate, dispelled Likud fears of an Arab onslaught, and moved quickly toward compromise and resolution. They talked of using economic growth to build constituencies for peace, and of assuring that the next generation of Israeli men would not serve in the military, as did they, into its middle age and beyond.

Some Arab leaders got infected by the same bug. The Jordanian leadership's visionaries dismissed the Arab-Israeli conflict as an anachronism which needs quickly to be settled so that the Middle East can gain stability and prosper. Egyptian and Saudi diplomats took a similar approach, as did many of their brethren from the Persian Gulf sheikhdoms and North Africa. Finally, in a move that took our collective breath away, Yasir Arafat too began talking the talk. The moment of peace seemed finally to have arrived that bright summer day in September 1993 on the White House lawn. Western analysts read great things into it. For example, Ben Lynfield wrote in the *Christian Science Monitor* that the PLO-Israel mutual recognition and declaration of principles "have changed forever the relationship between Jews and Arabs in the Middle East."

As economics seem to loom larger and military strength smaller, Middle Easterners give off a sense of being aware that they are being left behind. The oil money was squandered, East Asia is taking off, and the West seems ever more distant. Even Saddam Hussein joins in this spirit, in his own bellicose manner: "If anyone imagines the Koreans can develop, the Americans can develop, and the Taiwanese can develop, but the Arabs cannot, then he is deluded." But another reality coexisted with these hopes, a reality of dark passions and downward trends. Consider: The ugly program of militant Islam is gaining strength among many of Israel's neighbors and among the Palestinians. The oil boom ended so long ago, the oil bust is now in its second decade, with no change ahead likely. Rogue regimes are entrenched in the Middle East and gaining in numbers. Sudan recently joined the ranks of Libya, Syria, Iraq, and Iran; Algeria could be next.

Moreover, a close look at Arab attitudes to Israel shows that not much has changed. A 1993 survey of one thousand Lebanese, Syrians, and Palestinians conducted by Hilal Khashan of the American University of Beirut (and published in the March 1994 issue of the *Middle East Quarterly*) makes this abundantly clear.

Khashan concludes from his research that "the respondents show little understanding of the meaning of peace [with Israel], much less an appreciation of its possible benefits." Rather, they tend to see peace as a moratorium in which to prepare for the next round of fighting.

Nor has Israel been immune to negative developments. The split between religious and secular has widened, as has the one between doves and hawks—and Baruch Goldstein's horrible act of vengeance exacerbates both these divisions. What would Israelis do to each other if spared the Arab threat? It could be that external challenge has kept the state together.

As Americans, there's little we can do if Middle Eastern leaders persist in deluding themselves that peace and economic growth are just around the corner. But we can ourselves understand that the Middle East is on a downward course and prepare accordingly. From our point of view, the Middle East increasingly stands out as a region that develops and exports problems, including political radicals, terrorism, drugs, unconventional weaponry, and conspiracy theories. We should recognize that this region resembles the Pacific Rim less than it does Africa; and we should ready ourselves for the many troubles yet to come.

(16 March 1994)

THE ARAB STREET VS. ISRAEL

with Tonya Ugoretz Buzby

Are the Arabs ready for peace with Israel? In survey research conducted in 1993, just before the signing of the Oslo accords, Hilal Khashan showed they were not. More than 90 percent of Muslim Lebanese, Syrians, and diaspora Palestinians, he reported, saw peace as an interim measure, something useful to allow them time to reorganize and strike at Israel later. Worse, he found that not one respondent gave a positive justification for peace with Israel.

Much changed on the Arab "street" over the next two years. The wall of rejection collapsed, replaced by a far more nuanced set of attitudes. While complex, even confusing, these changes deserve careful attention.

The June 1995 issue of the *Middle East Quarterly* contains reports on two polls: one an update by Professor Khashan, the other a distillation (by Lauren G. Ross and Nader Izzat Sa'id) of fifteen public opinion surveys carried out monthly by a Palestinian organization on the West Bank and in Gaza. Although asking quite different questions of two distinct populations, the polls send a single message: while many Arabs now accept formal peace negotiations and treaties with Israel, they continue to harbor strong antagonism toward Israelis. Let's look at each of these elements separately.

Accept negotiations and treaties. The reality of Arab leaders' talking peace with Israel is taking hold in the Middle East. Where once Arabs opposed the Oslo accord signed on the White House lawn, the barrage of information on peace with Israel since 1993 has induced many of them to accept negotiations. Among Syrians, for example, approval for the peace talks has increased from 28 percent to 45 percent—a striking change in so brief a period. Among Palestinians living in Amman, support has more than doubled, from 26 percent to 63 percent. Further, over 40 percent of Palestinians in the West Bank and Gaza support the negotiations. Their number is likely to grow, for nearly 30 percent of the remainder is undecided, including many pragmatists withholding support until they see tangible results.

Maintain strong antagonism. These encouraging shifts do not mean the end of Arab animosity toward Israelis, however. Formal negotiations and agreements remain isolated to the political arena, with no basic shift in attitudes, emotions, or actions. Khashan's survey shows that 87 percent of respondents believe Israel pursues peace with ulterior motives, such as to achieve economic predominance, seize control of water resources, or establish a "Greater Israel." Ross and Sa'id find that 70 percent of Palestinians in the West Bank and Gaza doubt Israelis are serious about achieving peace. Consistent with these profound suspicions, 65 percent of Levant Arabs say they would abandon the peace were Israel weakened, and 39 percent of Palestinians still support the total destruction of Israel.

The hostility is pervasive. Overwhelming majorities of respondents in the Levant refuse to look at Jewish history from an Israeli perspective (94 percent) or send their children to an Israeli university (93 percent). Palestinians show even stronger antagonism. Fully 46 percent of those questioned support armed attacks against Israeli targets; among Fatah sympathizers—in other words, those who support negotiations with Israel—an astonishing 40 percent support such violence. A plurality of the Palestinian population, in other words, advocates both the peace process and violence against Israelis.

Clearly, this means that support for the peace process does not signal a change of heart in Arab attitudes toward Israel. Many supporters of peace are simply lying low until Israel weakens militarily. Yes, they seem to be saying, we realize there is no choice other than official reconciliation with Israel; we accept that. But no, we will not interact with Israelis—indeed, we continue to see violence against them as legitimate.

This bifurcation of opinion has three direct implications for U.S. diplomacy:

- *Narrow the chasm in Israeli politics.* Israel's Labor Party emphasizes the positive side of relations with the Arabs almost to the exclusion of the negative; Likud does the reverse. The middle ground of ambivalence and uncertainty hardly exists these days, yet it is the most constructive approach. Rather than side with one party (Labor) against the other (Likud), American leaders should use their influence to inject balance and help find a realistic common ground.

- *Press Arab leaders to push for reconciliation.* "Real peace requires more than mutual recognition on the political level," Khashan has written; "it requires a reconciliation of the heart, an acceptance of the need to compromise goals and aspirations even at the level of the individual." Unfortunately, the Arab media does not even debate the issue of peace but condemns it outright, making it difficult for Arabs to form positive impressions about Israeli intentions. Virtually all the Arab regimes, including the Palestinian Authority, control their press, educational materials, and other vehicles of opinion. However regrettable this state of affairs, it does exist, so we might as well push it in a positive direction by urging Arab leaders to use these resources to call for reconciliation with Israel.

- *Fortify U.S.-Israel ties.* Make it clear that Israel is here to stay. Unless Arab populations perceive Israel not just as powerful but as unbeatable, their dream of destroying the Jewish state will live on. Strong ties between the United States and Israel do much to further this impression, so these must steadily be enhanced. In this light, current congressional action to move the U.S. embassy from Tel Aviv to Jerusalem, far from impeding the peace process, gives it an important boost.

(8 June 1995)

Two-Faced Yasir

with Alexander T. Stillman

When Yasir Arafat shook hands with Israel's Prime Minister Yitzhak Rabin in September 1993, he made two main promises: to include in his public statements that the PLO "encourages and calls upon" Palestinians to take part in "rejecting violence and terrorism"; and to "achieve coexistence" with Israel—implying an acceptance of the Jewish state as a permanent fact of life.

Israelis vociferously disagree on how well he has kept those promises. At one end of the spectrum, Foreign Minister Shimon Peres declares Arafat to be "the one and only Palestinian leader with whom Israel can and should negotiate." At the other end, a Likud Party statement calls Arafat someone "who continues the Nazi way."

Who's right? Has Arafat in fact fulfilled his obligations or not? There is no easy answer, for Arafat is a study in contradiction. Accepting the Nobel Prize in Oslo, he seemed genuinely to advocate peace and stability:

> Like their Arab brethren, the Palestinians, whose cause is the guardian of the gate of the Arab-Israeli peace, are looking forward to a comprehensive, just, and durable peace on the basis of land for peace and compliance with international legitimacy and its resolutions. Peace, to us, is a value and an interest. Peace is an absolute human value which will help man develop his humanity with freedom that cannot be limited by regional, religious, or national restrictions.

But in Gaza a few months later, he repeatedly called for jihad against Israel:

> We will go on with the jihad, a long jihad, a difficult jihad, an exhausting jihad, martyrs, battles. But this is the path of victory, the path of glory, the path of jihad, not just for the Palestinian people but for the entire Arab nation.

In an effort to see beyond the contradictory evidence of specific speeches, we have systematically analyzed 244 public statements (including speeches, press conferences, and interviews) made by Arafat in the year starting July 1, 1994, just as he took control of the Gaza Strip and Jericho, and ending on June 30, 1995. Expecting that he speaks differently to Westerners and to Muslims, as in the examples above, we categorized these statements by their primary audiences (speeches by where delivered, press conferences by composition of the press corps—almost always Western—and interviews by the language of the journalist's media). In all, slightly over half (126) were addressed to Westerners and slightly fewer (118) to Muslims.

Rejecting violence. Fifty-one statements are pertinent to assessing whether Arafat kept his promise to discourage violence against Israelis, thirty-eight addressed to Westerners and just thirteen to Muslims. Not only did Arafat take up this subject with Westerners three times more often than with Muslims, but the former heard a message significantly different from the latter. In just over half of his statements to a Western audience, Arafat condemns violence. For example, to an Israeli journalist, he abhorred the suicide bombing by Islamic Jihad in November 1994:

> We hold a very grave view of the attack in Netzarim. ...We totally reject such acts. It has been decided to take the appropriate steps in reaction. Such steps are the arrests carried out among the Islamic Jihad activists. We have arrested 136 Islamic Jihad members.

A month later, responding to the suicide bombing of a Jerusalem bus, Arafat (through his spokesman) called the incident a "criminal act" and wished the wounded "a speedy recovery."

To Westerners, thus, Arafat fulfills his promise. What about Muslim audiences? On the thirteen occasions Arafat mentioned terrorist violence, he not once condemned its practice against Israelis. Rather, his statements fell into one of three categories: avoiding the subject, placing responsibility for the violence partially on Israel, or calling for more violence.

First, Arafat is a master of avoidance, achieving this sometimes through silence. For example, he immediately condemned the terrorist attack in Netzarim to Israelis, but in not one of his nine statements to Arab audiences in the week that followed did he so much as mention the atrocity. At other times, he wiggles out of questions: when a London-based Arabic newspaper asked him in February 1995 whether Hamas's violence against Israelis were legitimate acts of jihad, Arafat insouciantly ignored the question:

> What I would like to say is that we all must respect the agreements concluded in the times of war and peace. ... I wonder why Hamas, Islamic Jihad, and the Syria-based and Jordan-based factions do not carry out their operations from Syria and Jordan, particularly since there are borders between Syria and Israel and between Jordan and Israel. Why are they making us look as if we are to be held responsible for this?

Arafat, it would appear, cares not to discourage violence but to make sure Jordan and Syria get blamed for it.

Second, Arafat hints that Israel's government is partly behind the violence against its own citizens. Why would it do that? To discredit the Palestinian Authority he heads, and so to slow down the withdrawal of Israeli troops from the West Bank. Along these lines, Arafat stated in April, 1995 that

> The target is not Israel, which is not against them [Hamas members engaged in violence]. These operations' objective is to allow Israel to use the issue of security or the lack of it as an excuse for stopping the implementation of what we agreed on.

Finally, Arafat sometimes invites more violence. At the Seventh Islamic Conference Organization Summit in December 1994, he called for continued jihad:

> Today, I come to you for the first time from Palestine, the homeland which has not yet been liberated from the Israeli occupation which is weighing heavily on our people. ... Let our jihad continue until an independent Palestinian state is established, with holy Jerusalem as its capital.

An Arab audience in May 1995 heard a similar appeal: "everyone should view himself as a recruit in the ferocious battle we are fighting to protect Jerusalem and our sanctities in it."

In sum, Arafat keeps his word in condemning the violence to Westerners—those least likely to strap on a bomb and blow up an Israeli bus in Jerusalem or Tel Aviv. But he fails to follow through with his fellow Arabs; to them he never condemns a specific terrorist attack against Israelis. Arafat thus keeps the letter but not the spirit of his promise.

Accepting Israel. What about accepting the State of Israel's permanence? Although Arafat refers to Israel in nearly all of his public statements (often as "the occupation"), only twenty or so of them are pertinent to this question. Just as with violence, Arafat sends a mixed message in these twenty statements.

To Westerners, he fully accepts Israel's permanency. For example, addressing Israeli youth in a July 1994 interview, he spoke of "a new era for our new generations," pointing to a break from the past. He went on: "a new era in the Middle East has started. And, we are neighbors, we can coordinate, cooperate, in all fields by all means for the sake of our new children." Similarly, responding to remarks by Faruq Qaddumi, head of the PLO's Political Department, about the "evil" enemy Israel and her existence (at Peres's demand that Arafat condemn Qaddumi's remarks), the PLO chairman deemed

Qaddumi's statement incompatible with the Palestinian Authority's commitment to the agreements with Israel and said: "I will abide by the agreements with Israel and I will honor all the letters I exchanged with Prime Minister Yitzhak Rabin concerning mutual recognition." On another occasion, Arafat spoke warmly of an enduring peace based in the holy city of Jerusalem: "There must be no walls between East Jerusalem and West Jerusalem, no Berlin Wall. Jerusalem will be a symbol of the peace of the brave, of coexistence between two peoples-the Israelis and the Palestinians."

To Arab audiences, predictably, Arafat sends a different signal. While he never denies Israel's permanency, he does hedge, stressing legal obligations rather than political attitudes. He talks dramatically of respecting the agreement with Israel, not of accepting Israel.

> We have signed the peace of the brave [he told a press conference on July 1, 1994]. Our views may differ, but if a Palestinian child signs an agreement on behalf of the Palestinian people, we will be committed to his signature. So it is the case if the signing is made by a Palestinian delegation or authority. We will build the peace of the brave and preserve it.

In a speech to an Arab audience in Gaza, Arafat said: "We call it [the Oslo accord] an agreement of the courageous, and we will honor this agreement of the courageous just as we have pledged." With Arab audiences, Arafat skips the more emotional sentiments he occasionally expresses to the West (mutual recognition, peaceful coexistence of Palestinians and Israelis) in favor of an official, legalistic endorsement of the agreement's sanctity.

Assessment. In hundreds of statements, Arafat has firmly established a record of sending substantially different messages to Westerners and Muslims. He condemns terrorism to those who do not engage in it, while avoiding the issue for those who do. He proclaims Israel's permanency to those who themselves accept this fact but hides behind legalism when addressing those who still reject it.

Arafat's conflicting signals confuse his listeners, prompting debate over his intentions and justifying two starkly divergent readings of his performance. Ambiguity prompts each side to hear what best suits it. Optimists point to the Western-oriented Yasir Arafat who condemns terrorism and speaks of co-existence with Israel. Pessimists conjure up the jihad-threatening Arafat who never condemns specific terrorist attacks against Israeli citizens to his fellow Arabs or commits to long-term co-existence with Israel.

Those embroiled in this debate find the Arafat of their predisposition. Committed to the peace process, Peres sees the pro-Western Arafat. Fearful of the peace process being carried out, Likud sees the Arafat who still hopes to destroy Israel.

Which is the real Arafat? A clue may lie in the revealing statement he made to a Spanish newspaper in October 1994, when asked if he differed from the Arafat of 1974, the one who appeared before the United Nations with an olive branch in one hand and a Kalashnikov in the other. "In no way at all," he replied. "I am not a chameleon, I cannot change my coat." By his own words, then, Arafat is the same person of twenty years earlier. The only difference is that, for the most part, he now holds up only an olive branch for the West and a Kalashnikov for his fellow Arabs.

(25 September 1995)

ISRAELI FATIGUE

Israel's forthcoming elections in June 1999 are being called a referendum on the peace process, but they are not. That issue is already decided. Five years of experience show that a substantial majority of Israelis want the Oslo process to proceed almost without regard to Palestinian behavior. Compliance is a virtually dead issue. The Oslo process moves unrelentingly forward because that's what the Israeli electorate wants—not because Prime Minister Binyamin Netanyahu is weak or the American government pressures him.

Why so? The key factor is a profound sense of fatigue. With the exception of the religiously observant, Israelis speak with near despair about the unpleasantness of their having to repress Palestinians, of having to serve in the military and, more generally, of being mired in a century-old tribal conflict.

Instead, they want to pursue more modern and exciting pursuits—the Internet, drip technology, cutting-edge social experimentation, and other pleasures of the late twentieth century. This longing for release leads to a willingness to try anything, even the rather unlikely proposition that ignoring aggression by Palestinians might prompt the latter to calm down and accept Israel's existence. If they achieve prosperity, the thinking goes, if they have reason to hope for the future, then they are more likely to become civilized neighbors.

Since the breakthrough 1993 agreement, relations between Israelis and Palestinians have been based on a very simple deal. Israel granted the Palestinians control over their own lives. In return, Palestinians accept the permanent existence of a Jewish state. Israel, the victor in war, gives material benefits to the losers; the Arab side merely has to promise to behave itself.

Reality is quite different. Israel, a law-abiding democracy, must do as it says, for its own citizens demand nothing less. And, indeed, some 97 percent of Palestinians now live under the Palestinian Authority. To be sure, Israel has not fulfilled all of its promises, nor has it always done so in a timely manner, but (to use a legal term) it has materially fulfilled its promises.

What about the Palestinians? Yes, they participate in joint security patrols and sometimes express peaceful intent. But these positive signs are nearly drowned out by their huge number of infractions. Yasir Arafat's speeches are replete with allusions to jihad. The PA's logo includes the entirety of Israel, implying that it ultimately seeks to do away with the Jewish State. The PA television station shows small children singing anthems full of martial threats and violent rhetoric. Survey data shows the population exceedingly unwilling to establish human ties with their Israeli neighbors. Worse, the PA brings in vast arsenals prohibited by the accords. There are also indications that the PA has, again in defiance of its agreements, begun to manufacture weapons. Not unreasonably, Israeli authorities conclude that the PA is preparing for battle.

In normal circumstances, when one party to a contract does not fulfill its obligations, the other side stops delivering what it promised. But a strange thing is taking place in this case: Israelis have generally chosen to ignore the Palestinians' dismal record. Instead, they keep handing over more territory and other benefits. Rather than take the obvious step of holding up negotiations until the Palestinians do as they promised, Israelis deem Palestinian behavior acceptable. They complain about Palestinian transgressions and they sometimes slow down negotiations, but at each decisive moment, they invariably go ahead and sign more agreements, give more rewards.

Nothing shows this pattern so clearly as the Israeli willingness on three different occasions to bargain for the same concession by the Palestinians. In agreements signed in 1993, 1997, and 1998. Arafat solemnly promised to annul the many phrases in the Palestinian National Charter that call for the destruction of Israel. It took Clinton going to Gaza in December 1998 to get it done, more or less.

The surprising thing is not that the Palestinians take advantage of Israeli patience but that Israelis let them to do so. The Israeli body politic has a reputation for emphasizing security issues, but a closer look reveals that in fact it is willing to overlook almost any terrorist act. Repeatedly, the Israelis announce that they can no longer accept Palestinians transgressions, only to accept them soon after. For example, a bomb went off in Gaza during the Wye Plantation negotiations of October 1998, killing a soldier. Netanyahu said he would stop negotiations. A few days later, he signed an agreement.

This puzzling behavior results from a near-consensus within the Israeli body politic to proceed regardless of Palestinian trespasses. By a 4-to-1 margin the Oslo process remains popular in Israel. Thus, the toppling of the Netanyahu government raises only the question of which politician will end up as prime minister and pace the future of the negotiations—not their outcome.

The implications of this consensus are not cheerful. If Israelis insist on pursuing the chimera of co-opting Palestinians by enriching them, they will sooner or later find themselves facing not just an overwhelmingly hostile people, but one that now has far greater means at its disposal. Eventually, Israelis will realize that, however unpleasant the prospect, they must resume their deterrence posture of old. They will have no choice but to stick to the dull but effective policy of making sure that anyone who threatens them pays dearly for his aggressiveness.

This is the bad news. The good news is that this tough approach will one day succeed. The Palestinians, will recognize the permanence of Israel. This may take decades, or even longer. When it does happen, then the time will be ripe to show magnanimity. In the meantime, the premature conclusion that Palestinians have closed down the conflict, when they in fact have not, is sure recipe for trouble.

(25 December 1998)

IMPLICATIONS OF ISRAEL'S RETREAT FROM LEBANON

A huge argument has raged since the signing of the Oslo accord in September 1993. Those concerned with the security of Israel have intensely disagreed among themselves whether our country's policies are leading to peace or to renewed war. Now, thanks to the dramatic recent developments in Lebanon, that debate is about to be settled. Before the end of 2000, one side will be proved correct and the other side wrong.**

The Left argues that Israel should give its enemies all of what they can legitimately claim: Lebanon, the Golan Heights, a Palestinian state in the West Bank and Gaza; then, backed by a strong warning against further force, it can expect them henceforth to live peaceably with the Jewish state. To be sure, unpleasantries (anti-Semitic statements, the celebration of killers of Jews, talk of eliminating Israel) will continue, but the Left counts on Israel's powerful military ensuring that these hostile intentions remain inoperative.

The Right worries that unilateral concessions do not reduce enmity to Israel but reward violence—thereby breeding more violence. The Right sees anti-Israel sentiments not as ineffectual dreams but as operational statements of intent. As for Israeli's military, it is powerful on paper but its utility is reduced by a low state of national morale and a reluctance to incur casualties. Israel's enemies understand this and perceive Israel as weak and vulnerable, and are therefore more likely to resort to force in order to impose their will on Israel.

The Left's optimism and the Right's pessimism over the years mostly pertained to the Palestinian Authority and Syria. The debate over policy went in circles because Israel never gave either Yasir Arafat or Hafez al-Assad everything they requested. This meant that neither Left nor Right could credibly claim corroboration for its views. They merely belabored the same arguments, unable to produce definitive proof for their claims.

But, as of the early morning of May 24, 2000, closure exists. As of that date, Israel has endeavored scrupulously to carry out United Nations Resolution 425 by evacuating all its soldiers from Lebanese

---

**Note added in 2003: As though on cue, Lebanese attacks across the border and the new round of Palestinian violence both began in late 2000.

territory and reverting to the old international border. Then, completing the Left's program, Prime Minister Ehud Barak strongly warned would-be aggressors to desist ("Shooting at soldiers or civilians within our borders will be seen as an act of war which will necessitate response in kind").

What will Israel's enemies in Lebanon (Syria, Iran, Hezbollah, radical Palestinian groups) now do? The Left counts on them to reward Israel for its complete withdrawal by henceforth living quietly side-by-side with it. The Right expects them to build on their victory in southern Lebanon by moving the battle to northern Israel. Both of these scenarios have vast implications.

Should the Lebanese border remain tranquil, Israelis can conclude that the policy of magnanimity works. Skeptics (like myself) will have to acknowledge that what they presumed to be unilateral concessions made by a state with low morale was in fact a subtle and effective approach to problem resolution. Israel will have shown it really can end its conflict by setting reasonable goals and filling them.

But if the Lebanese border remains hot, with rockets, terrorists, or other forms of aggression directed towards Israel proper, then Israel's policy since 1993 will have proven hollow—a case of wishful thinking, perhaps even self-delusion. Those who encouraged this approach (foremost among them, the Clinton administration) will be morally bound to admit they backed a failed policy, and will be forced to adopt a more conventional and much tougher approach to solving the problem of Arab aggression against Israel.

What happened in Lebanon will also affect Palestinian and Syrian relations with Israel. They have a choice: They can fulfill the Left's expectations—that is, note that Israel intends to treat them fairly, respect Israel's arsenal, and agree to live as good neighbors. This conclusion will lead to a diminishment in bloodshed along with a revival of the Palestinian and Syrian diplomatic tracks.

But if, as the Right predicts, Palestinians and Syrians conclude from the Lebanese conflict that violence works, negotiations will falter and they will emulate the Lebanese by resorting to terrorism and confrontation.

In short, this is a pivotal moment in Arab-Israeli relations, both in terms of resolving the Israeli debate and drawing the main lines of future Arab policy.

(7 June 2000)

THEY HAD A NAME FOR IT

with Mimi Stillman

In its short history, Israel has dealt with its enemies along the lines of two very different doctrines.

From 1948 until about 1993, it discouraged opponents from taking hostile steps by threatening painful retaliation. This doctrine has a well-known name: deterrence. Deterrence worked well for Israel, winning it the grudging acceptance of its enemies over a forty-five-year period. But deterrence also had many drawbacks, being slow moving, expensive, and passive. It was also harsh and internationally unpopular.

Around 1993, Israelis tired of deterrence in favor of a doctrine that had the attractions of being faster, cheaper, more activist, gentler, and more acceptable around the world. Rather than threaten foes, this new policy has three main elements, which are basically the same whether Labor or Likud is in charge.

- It bestows on the Arabs what Israel deems they legitimately can claim. In this spirit, the Lebanese were handed a complete evacuation of Israeli forces from their territory; the Palestinians already have autonomy and look forward to a state of their own; Syrians need only say "yes" to find the whole Golan Heights under their control.

- Although Israel formally requires its negotiating partners to sign agreements, it barely insists on their fulfillment. It has taken no serious steps to enforce the ban on jihad rhetoric, to have terrorists handed over, or to restrict the size of the Palestinian arsenal.

- There must be an indication that no more violence will be tolerated.

A subtle logic underlies this doctrine: Israel's generous—indeed, nearly unilateral—fulfillment of Arab wishes, plus the ignoring of provocative acts and aggressive statements, is done with an eye to establishing economic growth and a friendlier atmosphere, thereby inculcating Arabs with a less radical and more settled outlook, leading, in turn, to improved relations with Israel.

The old doctrine was called deterrence; does the new one have a name? Well, yes, it does. It is called appeasement.

Lest this characterization seem unfair, here—from the authoritative *Encyclopedia of U.S. Foreign Relations*—is an objective description of appeasement as the term was used before the mid-1930s. Until then, we learn, it

> primarily referred to timely concessions to disgruntled nations whose grievances had some legitimacy, in the hope of defusing difficulties and promoting peace and goodwill. Acting from a position of strength, the appeasing power was motivated not by fear or weakness but by a sense of statesmanship and a perception that limited concessions would not endanger its vital national interests.

Sound familiar? The doctrine describes Israel precisely—the sense of strength, the one-way transfer of assets, the perceived non-vital nature of the concessions.

But wait, there's more. The encyclopedia goes on to explain what happened in the 1930s. The leaders of Great Britain and France, faced with aggressive regimes in Germany, Italy, and Japan, and haunted by terrifying memories of World War I, "sought to reduce tension by a new type of appeasement that included overlooking blatant violations of the peace settlement." That too describes Israel to a tee.

And more yet: Concessions by Britain and France "invariably resulted in increased demands, heightened tensions, and threats of war." Israel knows about that too—think of Hezbollah's recent blood-curdling threats, subsequently echoed by Hamas.

Some of the specifics from the 1930s are also uncannily close. Here are three:

- Britain's prime minister, Ramsay MacDonald declared that security must be sought, "not by military but by moral means." Shimon Peres, father of the Oslo process, couldn't have said it better.

- A later British prime minister, Neville Chamberlain, seeing Hitler's insistence on a part of Czechoslovakia as "the Führer's last demand," agreed to his taking over that valuable piece of territory. Shades of Israeli policy toward Syria and the Golan Heights.

- Chamberlain tried, writes the eminent historian Donald Kagan, "to win German good will and good behavior by offering economic incentives." That pretty much describes Israeli policy toward the Palestinians.

And the future? According to the same encyclopedia, "As successive failures strengthened the determination of the appeasers to succeed through intensification of their efforts, a policy that was conceived with honorable objectives degenerated into one of intrigues and machinations, and, at length, humiliating surrender."

Fortunately, Israel is far from a humiliating surrender and at any time can improve its prospects by abandoning the doomed doctrine of appeasement and reverting to that old standby, deterrence. To be sure, the latter is slow, harsh, and unpopular. But it does work.

(5 July 2002)

A PERVERSE DYNAMIC AT WORK

The summit meeting at Camp David in July 2000, when President Clinton spent two weeks trying to broker a deal between Israel's Prime Minister Ehud Barak and the Palestinian leader Yasir Arafat, had a topsy-turvy quality to it, as two facts suggest.

- Israel, the major power of the Middle East, the victor in war, the economically prosperous and politically stable country, did all the giving while the Palestinians—losers, weak, poor, and unstable —were to get the practical benefits. Lest this seem like an exaggeration, consider the issues under discussion at Camp David: Jerusalem, borders, Jewish settlements, Palestinian refugees. In every one of these, Israel gives and the Palestinians take. Issues that would benefit Israel—normalizing relations, changing school textbooks, the Arab League declaring a formal end to the conflict—were not even on the table. The old "land-for-words" formula of UN Resolution 242 is apparently defunct, replaced by Oslo's "land-for-nothing" logic.

- Stranger yet is the fact that the Israeli side made almost every concession at Camp David. It made a heart-wrenching Zionist compromise on Jerusalem, a strategic one on the Jordan River front, and a political one on the return of Palestinian refugees. Despite the remarkable nature of these steps, much at variance with traditional policy, polls showed Israeli public opinion, with reservations, endorsing the prime minister's efforts.

In contrast, the Palestinian side mounted a wall of opposition to Yasir Arafat's presence at the negotiations, seeing in this alone something terrible. Hamas, the leading militant Islamic group, declared the Camp David meeting to be nothing less than "a new Zionist and American conspiracy" against "the rights of our people." Islamic Jihad, a yet more radical group, concurred: "The summit is in the Israeli interest and Israel and the United States will try to pressure the Palestinians and impose Israel's position on them."

The prospect of Arafat making any concessions was anathema to his constituency. On the issue of refugees returning to Israel, for example, one member of the Palestinian Legislative Council, Hussam Khadir, warned Arafat that "A pistol bullet has been passing from generation to generation and its last destination will be the heart of those who cede the refugees' right to return." With this kind of threat hanging over the Palestinian delegation, it is not surprising that they stood tough on nearly every point.

Whatever the summit might have achieved would have been unwelcome to Palestinians. "I consider any agreement that might be reached at Camp David to be a failure because it is not what the Palestinians are looking for," Sheikh Ahmed Yasin of Hamas proclaimed. Like Hafez al-Assad four months earlier, the Palestinians would not take yes for an answer.

All this is really very odd. Not only is the stronger power unilaterally handing over its trump cards, but the recipient is loath to take them. What explains this upside-down circumstance?

Palestinians have, over the seven years of the Oslo process, grown accustomed to taking from Israel and offering very little by way of compensation. In fact, they have come to take this for granted. They expect more of the same—land, autonomy, tax income—culminating in the declaration of a Palestinian state.

As the Palestinians have become the beneficiaries of Israeli largesse, their earlier fear of Israel has been replaced with a disdain that borders on contempt. The result is plain to see. The Barak government signals a willingness to turn over about 90 percent of the West Bank, a much larger percentage than ever previously discussed, and the Palestinians react with indifference. Why bother with this, they ask each other. Why settle for anything less than full control of the land?

At the very least, they can hold out for a better offer. Or they can turn to the alternative, the one that Hezbollah trailblazed in Lebanon. Instead of the indignity of negotiations, Palestinians can resort to the (for them) more noble and redeeming use of violence to extrude the Zionists from every last meter of what they consider to be their land.

A perverse dynamic, in other words, is at work here. The more that Israelis are reasonable and flexible, the less likely Palestinians are to accept a compromise with them. The grander Barak's gesture, the more trivial and even unwelcome it appears to his opponents.

This self-defeating logic is likely to continue until Israel again shows the kind of fortitude that it once made famous.

(2 August 2000)

OSLO'S NINE LIVES

At first glance, it appears that the Palestinian violence that began three weeks ago, in late September 2000, has had a profound impact on the Israeli psyche.

The Left has acknowledged its disarray, shocked by the actions of Palestinian Authority Chairman Yasir Arafat and the Palestinians. Amos Oz, the famed author, spoke for many when he admitted being "somewhat shaken" in his old assumption that the Palestinians "are as eager as we are to reach" a solution to the conflict. Others put it more strongly. "Complete failure" is how Sarah Ozacky-Lazar, co-director of the Jewish-Arab Center for Peace at Givat Haviva, dismisses her own multi-year efforts at Palestinian-Israeli conciliation.

Along similar lines, the Barak government has engaged in some unusually public soul-searching. Rarely does an official so candidly —and promptly—confess the error of his government's ways as did Nahman Shai, the government spokesman. Speaking about Arafat in the aftermath of the Arab summit in Cairo, Shai said: "For the past seven years he was the partner for peace. We were absolutely sure and convinced he was going to make peace with us. But in a few weeks everything collapsed, everything was brought down by him."

But what does this all amount to? The logical implication of this grand mea culpa would be a turnabout in policy, interpreting the past month's violence as part of a long-term effort to eliminate Israel. It would mean giving up on Arafat and the Palestinians as Israel's "partner for peace," at least for this generation. There are some signs of this: Prime Minister Ehud Barak has said "you have to be blind, both in diplomacy and security, in order to continue the negotiations as if nothing happened."

But the true meaning of October's violence appears, in fact, not to have sunk in. Israeli leaders and voters are not yet willing to draw the necessary conclusions.

Read the fine print: Barak has by no means given up on negotiation with Arafat, only called for a "time-out ... to reassess the peace process in response to the events of recent weeks." Translation: once the Palestinians stop the violence, the prime minister is still ready to resume bargaining with them. Confirming that the "time-out" is intended to assuage Israeli anger, not to signal a serious change in policy, the prime minister is continuing to permit the transfer of about $10 million a month in tax payments to the Palestinian Authority, as well as millions of cubic meters of water and all of its electricity.

Other Labor Party leaders are indignant at even this symbolic "time-out." Acting Foreign Minister Shlomo Ben-Ami retorted that "life does not take a time-out," and wants to resume negotiations where they left off in July at Camp David. Regional Cooperation Minister Shimon Peres, Justice Minister Yossi Beilin, and other ministers also joined in opposing any slowdown in diplomacy.

Nor is it only the political class that clutches at the illusion that more concessions will win Palestinian cooperation. A poll of Israelis published on October 13 found that 63 percent of the electorate still wants negotiations with the Palestinians to go on—a number not much lower than at the height of the peace process euphoria.

Israel suffers from a wide array of assaults—stone-throwing kids, gun-shooting "policemen," lynched and abducted soldiers, vicious anti-Semitic rhetoric, and Jewish institutions under siege on four continents—and responds with a mock ultimatum accompanied by pleas that everyone return to the bargaining table.

The errors begun at Oslo live on. Like a cat, Oslo has nine lives, with several of them still remaining. The Israeli fatalities of the past month have not been enough to wake the country from its stupor. How many more deaths will it take?

The bad news is that Oslo actively harms Israel, eroding its deterrence capabilities, and making it evermore difficult for its government to defend the country's interests. Unprovoked violence, political disrespect, and surging ambitions among its enemies will continue, perhaps increase, as long as the illusion endures that the goodwill of the Palestinians can be bought.

The good news is that Israel's mood of accommodation and weakness cannot endure. As things continue to get worse, even the most thick-headed politician will see that fortitude, as opposed to begging for the chance to make more unilateral concessions, is the country's only sensible strategy. Democratic states are notoriously slow to stand up for themselves, but when they do, watch out.

(25 October 2000)

WINDS OF WAR

The outbreak of Palestinian violence in late September 2000 fundamentally altered the atmosphere of Arab-Israeli relations from what it was before. In fact, it has created a situation that resembles the bad old days of pre-1967.

Back then, Israel's enemies widely believed that they could, with one good blow, dispatch the Jewish state. Their overconfidence explains why, with no one planning or wanting it, full-scale war broke out in June 1967. Israel's astonishing victory in the Six-Day War then seemingly destroyed Arab exuberance and forever closed the question of its permanent existence.

But it was not to be. The Oslo process, along with other signals of Israeli demoralization over the seven years of the Oslo period, reignited Arab overconfidence and wakened the sleeping dogs of war. In the two months since the violence began, the enemies of Israel are again tempted by the military option in ways reminiscent of the years before 1967.

In brief, the security that war had achieved for Israel, diplomacy has undone.

Listen to how, over the past two months, making war on Israel has become a real choice for the Arab states and Iran.

As usual, Iraq acts the boldest, calling for a jihad to "liberate Palestine" and "put an end to Zionism." Saddam Hussein has noisily recruited two million volunteers to fight Israel and sent a division of soldiers to his border closest with Israel. Iran's supreme leader, Ayatollah Ali Khomeini, has called Israel a "cancerous tumor" that must "be removed." The untried Syrian regime of Bashar al-Assad has rattled sabers with talk of war.

In Cairo, reports the Middle East Newsline, the current debate is about "whether the Israeli-Palestinian mini-war will escalate into a regional confrontation. At that point, the question is whether Egypt will enter the fray." Egyptian President Hosni Mubarak denies plans to make total war ("A war until the last Egyptian soldier is definitely not in the cards") but makes ominous-sounding threats about "entering the tunnel of the unknown." Israeli analysts recognize this danger. For example, Yuval Steinitz, the thoughtful Likud member of the Knesset's Foreign Affairs and Defense Committee, observes that "Egypt is preparing for a conflict with Israel, though not necessarily an all-out war."

The U.S. government has, in the person of its ambassador to Israel, Martin Indyk, acknowledged this danger. Indyk noted how the Israeli-Palestinian clashes of recent weeks have caused some in the Arab world to float the idea of resorting to a military option against Israel. He calls these "a very dangerous challenge."

How might a full-scale war actually come about? Hezbollah, the Lebanese militant Islamic organization that expelled Israel's forces from south Lebanon earlier this year, is probably the key, for Israel has promised to punish Hezbollah aggression by hitting Syrian targets.

Here is one scenario of a conflict starting without anyone intending it to (as in 1967) from the *Jerusalem Report*'s cover story of November 20, 2000, "What Could Trigger War": Palestinian snipers kill Jewish children, Israeli forces respond with artillery shells, one of which goes astray and kills twenty Palestinian children. Furious demonstrators pour into the streets across the Middle East. Riding these sentiments, Hezbollah attacks northern Israel. As promised, Israel retaliates against Syrian targets, prompting a mobilization of Syrian, Egyptian, and other forces, including Israel's. At this point, concludes the *Report*, "All-out war on all fronts is one pull of the trigger away." Who would pull the trigger? Saddam is a likely candidate. A Palestinian source notes that "What Saddam wants is to spark a regional war which he can lead." Israelis agree: a senior military officer expects that the Iraqis "would love to participate" in a conflict against Israel.

If such a descent into war is not to take place, Israel must carefully calibrate its actions to achieve two nearly contradictory goals: deter potential enemies (be willing to use force and lose lives); and not agitate the Arab street (deploy violence in an intelligent and controlled way).

This is an exceedingly difficult pair of objectives and they are getting even harder to achieve as each new day of violence simultaneously diminishes Israeli deterrence and heightens Arab anger. To be sure, the government of Israel has taken some steps (for example, sending a private warning to Damascus and reinforcing troops on the Golan Heights) but such easy gestures alone will not suffice. The sooner Israel begins the effort to seriously dissuade its potential enemies, the better its chances to dispel the winds of war.

(20 December 2000)

Oslo Diplomacy: An Israeli Choice

Through the over seven years of the Oslo process, one issue has kept coming up: Are Israel's concessions the result of its own sovereign decisions, or are they due to U.S. government pressure? Now, in January 2001, as the Clinton administration enters its final lap, a definitive answer is finally at hand.

It was pretty clear from the start that the decisions were made in Israel; sure, American politicians appreciate the giveaways, but they do not demand them. Symbolically, the diplomacy got started in the cool woods of Norway, far from madding Washington and without even any American knowledge.

Also, as Aaron Miller of the State Department points out, the U.S. government gets involved not of its own volition but at the request of Israeli politicians. In September 1996, widespread Palestinian violence followed the opening of a Temple Mount tunnel and saw Prime Minister Binyamin Netanyahu rush to Washington to engage the Americans in solving this problem. Likewise, it was Prime Minister Ehud Barak who pressed President Clinton to convene the Camp David II summit in July 2000; and it was Barak's insistence that the president offer "bridging proposals" that explains the current flurry of diplomacy.

The amazing prospect of a caretaker prime minister, one lacking any sort of parliamentary or public mandate, and relying on speed diplomacy to solve his country's deepest problems in advance of an election, further confirms where the diplomatic initiative is coming from—namely, Israel. Ehud Olmert, the mayor of Jerusalem, got it right: "The initiative to divide Jerusalem is not the fruit of American pressure but the fruit of Barak's own capitulation."

The idea that Washington pressures Israel to make concessions has some grounding in reality—it just happens to be out of date.

The American "land for peace" policy that emerged in the aftermath of Israel's victory in 1967 was for twenty years (1973-93) a source of tension with Israel. During that period, Arab states and the Palestinians increasingly talked about "peace" with Israel, understanding this was a prerequisite to the voluntary return of lands they had lost in 1967. At the same time, Israelis suspected the sincerity of their statements, which were usually issued through gritted teeth, in English, freighted with conditions and angry demands. Washington pressed a reluctant Israel to accept those statements as valid, and to respond by turning over land in exchange.

Then came a historic shift. In 1992, Yitzhak Rabin came to office intent on trading the territories for peace agreements. His intensive efforts notwithstanding, he managed no land-for-peace exchange. Rabin concluded that persisting in this approach would leave Israel without agreements and with the territories he was trying to unload. So, as Douglas Feith points out, Rabin tried something very different: "Seeing that he could not insist on a secure peace while bringing the occupation to a prompt end, Rabin decided, fatefully, that the latter took priority." In other words, he began a policy of unilateral withdrawal, which yet remains in effect.

With this shift, the government of Israel effectively abandoned its old worries and adopted the carefree American approach. Out went two decades of doubts; in came a willingness to ignore Arab statements and actions. Which brings us to the present and the strong, autonomous Israeli desire for paper agreements, independent of U.S. pressure.

For those skeptical of the Oslo process, it is consoling to blame Israel's downward spiral of the past seven years on Americans. For one, this implies that the old Israeli spirit is still alive, submerged somewhere under American demands. For another, it suggests that a change in Washington could lead to improved Israeli policies.

But these cheery illusions can no longer be indulged. Reality must be faced. Israelis are making their own choices and forging their own destiny.

(3 January 2001)

TWO MISTAKEN ECONOMIC ASSUMPTIONS

The election of Ariel Sharon to replace Ehud Barak in February 2001 allows us to look back with amazement at the previous seven and a half years, when the Israeli government pursued a course without parallel in the annals of diplomacy.

The best known of its negotiations were with Yasir Arafat and the Palestinians, but these were paralleled by no less important discussions with the Syrians and Lebanese. In all tracks, the Jewish state pursued a similar approach, which might be paraphrased as follows: "We will be reasonable and will give you what you can legitimately demand; in turn, we expect you to have a change of heart, ending your campaign to destroy Israel and instead accepting the permanence of a sovereign Jewish state in the Middle East." In brief, the Israelis offered land for peace, as the U.S. government had long pressed them to do.

This policy prompted Israel to take a series of steps that struck some observers as bold and others as foolhardy: to the Palestinians it offered a state, complete with Jerusalem as its capital and sovereignty over the Temple Mount. To the Syrians, it offered full control over the Golan Heights. To Lebanon, it not only offered but actually carried out a complete and unilateral withdrawal of Israeli forces from the southern part of that country in May 2000.

These concessions won Israel in return precisely nothing. Reaching out a hand of friendship won not Arab acceptance but ever-increasing demands for more Israeli concessions. Palestinians and Syrians disdained successive Israeli offers, always demanding more. Lebanese took everything Israel gave and made more demands.

Worse, the jaw-dropping array of Israeli concessions actually increased Arab and Muslim hostility. When the Oslo process, as that episode of diplomacy is called, began in 1993, Israel was feared and respected by its enemies, who were beginning to recognize Israel as a fact of life and reluctantly giving up their efforts to destroy it. But those efforts revived as Arabs watched Israel forsake its security and its religious sanctities, overlook the breaking of solemn promises, and make empty threats. The impression was of an Israel desperate to extricate itself from further conflict.

What Israelis saw as far-sighted magnanimity came across as weakness and demoralization. Combined with other sources of Arab confidence—especially demographic growth and resurgent faith—this led to a surge in anti-Zionist ambitions and rekindled the hopes of destroying the "Zionist entity." Steps intended to calm the Palestinians instead heightened their ambitions, their fury, and their violence. For all its good will and soul-searching, Israel now faces a higher threat of all-out war than at any time in decades. No doubt that is why Sharon was elected by so wide a margin.

Land-for-peace contained a plethora of errors, but the two most fundamental were economic. One overestimated Israeli power, the other misunderstood Arab aspirations.

First, the Oslo process assumed that Israel, by virtue of its economic boom and formidable arsenal, is so strong that it can unilaterally choose to close down its century-old conflict with the Arabs. Israel's GDP is nearly $100 billion a year and the Palestinians' is about $3 billion; Israel's per capita income of $16,000 is slightly higher than Spain's, while the Syrian per capita income of about $800 compares to that of the Republic of Congo. The Israel Defense Forces deploy the finest aircraft, tanks, and other materiel that money can buy; the Palestinian police force has rudimentary weapons.

This material strength, it turns out, does not permit Israel to impose its will on the Arabs. In part, it cannot do this because the Arabs initiated the conflict and have continued it; only they, not the Israelis, can end it. The key decisions of war and peace have always been made in Cairo, Damascus, and Baghdad, not in Jerusalem and Tel Aviv.

However formidable Israel's strength is in planes and tanks, its enemies are developing military strategies that either go lower (to civil unrest and terrorism, as in the recent Palestinian violence against Israel) or higher (to weapons of mass destruction, as in the Iraqi threat).

Finally, a high income or a mighty arsenal is not as important as will and morale; software counts more than hardware. In this respect, Israelis do not impress their opponents. In the words of philosopher Yoram Hazony, Israelis are "an exhausted people, confused and without direction." Loud announcements for all to hear that Israelis are sick of their conflict with the Arabs—how they loath reserve military duty that extends into middle age for men, the high military spending, the deaths of soldiers, and the nagging fear of terrorism—do not inspire fear. How can an "exhausted people" hope to impose its will on enemies?

Thus is Israel's hope to coerce its enemies illusory.

A second assumption behind the Oslo diplomacy was that enhanced economic opportunity would shift Arab attention from war to more constructive pursuits. The logic makes intuitive sense: satisfy reasonable claims so the Palestinians, Syrians, and Lebanese can look beyond anti-Zionism to improve their standard of living. If they only had a nice apartment and a late-model car, the thinking went, their ardor for destroying Israel would diminish.

There is little evidence for this expectation. As shown by the Arab readiness to accept economic hardship in the pursuit of political aims, politics usually trumps economics. The Syrian government has for decades accepted economic paralysis as the price of staying in power.

More dramatic is Palestinian refusal to give up the "right of return." To fend off Palestinian claims to territory and buildings abandoned by their ancestors in Israel over fifty years ago, the idea was sometimes bruited of buying them off, in return for giving up a distant and seemingly impractical aspiration. No deal. A reporter in Baqaa, a Palestinian camp in Jordan, recently found no one willing to take cash in return for forgoing claims to Palestine. As one middle-aged woman put it: "We will not sell our [ancestral] land for all the money in the world. We are Palestinians and we'll remain Palestinians. We don't want compensation, we want our homeland." The owner of a pharmacy concurred, adding, "Even if Arafat agreed to compensation, we as Palestinians can't agree to it."

Israelis had devised an elegant push-pull theory of diplomacy: between Israeli strength and Arab hopes for a better future, they figured the Arabs would find themselves compelled to shut down the long anti-Zionist campaign. Both assumptions, however sensible sounding, were dead wrong.

In this, the Oslo process belonged to a tradition of failed diplomacy that relies on granting an opponent some of what he wants in the hope that this will render him less hostile. It did not work for Neville Chamberlain with Hitler; nor for Richard Nixon with Brezhnev. The Israelis offered far more than either of these and ended up with even less.

(March 2001)

8

THE OSLO WAR

LIFT THE "SIEGE"?

In the nearly six months since starting the sustained violence against Israel in September 2000, the Palestinian Authority has been left economically destitute. Per-capita income has fallen about one-third, from $2,000 to $1,400. The population living below the poverty line has gone up by 50 percent. Unemployment has gone up four-fold, from 11 percent to 45 percent. Recipients of United Nations aid to alleviate hardship has increased tenfold, from 8.5 percent to 85 percent.

The U.S. ambassador to Israel, Martin Indyk, finds the Palestinian economy "on the brink of collapse." A UN source predicts that, if nothing is done, the PA "could collapse by the end of March." To prevent this, Israel is being pressed from all sides, in U.S. Secretary of State Colin Powell's words, to "lift the siege."

The assumption behind this pressure, as explained by London's *Independent* newspaper, is that economic problems are causing the PA territories to slide into an anarchy that undercuts PA Chairman Yasir Arafat's ability to negotiate with Israel "over restoring calm." Implicitly, those calling on Israel to ease the economic pressure are saying that no matter what the PA does—break its word, incite hatred, sponsor violence—Israel's enlightened self-interest requires it to assure that Palestinians economically fare decently.

This, to put it mildly, is a highly original argument.

When the UN had a problem with Rhodesia, South Africa, Libya, Iraq, and Afghanistan, it pursued exactly the opposite approach and imposed an embargo to cripple those countries economically. The goals are multiple: weaken the military machine, punish the leadership, demoralize the regime's supporters, turn the population against its rulers. The U.S. government uses the same tactics: generations-old embargoes remain in place on North Korea and Cuba.

Nor is this anything new, for conflict has always had an economic angle. Ancient armies cut supply routes. Medieval cities were starved into submission. Two centuries ago, during the Napoleonic wars, the British Navy established a naval blockade to cut France off from supplies. World Wars I and II witnessed extensive use of economic deprivation.

What Israel is doing—withholding tax money, denying entry to laborers, and restricting movement—fits into an ancient, sensible, and somewhat effective method of warfare. Why, then, is it expected to do otherwise and fund its enemies?

The reason, ironically, has little to do with the UN or U.S. and much to do with Israelis themselves. They developed the "new Middle East" notion (which others now echo) that Israel's long-term welfare and security lies not in depriving its enemies of resources, but in helping them develop their economies. This, the American analyst Patrick Clawson writes, is "a vision of the Middle East that looks for all the world like the French plan for Europe after World War II: use economic cooperation as the starting point for cementing ties and reconciling peoples, with the goal being a common market that in turn leads to close political ties."

But Germans were incorporated into the French vision, it bears noting, not while Hitler ruled, but after the Nazi defeat. The French plan built up the former enemy only after he was crushed, acknowledged his errors, and had a totally new government. By similar token, American aid will flow to Iraq only when Saddam Hussein is history.

In contrast, the "new Middle East" idea offers economic help even before the war is over. It is tantamount to sending the enemy resources while fighting is still under way—not a hugely bright idea so long as, in Efraim Inbar's words, "Arafat and his coterie are part of the problem and not of the solution." Accordingly, the strengthening of Arafat will hardly "restore calm." Rather, it will provide him with the resources for a bigger arsenal and a more long-lasting intifada.

Until the Palestinians do give up their war against Israel, they need to be shown that their aggression carries a heavy price. The higher that price, long experience shows, the sooner they are likely to give up their hostile ways. Thus all who hope for a resolution of the Palestinian problem should urge the Sharon government to squeeze the PA just as hard as it can. Ironically, this is in the long-term interests of everyone, including the Palestinians themselves, who only in this way will give up on their urge to destroy Israel in favor of other, more constructive pursuits.

(14 March 2001)

THE LEFT'S ONGOING OSLO DELUSION

What do you do when everything you predicted fails to happen?

This is the quandary of the Israeli Left and its Diaspora allies. They were sure that if only Israel made extensive compromises, Palestinians would respond by accepting the permanent existence of a sovereign Jewish state in the Middle East. This certainty inspired the seven-year-long Oslo effort from September 1993 until September 2000 (yes, also during Binyamin Netanyahu's three years), when Israeli governments pursued a policy of niceness.

But instead of winning Palestinian acceptance, Oslo's painful concessions had the reverse effect. The more Israel showed flexibility, the more Palestinians smelled blood and became enraged at the very existence of the Jewish state. This culminated in the violence of the past seven months.

Explaining what went so terribly wrong with their plans, the extreme elements of the Israeli and Jewish Left blame only Ehud Barak; in a full-page *Ha'aretz* advertisement, Uri Avnery's Gush Shalom faults him for a "total ignorance of the Palestinian narrative and with disrespect to its importance"—whatever all that means. Slightly less extreme leftists blame politicians on both sides: "The government ambassadors have failed," announces a coalition of American Jewish groups in a full-page *New York Times* advertisement. The moderate Left blames Arafat, though it cannot quite agree on the reasons for his misbehavior: either he is too set in his violent ways, or he is a bad character ("either stupid, evil or both"), or he engages in "terrible foolishness and recklessness."

Despite these differences, the entire Left shares one key belief: that Oslo failed due to the personality and actions of leaders—and not because of its inherent faults. The Left still thinks that Israel making concessions will resolve the Arab-Israeli conflict. And so it hopes that the Oslo process will soon be resumed, with just some minor adjustments: emphasizing the role of confidence-building measures; treating Palestinian violations of promises with greater seriousness; inviting international monitors; withdrawing settlers; replacing Arafat (the *Jerusalem Report* urges "would-be Palestinian leaders of vision and guts to stand up and be counted"); waiting until Arafat dies; ignoring politicians and initiating people-to-people exchanges.

My favorite is the "Olive Trees For Peace" initiative that calls on Jews to purchase olive trees and replant them in Palestinian villages.

These suggestions reveal how astonishingly little the Left learned from the collapse of the Oslo process. Instead of advocating a change in course, it wants Israel to revert to the discredited policy of nice-ness. If a mistake is worth making once, the Left seems to think, it is worth making again and again. The Oslo process did not fail be-cause of poor implementation. Rather, its basic assumption—that a policy of niceness would seduce Palestinians into accepting Israel—proved profoundly wrong.

If Israel truly wants to end its problem with the Palestinians, it must adopt the opposite approach: convince Palestinians not of its niceness but its toughness. This means not replanting Arab olive trees but punishing violence so hard that its enemies will eventually feel so deep a sense of futility that they will despair of further conflict.

A historical analogy comes to mind: when World War I ended, German armies remained intact and their capital city unoccupied. Not convinced they had really lost the war, Germans harbored a deep discontent that led to the rise of Hitler. In contrast, Germans emerged from World War II utterly defeated and without any illu-sions to confuse them. This time, understanding the need for a fresh start, they turned to Konrad Adenauer and built a peaceful, success-ful country.

The Palestinian Authority is hardly Germany, but the analogy does hold: Palestinians will not give up on their aggressive ambitions vis-à-vis Israel until fully convinced that these cannot succeed. Only then can they build a polity and an economy commensurate with their dignity and talent. Ironically, then, Palestinians need almost as much to be defeated by Israel as Israel needs to defeat them.

It's time for the Left to recognize the vastness of its error in the Oslo process and adopt the tough-minded policies that will finally liberate Israelis and Palestinians from their mutual conflict.

(25 April 2001)

ISRAEL'S LEBANON LESSON

Rocket attacks coming out of Lebanon and directed against Israeli troops in May 2002, followed by a tough Israeli response, serve as a poignant reminder that Israel's withdrawal from Lebanon a year ago did not exactly live up to its expectations.

It may be useful to recall just how high those expectations were. By a nearly four-to-one margin, Israelis endorsed the retreat from Lebanon as an excellent strategic move. On the left, Internal Security minister Shlomo Ben-Ami thought that Syria's president was "very stressed by Israel's decision to withdraw from Lebanon." On the right, foreign minister David Levy declared that the pullout would weaken Syria's position.

Others speculated further. Dan Margalit of *Ha'aretz* forecast the withdrawal would "spur Syria to come back to the negotiating table." Novelist Amos Oz boldly predicted about Lebanon's most aggressively anti-Israel organization: "The minute we leave south Lebanon we will have to erase the word Hezbollah from our vocabulary."

A year later, how do things look?

The idea that an Israeli retreat would scare Damascus into restarting negotiations turns out to be as silly as it sounds. President Hafez al-Assad went to his grave without returning to the bargaining table and his son Bashar has so far shown no willingness to talk.

The expectation that Israel would enjoy a peaceable northern border proved similarly misguided. Hezbollah concocted a new claim to a piece of Israeli-held land (the Shaba Farms) to justify continued hostilities. No longer restrained by Israel's security zone in Lebanon, it threatens to use Katyusha rockets against Israel proper, prompting an alert as far away as Israel's third-largest city, Haifa. In the course of a year, Hezbollah attacked Israel seven times, attempted many infiltrations, abducted three Israel soldiers and killed two others. In response, Israel's government deployed helicopter gunships and attacked a Syrian radar site, killing three Syrian soldiers.

In brief, "Hezbollah" has hardly been erased from the Israeli vocabulary.

But the greatest consequence of the Israeli retreat was felt among the Palestinians. That impact is partly practical, with Hezbollah providing instruction and arms to the Palestinian Authority. For example, Hezbollah reached an agreement with the PA "to train fighters and provide weapons against tanks and aircraft," reports the Middle East Newsline. Palestinians took up Hezbollah's distinctive tactics and tools—suicide bombings on the one hand, roadside bombs detonated by mobile phones on the other. They even adopted the Hezbollah technique of filming themselves carrying out attacks on Israelis, then making the film available to the Arab and Muslim media.

The impact is also psychological. Palestinians watched Hezbollah impose every last one of its demands on Israel, without having to sit around a table with Israeli diplomats; this served as an object lesson. Palestinians concluded that if they used enough violence, they too could get all they wanted from Israel without having to compromise. This "Lebanonization" of the Palestinians has had major consequences.

Prime Minister Ariel Sharon draws a connection between the Israeli retreat from Lebanon and "what happened later on" with the Palestinians. The head of Israel's former Lebanese allied force puts it more strongly; Israel's every concession to Hezbollah, he says, has been "very costly" for it in dealing with the Palestinians. Specifically, Hezbollah's success first inspired the Palestinians to turn down even the amazingly generous terms that Prime Minister Ehud Barak subsequently offered them, confident that they could do better on the battlefield. It prompted the Palestinians to abandon the bargaining table and revert to violence against Israel. It also helps account for the escalation in that violence, which started with rocks and now includes long-distance mortar shellings.

The great majority of Israelis a year ago lived in the sweet delusion that unilateral concessions to neighbors would eventually win acceptance and quiet. After eight months of Palestinian violence—partly attributable to Israel's withdrawal under fire from Lebanon—the hollowness of this hope is becoming increasingly apparent.

As they shudder back to reality, Israelis can console themselves with the knowledge that, by abandoning their Lebanon delusion, however painful that process is, they are taking the necessary first step toward dealing with today's crisis. The second step will be to understand that acceptance by neighbors will result not from Israel's making unilateral concessions, but from its being respected and feared.

(23 May 2001)

"It's 1967 All Over Again"

I warned in December 2000 of the "winds of war" blowing in the Middle East.* A few days ago, the far-left Israeli politician and member of parliament, Naomi Chazan, echoed my warning, down to using that same English-language expression.

But we understand the dangers a bit differently. For her, the danger stems from "the failure of the cease-fire and the absence of any movement on the diplomatic front." In contrast, I emphasized "Israeli demoralization over the past seven years, [which has] reignited Arab overconfidence." Not surprisingly, we recommend polar-opposite policies. Chazan's solution lies in Israel resuming what I call "Oslo niceness"—overlooking Palestinian violence, promoting the Palestinian economy, withdrawing forces from the territories, and recognizing a Palestinian state.

But haven't we already seen this movie? Oslo niceness between 1993 and 2000 brought Israel to its present predicament. Arabs and Iranians watched as a majority of Israel's population clamored to hand over territory in return for scraps of paper and (correctly) concluded from this that morale in the Jewish state had deeply eroded.

They also (wrongly) concluded that the state was therefore militarily vulnerable. With this, the grudging acceptance that Israel had won from many Middle Easterners, via six wars and six victories, was rapidly undone. As Arabs and Iranians smelled blood, their ambition to eliminate Israel, previously in remission, resurfaced rapidly and widely.

Survey research shows its extent. The (Arab-run) Jerusalem Media and Communication Center revealed in June that 46 percent of Palestinians want the current violence to lead to the "freedom of all Palestine"—code words for the destruction of Israel. A nearly simultaneous Bir Zeit University poll found an even more resounding 72 percent of Palestinians supporting the "liberation" of Israel.

---

*See "Winds of War," pp. 157-59.

These vaulting hopes have spawned an Arab war fever reminiscent of the terrible days of May 1967. Ze'ev Schiff, dean of Israeli military correspondents, finds that, just as "on the eve of the Six Day War, Arab leaders are issuing threat after threat against Israel, stirring their own passions and those of their audiences." A few sober-minded Arabic-speakers share this concern. "It's 1967 all over again" is the title of a dissident's article coming out of Damascus, full of worries about a repeat disaster.

Unless Israel sends clear signals of strength, the current bout of saber rattling could, 1967-style, lead inadvertently to another all-out war. Although elected to send precisely those signals of strength, Ariel Sharon began his prime ministry by unexpectedly continuing his predecessors' passive response to Palestinian violence (though this then changed somewhat).

Whatever Sharon's reasons for inaction—win Western favor, maintain his coalition government, redeem his reputation—such a soft policy has major implications. If even this most feared of Israeli leaders absorbs the death of twenty-one young people without retaliation, as he did in June 2001, it confirms the belief that Israel is nothing but a "paper tiger." Or, in the evocative metaphor of Hezbollah's leader, it is "weaker than a spider's web."

To combat this perception, Israel needs to take more active steps. With a nod to Brig.-Gen. (res.) Effi Eitam and Haifa University's Steven Plaut, here are a few suggestions. Bury suicide bombers in potter's fields rather than deliver their bodies to relatives (who turn their funerals into frenzied demonstrations). Freeze the financial assets of Palestinian Authority Chairman Yasir Arafat, the PLO, and the PA. Prevent PA officials (including Arafat) from returning to the PA. Permit no transportation of people or goods beyond basic necessities. Shut off utilities to the PA.

Then: Implement the death penalty against murderers. Seize weapons from the PA and make sure no new ones reach it. Re-occupy areas from which guns or mortars are fired. Raze the PA's illegal offices in Jerusalem, its security infrastructure and villages from which attacks are launched. Capture or otherwise dispose of the PA leadership. Destroy the PA. Reach separate deals with each Palestinian town or village.

Sharon, in short, has no lack of choices. The hard part is finding the political will to act on them. The stakes are high. Unless Israel take steps to deter its potential enemies by reasserting its strong image, today's war fever could lead to tomorrow's war.

To help avoid such a war, the outside world (and especially the U.S. government) should do two things: end its repetition of the illogical mantra that "there can be no military solution to this conflict" and, instead, urge Sharon to take the steps needed to resurrect Israel's once-fearsome reputation.

(18 July 2001)

THE ARABS STILL WANT TO DESTROY ISRAEL

In June 2001, Palestinian television broadcast a sermon in a Gaza mosque in which the imam, Ibrahim Madi, made the following statement: "God willing, this unjust state Israel will be erased; this unjust state the United States will be erased; this unjust state Britain will be erased."

The sheikh's gentle homily comes to mind again as Palestinians' efforts to build their arsenal and persistent attacks on Israeli civilians have again been exposed of late. The most recent assault was at a ballroom last night [January 17, 2002], when a Palestinian used hand grenades to kill five and wound more than thirty Israelis, a much smaller number than would have been the case had the explosives on the terrorist's body gone off as intended.

And while the American and Israeli situations might seem completely different, Sheikh Madi's remarks established that the forces of militant Islam see them as akin. So if a reminder is needed that the war on terrorism goes beyond the campaign in Afghanistan, the Palestinians offer a powerful mnemonic. Militant Islamic rule in Afghanistan may be history but militant Islam is not.

Osama bin Laden years ago declared a jihad against all Christians and Jews while his friend Mullah Omar, the Taliban dictator, talked publicly about "the destruction of America," which he hoped would happen "within a short period of time." That militant Islamic leaders wish the same for Israel should hardly be news. The most powerful of them all, Iran's supreme leader Ayatollah Ali Khamene'i, recently called for "this cancerous tumor of a state be removed from the region."

There are differences in the situations, to be sure. The jihad against the U.S. is newer, less advanced, and has less supported from non-militant Islamic elements. But especially now, as the U.S. has formally declared war on terrorism, the common cause against the two states is growing.

As far as being a target nation goes, Israel is a bit further along the learning curve. The attempt to destroy the Jewish state has gone on since it came into existence in 1948. For over a half century, the majority of Arabs have persisted in seeing the state of Israel as a temporary condition, an enemy they eventually expect to dispense with, permitting Israelis to, at best, live as a subject people in "Palestine." At worst, who knows?

When Israel first came into existence, the Arabs casually assumed they would destroy it. But Israel did something right. For forty-five years the state defended itself with a toughness and determination that had, by 1993, left the Arabs reeling. It was a moment when Israel should have pushed its advantage, to get recognition once and for all of its right to exist. Instead, the Israelis made what has turned out to be the historic mistake of easing up. Rather than go in for victory, they offered advantageous deals to their two main enemies, the Syrians and Palestinians.

Predictably, these offers backfired: Rather than being seen as far-sighted strategic concessions intended to close the conflict, they were interpreted as signs of Israel's demoralization. The result was renewed Arab hopes of destroying Israel through force of arms and an upsurge in violence. Diplomacy, in other words, unintentionally revived Arab dreams of obliterating the Jewish state.

Obviously, this wall of Arab rejection harms Israel, denying its bid to live as a normal nation, subjecting its population to homicidal attacks, and compelling it to take tough steps against neighbors. But Israel is prospering despite these attacks, boasting a high standard of living, a democratic policy, and a vibrant culture.

The great irony is that Arabs are paying the higher price for their destructive urge. The Arab focus on harming the Jewish state prevents a talented and dignified people from achieving its potential. It means they neglect improving their own standard of living, opening up their own political process, or attaining the rule of law. The result is plain to see: Arabs are among the world leaders in percentages of dictatorships, rogue states, violent conflicts, and military spending.

Getting Arabs to reconcile themselves to Israel's existence is easier to say than to do. But it is, and will remain, the only solution. Only such a change of heart will close down the century-old conflict, permit Israel to attain normality, and give Arabs a chance to advance down the path to modernity.

But this interpretation of the Arab-Israeli conflict puts the onus on Arabs, something we're not altogether accustomed to doing these days. Conventional wisdom has shifted so far that even Israelis tend to consider Arab acceptance of Israel a fait accompli, shifting the burden of action to Israel in the form of concessions (handing over the Golan Heights, parts of Jerusalem, etc.). But if that position was credible in 1993, surely today's inflamed rhetoric and the drumbeat of Palestinian violence proves it to have been a mirage.

Israel now has the unenviable task of convincing the Arabs that their dreams of destruction will fail. Translated into action, that means resolve and toughness. It means becoming feared, not loved. The process will be neither domestically pleasant nor internationally popular. But what choice is there? The failure of the Oslo negotiating process showed nothing so much as that attempts at a quick fix are doomed to fail.

Understanding the conflict in this way has profound implications. It means that the outside world, always anxious to solve the Arab-Israeli conflict, can be most helpful by simply coming to terms with the basic fact of continued Arab rejection of Israel. It must acknowledge Israel's predicament, tolerate its need to be tough, and press the Arabs to make a fundamental change in course.

For many governments, even the American one, this approach requires a reversal from the current policy of premising a breakthrough on concessions from Israel. Such a reversal in policy will not come easily, but it is a near-prerequisite for anyone serious about closing down the Arab-Israeli conflict.

(18 January 2002)

THE *ONLY* SOLUTION IS MILITARY

"We are in a war," Israel's prime minister, Ariel Sharon said in February 2002, referring to his country's fight with the Palestinians.

The Palestinians agree: "This is war," responded Al-Fatah's commander on the West Bank, Husayn Shaykh.

In fact, Israelis and Palestinians have already been at war for over a year, but their leaders finally acknowledging this fact makes it easier squarely to assess the situation. War has clearly established patterns, and these provide insights into the Levantine situation:

- What each side seeks—to achieve victory and avoid defeat—is primarily psychological in nature. Victory consists of imposing one's will on the enemy (Israel wants its neighbors to leave it alone; the Palestinians want to destroy Israel) by convincing it that his cause is hopeless. Defeat means accepting that one's cause is hopeless.

- Will, fortitude, and morale are often more important for victory than are objective factors such as the economy, technology, arsenal, number of casualties, or votes at the United Nations. In many cases, these latter count mainly in so far as they affect a combatant's mood.

- Resolution occurs when one party realizes it can no longer pursue its aims and gives them up. This usually follows its unambiguous vanquishment, either a military collapse (as in World War II) or internal rot (as in the Cold War). "In every case I can think of," writes strategist Michael Ledeen, "peace has come about at the end of a war in which there was a winner and a loser. The winner imposed terms on the loser, and those terms were called 'peace.'" Resolution can follow from other reasons—e.g., when a bigger enemy turns up. Worried about the common German menace, Britain and France buried their historic enmity in 1904.

- Stalemate, conversely, keeps conflict alive by letting both sides hope to win another day. The Germans lost too narrowly to give up in their first attempt to dominate Europe (World War I), so they tried again (World War II); when they were decisively defeated and gave up. Many unresolved conflicts loom in today's world. The Korean War ended inconclusively in 1953; a half-century later, another round remains likely—unless the North Korean regime collapses first. The Iran-Iraq conflict ended in 1988 with neither side feeling defeated, so more hostilities are likely—again, unless one regime first disappears. So too in the Arab-Israeli conflict: The Arabs lost many rounds (1948-49, 1956, 1967, 1970, 1973, 1982) but never felt defeated, so they keep coming back to try again.

- Diplomacy rarely ends conflicts. Hardly a single major interstate conflict has concluded due to someone's clever schema. The idea that a "peace process" can take the place of the dirty work of war is a conceit. Again, to quote Ledeen, "Peace cannot be accomplished simply because some visiting envoy, with or without an advanced degree in negotiating from the Harvard Business School, sits everyone down around a table so they can all reason together." The oft-heard mantra that "there is no military solution" (repeated recently, for example, by former Sen. George J. Mitchell), in short, has things exactly wrong.

Applying these rules of war to the Palestinian-Israeli conflict offers some useful insights. Palestinians were winning until about a year ago, now Israel is. Until Prime Minister Ariel Sharon took over, Israel was politically divided and militarily demoralized, avoiding reality, and indulging in escapism (like "post-Zionism"). Meanwhile, Palestinians exulted in their successes. Smelling victory, they showed impressive stamina and great capacity for self-sacrifice.

A year later, circumstances have flipped. Palestinian violence had the unintended effect of uniting, mobilizing, and fortifying Israelis. "Specialists in terrorism have been surprised—some of us are even amazed," admits Ely Karmon of the Interdisciplinary Center in Herzliya, "by the endurance, the patience, the relative calm of the Israeli public to what has happened in last year and a half." Contrarily, the Palestinians' morale is plummeting and despair is setting as Yasir Arafat's ruinous leadership locks them into a conflict they cannot win.

History teaches that what appears to be endless carnage does come to an end when one side gives up. It appears increasingly likely that the Palestinians are approaching that point, suggesting that if Israel persists in its present policies it will get closer to victory.

(25 February 2002)

ENDING THE PALESTINIAN VIOLENCE

The Palestinian campaign of terrorism rolls on, with twenty-two Israelis murdered in Tel Aviv in early January 2003. And even without counting minor incidents involving rocks and firebombs, the Palestinians average more than ten attacks on Israelis *every* day. Which makes this a particularly apt moment to review my assessment of a year ago, that Prime Minister Ariel Sharon's tough response will cause the Palestinians to give up on violence.*

To begin with: while the violence continues, it declined throughout 2002: Attacks dropped by a third from the year's first quarter to

---

*See pp. 175-77.

its last (from 1,855 to 1,246)—and fatalities fell by more than half (from 157 to 70).

More significant are the many signs pointing to a realization among Palestinians that adopting violence has been a monstrous error. What the Associated Press calls a "slowly swelling chorus of Palestinian leaders and opinion-makers" is expressing disillusion with the poverty, anarchy, detention, injury, and death brought by twenty-seven months of violence. Mahmoud Abbas, the No. 2 Palestinian leader after Yasir Arafat, concedes "it was a mistake to use arms ... and to carry out attacks inside Israel." Abdel Razzak al-Yahya, the so-called interior minister, denounces suicide bombings against Israel as "murders for no reason," demands an end to "all forms of Palestinian violence" and wants it replaced it with civil resistance. Bethlehem Mayor Hanna Nasser finds that the use of arms did no good and insists that the Palestinian struggle "has to be a peaceful one."

Other developments confirm this sense of dismay and a willingness to rethink:

- *A sense of despair*: "It's over," a man in Ramallah says of the violence. "We didn't achieve anything." A Gazan is so numbed by the downward spiral, he utters the unmentionable: "To be honest, I think reoccupation [by Israel] would be better" than the current situation.

- *Regretting missed diplomatic opportunities*: "Didn't we dance for joy at the failure of Camp David?" asks Nabil Amer, formerly one of Arafat's chief aides. "After two years of bloodshed, we are now calling for what we rejected."

- *Less support for terrorism*: Asked by a Palestinian pollster if the Palestinian Authority should, once it reaches an agreement with Israel, arrest those setting off to engage in violence within Israel, 86 percent of Palestinians said "No" in December 2001. The number fell to 76 percent in May 2002, then to 40 percent in November 2002 – still very high, but the trend is clear.

- *Fear of retribution*: On occasion, prospective suicide bombers have turned themselves in, or were turned in by their parents, out of fear that the family house would be destroyed in retaliation.

- *Blaming Arafat*: When the violence began, Palestinians held Israel responsible for their many woes. But as time went by, says the pollster Khalil Shikaki, they turned "very strongly" against Arafat and the PA. One conspiracy theory holds that Arafat initiated the violence less to defeat Israel than to deflect growing discontent over the PA's failures.

- *Emigration*: Fed up with their self-inflicted misery, some 10,000 Palestinians a month left the West Bank and Gaza during 2002, while many more tried to flee. At one point, more than 40,000 would-be emigrants were camped out near Jericho, hoping to enter Jordan.

Perhaps the most affecting sign of a change came last month, when Ahmed Sabbagh, a self-described "heartbroken" Palestinian father, took the occasion of the death of his son Ala, a leading terrorist, to launch an unprecedented appeal to Israelis "to open a new page with the Palestinian people and to achieve peace based on mutual respect and justice."

Israelis are beginning to note the change on the Palestinian side. Former Mossad head Ephraim Halevy has commented on "the buds of Palestinian recognition" of the mistake in turning to violence. The chief of Israel's Ground Forces Command, Yiftah Ron-Tal, went further and in November predicted within months "a decisive victory" for Israel.

The Bush administration should take two steps to speed this process: Let Israel respond as it sees best, and stop bestowing undeserved gifts on the Palestinians (the latest: the "roadmap" and its promises of a state in 2003).

The sooner Palestinians realize how counterproductive their violence is, the sooner they will end it.

(7 January 2003)

9

SYRIA VS. ISRAEL

HAFEZ AL-ASSAD VS. THE OSLO ACCORD

In a little-noticed event, on December 14, 1993, the United Nations General Assembly broke with decades of relentless attacks against Israel. On that day, it voted by an overwhelming 155 to 3, with one abstention and twenty-five states not voting, to express "its full support for the achievements of the peace process thus far." The resolution specifically praises the Oslo accord three months earlier between Israel and the Palestine Liberation Organization (PLO). Israel's ambassador to the U.N. hailed this vote as "a turning point in the U.N.'s attitude toward the Middle East and Israel."

Just which were those three retrograde states voting against the resolution, and which one abstained? Iran, Syria, and Lebanon voted no; Libya abstained; Iraq was the only Arab state among those not participating.

Syria and Lebanon? Wait a minute; haven't U.S. government officials repeatedly assured us that Damascus has turned a new leaf? Or, as a senior administration official dealing with the Middle East told me recently, "Assad has made a strategic decision to make peace with Israel. His actions indicate this. The words coming out of Damascus point to this." If that's so, then what's going on?

Actually Syria's vote in the U.N. against the Oslo accord is completely consistent with recent statements by President Hafez al-Assad. He scorns that deal as having no consequences. To an American reporter's breathless question as to whether he felt "the earth move" when Rabin and Arafat shook hands, Assad replied: "No, we did not feel the earth move. I did not consider it a significant event. Nor do I think it will have great effect."

Assad makes no bones about his dislike of the accord. "What happened was regrettable. No one expected it," he told an Egyptian newspaper, referring to the accord. On another occasion he observed that "there is nothing good in it." Nor is Assad just grousing; all the Palestinian groups he sponsors—about a dozen groups in all and including such notorious figures as George Habash, Ahmad Jibril, and Abu Nidal—are actively engaged in trying to sabotage the accord.

Further, Assad believes he can scuttle the accord should it threaten his interests. He has explicitly stated as much. Oslo "cannot pose any danger to us. Had we wanted to obstruct it, we would have foiled it. If it becomes clear to us that its harm is great, we will do so." In other words, Assad has not yet made a serious effort to bring down the accord; he'll only do that when he needs to.

Before dismissing Assad's threat as idle words, it's worth remembering that this man has a long record of related accomplishments. For example, when he disliked a U.S.-brokered agreement between Israel and Lebanon in 1983-84, he scuttled it in less than a year. Nor does he boast idly. As on of his aides rightly puts it, Assad "carefully weighs every word and statement he makes. He only says what is necessary; there are no slips of the tongue."

Also very interesting: since September 13, 1993, Assad has stopped talking about the rights of Palestinians. Instead he now stresses the importance of Syria getting the Golan Heights back from Israel. In one revealing comment, worth quoting at length, he brought up statements by Israelis, including Foreign Minister Shimon Peres, asking in effect, "Why are you Arabs boycotting us? You have been saying the Palestine question is the core of the conflict. Here we are now, we have reached an agreement." Assad responded with impatience, accusing them of insulting his intelligence.

> Of course, we have said, and we still say, that the Palestine question is the core of the conflict. It is the core of the conflict in that it was the starting point of hostility. Hence we called it the core of the conflict, but it is not the conflict.... The Israelis know they have fought states. All the wars that were fought between Arabs and Israel were wars with states bordering Palestine. As a result of these wars, the core of the conflict that started in Palestine expanded to mean that every occupied Arab territory has become the core of the conflict.

This frank admission rips the veil of a quarter-century's hypocrisy and points to Assad's real concerns—not Palestinian nationalism but getting back the territory he personally helped lose to Israel in 1967. It also serves notice to Yasir Arafat that Assad feels free to oppose his accord with Israel.

Arafat, by the way, fully understands Assad's anger—he feels the heat as rival Palestinian leaders mock his efforts and his supporters get murdered. In protest, he complains about Assad's "intolerable interference in Palestinian affairs," but to little effect.

American officials, on the other hand, insist on seeing Syria as helpful to Israel-PLO efforts to reach an agreement. The same senior administration official quoted above observed that "the Iranians are the only ones, except for the Libyans, actively to oppose the Israel-PLO accord." It was this inability to see Damascus' opposition to the accord that lay behind the U.S. government decision, a mere eight days before the U.N. vote, to make an exception to long-standing policy and permit Syria to acquire three Boeing airliners from Kuwait.

The same blindness also lay behind President Clinton's decision to meet one-on-one with Hafez al-Assad in January 1994. That meeting is a terrible idea. It ignores the fact that Assad responds to U.S. concessions by thumbing his nose. It rewards him for sponsoring a dozen Palestinian groups trying to sabotage the Israel-PLO accord. And it signals that Washington tolerates his threat to scuttle a top U.S. foreign policy priority.

(24 December 1993)

JUST KIDDING: SYRIA'S PEACE BLUFF

With near clock-like precision, Syrian-Israeli diplomacy makes front-page news every few months. Invariably, it's some new offer, and almost always it comes from the Israeli side. Most recently, in a December 1995 meeting with President Clinton and address to a joint session of Congress, Prime Minister Shimon Peres reiterated his government's intent to withdraw from the Golan Heights. Then, with equal regularity, the Syrian-Israeli issue disappears for several months.

This odd pattern raises the question: Are Jerusalem and Damascus inching closer to a peace agreement, or has their four-year effort to make peace stalled?

The answer, actually, is yes and yes. Negotiations have made great progress, narrowing differences to very manageable proportions. At the same time, the signing of a Syrian-Israeli peace treaty appears as remote as ever.

On the positive side, the Syrian and Israeli governments—despite their tense relations—have quietly established the general contours of an agreement. In the four principal areas of negotiations, the two sides have no profound differences.

- *Extent of the Israeli withdrawal from the Golan Heights*: On this key issue, the two sides barely disagree. Peres has said that "The Golan Heights is Syrian land, and we are sitting on the Syrians' land"; he has made clear his willingness, in the context of an overall agreement and subject to a national referendum, to leave the heights. The only question is where exactly the future border will run. Israelis insist on the Mandatory (or international) border of 1923; Syria's President Hafez al-Assad demands a withdrawal to the June 4, 1967 border. The difference between the two amounts to just twenty-five square miles—hardly a deal breaker.

- *Timetable of the Israeli withdrawal*: Jerusalem started with a target of eight years in three stages while Damascus spoke of a complete withdrawal in six months. By the beginning of 1995, the one side had gone down to four years and the other had increased to eighteen months. A compromise here—akin to the three-year withdrawal from the Sinai agreed to with Egypt—seems likely.

- *Security arrangements* (i.e., preventing a surprise attack on Israel): The Golan Heights has great practical value to Israel and great symbolic value to Assad (who was Syria's defense minister when they were lost in 1967). On the question of demilitarization, the Syrians began with a call for exact symmetry while the Israelis sought a nine-to-one ratio. By mid-1995, the Syrians offered a ten-to-six ratio and the bargaining was underway. The issue of Israel's maintaining an early warning station or two on Mt. Hermon remains highly contentious. The late Yitzhak Rabin declared that "on this issue there will be no compromise," while Assad made it equally clear he had to have all Israelis off the Golan. Assad did hint, however, that he might accept Israeli airborne surveillance.

- *Normalization*: Jerusalem demands full normalization after the first stage of withdrawal. Rabin once defined this to include "an Israeli Embassy in Damascus, a Syrian Embassy in Israel, an Egged [i.e., Israeli] bus traveling to Aleppo, Israeli tourists in Homs, Israeli ships at Tartus, El Al planes landing, and commercial and cultural ties—everything, and in both directions." Assad initially refused to discuss normalization, saying this would only follow a complete withdrawal. With time, he made two concessions. First, he signaled that Israel would receive much of what it sought, talking on one occasion about "normal peace, of the type existing between 187 countries in the world" and on another about "good relations with Israel, like Egypt and Jordan have." Second, he agreed to establish low-level diplomatic relations after a first, partial withdrawal of Israeli forces.

Only relatively minor differences may separate the two sides, the sort that could be dealt with in a matter of weeks or maybe months; nonetheless, a Syrian-Israeli agreement seems not likely then or, indeed, so long as Hafez al-Assad remains in power.

Here we enter the realm of speculation: Assad totally dominates his government and no foreigner knows his exact intentions. All we can do is scrutinize his record and interpret his past actions. They can be read in two contrary ways: either that he seeks a lasting peace with Israel or that he wants only to appear to seek such a peace. The latter strikes this observer to be more likely.

Key to this reasoning is that Assad is recognized by few of the world's Muslims as a fellow believer. Rather, they see him as an 'Alawi, an adherent of a small, secretive post-Islamic religion found almost exclusively in Syria. This affiliation renders Assad an outsider in his own country. That 'Alawis have ruled Syria since 1966 has aroused great resentment on the part of the majority Sunni Muslim population.

As a small minority, 'Alawis fear they cannot rule indefinitely against the wishes of almost 70 percent of the population. Were the resentful majority of Sunnis to reach power, they would probably exact a terrible revenge. At any rate, that is the worry 'Alawis express in private. To assure the survival of his community, Assad must be a pragmatist who pursues interests rather than ideals. In this spirit, he appears to pursue two chief goals: control Syria during his own lifetime, then pass power on to his family and co-religionists.

Accordingly, the Assad regime approaches foreign relations less with an eye to achieve abstract goals than to survive. It does whatever is necessary to stay in power, whether that means starting a war with Israel or becoming an American ally. Assad's real interests concern not ideology but self-interest. A policy like anti-Zionism is an instrument, not an end in itself.

In this context, peace with Israel poses three threats.

- It would alienate such key constituencies as military and security personnel, Ba'th Party members, and government employees, most of whom appear intensely to dislike the rupture peace would cause.

- Other Syrians (especially businessmen and liberals) may harbor too great expectations of peace that go far beyond relations with Israel. They understand it would mean that their country sheds totalitarian rule, with its repression, poverty, and isolation, and moves into the American camp. As a young professor at Damascus University puts it, "We will expect democracy if peace comes." Assad probably fears that *perestroika* would do to him what it did to his Eastern European colleagues—cause him to lose control.

- Assad has relied on the tools of the police state through his twenty-five year reign. The prospect of greater openness, more democracy, and even flocks of Israeli tourists in the souks of Aleppo must frighten him terribly. He surely fears such changes would endanger the position of his family and of the 'Alawi community.

If he does not in fact seek peace with Israel, why, then, does the Syrian president pursue negotiations with Israel in an apparently serious manner? He has, after all, come within striking distance of a peace agreement.

In all likelihood, he negotiates as a way to improve his standing in Washington. If peace itself spells little but trouble, the peace process brings many benefits. Assad's goal, then, is not peace but a peace process. He participates in negotiations without intending that they reach fruition. Engaging in apparently serious talks wins him improved relations with the West without having to open up his country. He can wink at Washington while maintaining his ties to Iran and hosting a wide range of terrorist groups. He offers the occasional flourish (such as his call last week to Clinton as the latter was eating lunch with Shimon Peres) but does not change the substance.

This approach worked best when the Likud was in power, for Yitzhak Shamir's government could be relied on to maintain a hard line. Matters became more complicated when Labor took over in 1992 and made the historic decision to return virtually all the Golan Heights. Faced with such flexibility, Assad has fallen back on stalling tactics.

Understanding Assad's lack of interest in a resolution with Israel helps clear up various mysteries, for example, why, until the final days of 1995, his negotiators met their Israeli counterparts in only one formal round of talks in twelve months; why he refuses unambiguously to signal his good intentions to the Israeli population; and why he claims to see no difference between a Labor and a Likud government in Israel.

That the point of the peace process is not to improve relations with Jerusalem but with Washington makes Assad susceptible to American pressure. U.S. policy should exploit his worries so that he sees complying with American wishes as the best bet to keep his family and people in power. Washington should abandon its soft, more-in-sorrow-than-in-anger policy toward Damascus that has been in place since 1984, and instead adopt a much tougher approach.

An authoritarian leader like Assad responds to pressures, not to jawboning or goodwill gestures. When Assad engages in activities contrary to American interests, he needs to hear about it. When he does something right, Washington should express less delight. Instead, with more equanimity, it should say, "Thank you; what will you give us next?" Hearing these words, worried about hostile actions that might follow, Assad will probably make real concessions to American sensibilities and interests, perhaps including real progress on a peace treaty with Israel.

(18 & 25 January 1996)

THE BRINK OF PEACE?

Itamar Rabinovich has unique credentials for writing about the failed talks Syria and Israel held from 1992 to 1996. He is a leading academic specialist both on Syria and on Arab-Israeli negotiations, and he served during that period as the Israeli ambassador to Washington and as Israel's chief negotiator with Syria.

The result, *The Brink of Peace: The Israeli-Syrian Negotiations* (Princeton, N.J.: Princeton University Press, 1998), stands as a model of its genre: a book in which in an aware participant provides the inside skinny and the larger story of what he calls "an absorbing saga," neither burdening the reader with unnecessary information nor skimping on important details.

And, as the title implies, Rabinovich also has a thesis to argue: that Hafez al-Assad, the Syrian president, had in principle accepted peace with Israel and that the two states reached "the brink of peace." The author explains that if Assad had only acted more urgently, the two sides could have reached a deal and their conflict by now would be well on the way to solution. Unfortunately, Rabinovich goes on, Assad conducted himself "as if time were no constraint." This left the Labor government of Yitzhak Rabin, Shimon Peres, and the author to go into the May 1996 elections without having secured a deal with Syria, and that was one reason why it lost to Binyamin Netanyahu and the Likud.

Rabinovich surmises that, after those elections, "Assad must have realized that he had badly miscalculated" and speculates that "Assad grasped fully" that he had missed a real opportunity to conclude a deal with Israel. With this, Rabinovich offers what might be dubbed the optimistic interpretation of Assad's intentions; the dictator of Damascus truly wished to close down the conflict with Israel but made tactical errors that prevented him from doing so.

There is also another interpretation, the pessimistic one, that holds Assad never sought to end the state of war with Israel but instead entered into negotiations with his old enemy only as a means to an end. In this view, Assad used the talks with Israel as a way of improving relations with the West. He understood that Washington demanded that he adopt a less hostile attitude toward the Jewish state, so he did what he had to do. But he had no intention of ever signing a peace treaty with Israel. Instead, he kept the talks going and going, viewing them as an end in themselves. He wanted not closure but protraction; he wanted not peace but peace process.

To his credit, while partisan to the optimistic view, Rabinovich does not shape his account to buttress his argument. In fact, he provides much evidence to support the pessimistic outlook. For example, he recounts how, on the issue of normalization (that is, what sort of peace the two countries would establish), Assad demanded that this topic only be discussed in the multilateral Arab-Israeli talks that he happened to be boycotting! Nor does Rabinovich sanitize Assad's outlook ("Israel remained a rival, if not an enemy, and the terms of the peace settlement should not serve to enhance its advantage over the Arabs, Syria in particular, but rather to diminish it") or hide his own perplexity at Assad's actions. His text is littered with phrases like "we were deeply puzzled," "It is difficult to understand Assad's conduct," and "Many of Assad's decisions during this period have yet to be fully explained." Rabinovich candidly sums up his own implicit dissatisfaction with the optimistic analysis: "when all is said and done it is difficult to understand why Assad, despite his suspicions, reservations, and inhibitions, failed to take the steps that would have produced an agreement."

The author recounts how this puzzlement led his own prime minister, despite his belief in the possibility of a treaty with Damascus, to adopt the pessimistic view that Assad did not want to deal with Israel. For Rabin, "Assad's negotiating style and the substance of his positions" showed that the Syrian president "was not interested in genuine negotiation but rather in an American mediation or arbitration." Indeed, Rabinovich himself accepts the pessimistic interpretation, concluding that "Assad was more interested in obtaining a clear Israeli commitment to a withdrawal from the Golan than in coming to an agreement." He even refutes his book's optimistic title when he concludes that "at no time" in his four years of negotiating "were Israel and Syria on the verge of a breakthrough."

Rabin and Rabinovich alike find themselves falling back on the pessimistic interpretation because, no matter how positive their outlook, this makes better sense. Assuming Assad had no intention of signing an agreement with Israel sweeps away the puzzlements about his actions and shows how his supposed miscalculations actually were canny decisions.

But however much logic takes him in the direction of pessimism, the author resists it. On what basis? In a key passage, Rabinovich explains how he can persist in his optimism:

> I was not perturbed by the fact that...Assad was primarily interested in transforming his country's relationship with Washington, and that his acceptance of the notion of peace with Israel was a necessary prelude to that transformation and not the product of a change of heart with regard to us. If a mutually acceptable compromise could be found and an agreement could be made, the change of heart would follow.

In other words, Rabinovich reasoned, Assad's intentions did not matter, for Israel could eventually co-opt the Syrians into a peaceful and civilized relationship. Our author, however, never explains the mechanics of how "the change of heart would follow," and not surprisingly, for it is a hope, not a plan. Rabinovich (and his political superiors) wanted a peace agreement with Damascus so badly, they willingly overlooked the problems staring them in the face in the belief that a "compromise" would eventually fix things for them. They may have looked like hard-nosed planners, but Rabin and his staff were in fact pinning their country's future on a wish and a prayer.

Wishful thinking gave Israel's negotiations with the Syrians (and by extension, the other Arabs, especially the Palestinians) an indulgent quality. Rabinovich's account shows, for instance, that his side omitted any mention of the fact that Israel had won all its wars against Syria, as though to do so would be ill-mannered and tactless—even if it was the inescapable premise of the two states' negotiations. Likewise, that Israel threw in its lot with the United States and Syria with the Soviet Union never seems to arise.

As a result, instead of Damascus petitioning its vanquisher, the talks exude a sense of parity, whereby the Syrians make demands and act as Israel's equal. Israel's leaders presumably let the Syrians get away with this (with American encouragement) in the expectation that on the basis of this make-believe status, "the change of heart would follow."

This same motive probably explains the Labor government's surprising tendency to accept Assad's positions as though he were sincerely pursuing amity rather than tactically finding a p.r. advantage. For example, when Assad suddenly came up with the idea of implementing a Syrian-Israeli agreement not over the many years Rabin had proposed, but in one fell swoop, Rabinovich portrays the proposal as a serious bid for peace ("He was evidently worried by the passage of time") instead of a coy trick to have Israel blamed for turning down a chance for instant resolution.

In the same spirit, Rabinovich shows Israeli leaders accepting at face value Assad's fatuous statements about the need to find a peace "with dignity." Rather than present Assad as a crafty thug desperate to hold on to power in the face of murderous domestic opposition, Rabinovich presents Assad's "philosophy" of the negotiations. Finally, a reader who knows nothing about Syrian politics could read clear through *Brink of Peace* without any clear sense that its totalitarian system differs from Israel's liberal democracy.

Rabinovich is a sophisticated historian and diplomat; the Rabin-Peres governments he worked for had an ambitious vision of conflict resolution. Unfortunately, their efforts were premised on hopes, not plans.

(16 November 1998)

Assad isn't interested

Does Hafez al-Assad want a peace treaty with Israel? Just about everyone says yes, the all-powerful president of Syria hopes to wind down hostilities with his lifelong enemy. They offer different reasons for this change on his part: Assad wants to jump-start the decrepit Syrian economy. He wants the return of the Golan Heights (which many Arabs still blame him for losing in 1967). He hopes to make himself acceptable to the West. He is taking care of unfinished business for his successor, perhaps worrying that that successor will not hold out for a good enough deal.

This last theory is especially popular at present [August 1999], imbuing a sense of urgency to the talks with Israel. Former secretary of state James Baker said, after meeting with Assad in June 1999 that "a window of opportunity now" exists but warned that it might not last long.

Whatever Assad's precise reason might be, all these analyses assume that some years ago—1988 according to one Israeli scholar—Assad made a strategic decision for peace. At that time, he resolved to forgo war against Israel and bargain his way to a settlement. His subsequent military buildup serves mainly to position Syria for an acceptable deal.

It sounds good. But there's one problem: If Assad ten or so years ago decided to wind down the conflict with Israel, how come nothing has happened? Negotiations began at the Madrid Conference in late 1991 and, it is fair to say, have gone just about nowhere until now. Hypothetical questions were discussed but nothing was fully resolved. Every time a breakthrough shimmered on the horizon, Assad took a step that derailed it. Now, diplomacy takes time, lots of it. But the pace of these negotiations is more reminiscent of *Waiting for Godot* and the theater of the absurd than of a powerful state resolved to make a deal.

What explains the torpid pace? Proponents of the conventional wisdom have no reply. For example, in his book on this subject, Itamar Rabinovich, Israel's chief negotiator with the Syrians, repeatedly throws up his hands in incomprehension at Assad's actions.

There might be a simple answer: Change assumptions. If one figures that Assad does not really want a deal, things fall into place. There is one major reason to think this is, in fact, Assad's outlook—

his fear that the Syrian population sees a treaty with Israel as not some technical arrangement with a neighbor but as a signal that their government has changed its fundamental orientation. That they would view a treaty with Israel as the ending of totalitarian rule and much else—the military losing its paramount position, economic controls loosening, freedoms increasing, and political participation growing.

For Assad, who has ruled Syria with an iron fist for nearly three decades, such expectations must be alarming. He knows how to rule as a dictator, not as a leader accountable to his electorate. At the same time, continuing to negotiate with Israel brings Assad one hugely important benefit. It permits him to escape being branded a "rogue" state by Washington. Unlike his colleagues in Iraq, Iran, Libya, and Sudan, he gets visited by American secretaries of state. While they suffer U.S. economic sanctions and even the occasional military punch, he is seduced.

Assad's actions since 1991 have been entirely consistent with this interpretation: make cosmetic changes in Syria, negotiate unendingly with Israel, and hope to pass a working package to his successor. Assad is playing at negotiations but has no intention of ever concluding a treaty with Israel. This explains why hopeful diplomatic signs never pan out, why negotiations close down just when they seem most productive, and why changes of government in Israel makes almost no difference to the process.

This being the case, Baker has it exactly upside-down. Far from this being a moment when a fleeting "window of opportunity" exists, Assad's frail health could make him all the more reluctant to take risky steps.

For Israel, this skeptical interpretation has two direct policy implications. First, go slow—there is no rush. Current trends (especially a precipitous decline in Syria's economy and Assad's expected demise) mean that holding out will be rewarded. Second, approach the negotiations with Assad more as a public relations exercise than as a serious forum for closing down the Arab-Israeli conflict.

And wait for his successor to begin the talks in earnest.

(29 August 1999)

Israelis Turn Threats into Concessions

The Syrian foreign minister recently gave an extraordinary speech.

His talks with Israel had ended on January 10, 2000, and were supposed to resume nine days later. But they did not, because his own side put unexpected preconditions on the next round—requiring that Israel make huge concessions before it even started. Then, to knock a few more nails in the coffin of the negotiations, Damascus published an outrageous Holocaust-denial article and Israeli soldiers were shot at in Lebanon (last count: seven dead).

In this context came the speech by Foreign Minister Farouk Shara in late January 2000. It has a distinctly schizophrenic quality. In the first half he presents Israel as a regional superpower ("Israel is stronger than all the Arab states combined") beholden to hugely aggressive ambitions to expand far beyond its current borders. Indeed, Israel is so expansive and aggressive, it threatens the very existence of the Arabs; in Shara's pungent words, it views the Arabs "as Indians that should be annihilated." Zionist power is so dangerous, in short, that Syria is better off ending the military conflict with Israel. This both neutralizes Israeli weapons and permits Syria to compete in the "political, ideological, economical, and commercial" arenas where it can do better in conflict against the Jewish state.

Then Shara abruptly switches gears and, in the speech's totally different second half, asserts that Syria under the leadership of Hafez Assad "is strong" and will never end the military conflict unless Israel agrees to return every meter of territory it took in 1967. He denies recent stories and leaks that suggest Damascus's flexibility—that it would accept restrictions on its military, grant early-warning stations to Israel, expel Palestinian extremists, or make curriculum revisions. And should the "expansionist racists" in Israel not take advantage of the deal Damascus is offering them, it will be their loss, because thanks to Syria's own resources, Arab and international support, "our position is stronger than Israel's despite all its weapons." Shara goes on to threaten Israel, announcing that the recovery of the 1967 lands is but the first stage toward "restoring Palestine in its entirety"—code words for the destruction of Israel.

For anyone hoping Israel will reach a settlement with Syria, the foreign minister's remarks would appear to be a significant setback.

He begins by accusing Israel of seeking to eliminate all Arabs; he ends trumpeting Syrian ambitions to destroy Israel.

Nonetheless, in a February 2000 article in *Ha'aretz*, "Decrypting the Damascus Code," Itamar Rabinovich—a leading academic specialist on Syria and Israel's former chief negotiator with Damascus— finds good news in Shara's speech. Rabinovich acknowledges it looks like a reversion to Syria's old rejectionist position, but he finds it is actually "an attempt, albeit clumsy, to prepare the groundwork for a settlement with Israel." How so? Rabinovich explains that where Shara seemed to be negative, he only "dug in his heels" as a bargaining position for future negotiations. In effect, "Syria is telling us for the second time through Shara that it wants to end the conflict with us and to replace it with a cold peace and with rivalry over the shape that the Middle East will take."

Now, I defer to no one in my admiration of Professor Rabinovich's academic work. I praised his 1984 study of Lebanon as doing "an excellent job" of explaining its topic. I then lauded his 1991 inquiry into early Arab-Israeli negotiations for its "fine research and sensible conclusions." And I wrote that his 1998 book on Syrian-Israeli diplomacy is "a model of its genre." But now this skilled and knowledgeable analyst is not seeing what is plainly in front of him. He has somehow turned Shara's threat about "restoring Palestine in its entirety" into a benign statement of a Syrian intent "to end the conflict." It appears that Professor Rabinovich, along with many other Israeli leaders, is engaged in wishful thinking. So badly do they want an Israeli agreement with Syria, they turn threats into concessions.

In a similar spirit, they insist that the Palestinian Authority has fulfilled its obligations. They even portray a unilateral Israeli retreat from Lebanon as a threat to Syrian interests. Such self-delusion is pleasant enough—until reality hits. And it always does hit. The only question is when and where, and how terrible the toll will be.

(29 August 1999)

A LESSON COURTESY OF THE TURKS

How can Israel staunch its wounds in southern Lebanon, where about a thousand of its soldiers have been killed over two decades?

One route—preferred by the Barak government and most Israelis —is to reach a deal with President Hafez al-Assad of Syria, the man who makes the key decisions in Lebanon. The goal of closing this deal helps explain why several Israeli governments have shown such extraordinary flexibility in dealing with the strongman of Damascus, even to the point of offering him the Golan Heights, hoping this will put a stop to missiles and terrorists crossing the border.

But this hope is premised on the dubious assumption that Assad would keep promises after getting back the Golan: a close look at his record shows a nearly perfect thirty-year history of breaking his word with everyone—Turks, Lebanese, Israelis, Jordanians, Russians, and Americans. Even after he has the Golan, there is good reason to suppose Hezbollah would still harass Israel.

Stronger medicine is needed.

Turkey's recent experience suggests what that might be. Starting in 1984, a Marxist-Leninist organization, the Worker's Party of Kurdistan (PKK), began using Syria as a launching board for terrorist attacks on Turkey. By 1987, this insurgency had grown so much that the Turkish president traveled to Damascus to demand its cessation; Assad duly agreed, and in July 1987, their two governments solemnly signed a security protocol promising to "obstruct groups engaged in destructive activities directed against one another on their own territory and would not turn a blind eye to them in any way." But this agreement did little good, as PKK attacks soon picked up again.

In fact, the situation got so bad that the Turkish president took the unprecedented step, in October 1989, of publicly threatening Damascus to live up to the 1987 agreement or find its water supply diminished. This warning did lead to a reduction in PKK attacks, but not for long.

By 1992, Turkish officials began speaking publicly about the PKK problem; the Syrians responded by signing a second security protocol. Within months, however, attacks resumed. In late 1993, a top Turkish official delivered a first military warning: "Turkey cannot tolerate terrorist attacks from any of its neighbors... The necessary answer will be given."

More rounds of talks and agreements followed, all to little effect. A pattern had evolved: Turkish threats, a Syrian lull, a resumption in attacks, followed by new Turkish threats and another cycle.

Turks grew increasingly agitated as Syrians made promises they did not carry out. Finally, in mid-September 1998, Ankara got serious and made a series of specific demands of Damascus (drop claims to Turkish territory, close down PKK camps, and extradite the PKK leader) and top officials delivered a volley of portentous messages. "We are losing our patience and we retain the right to retaliate against Syria," the president announced. The prime minister accused Syria of being "the headquarters of terrorism in the Middle East" and warned Damascus that the Turkish army was "awaiting orders" to attack. The chief of staff described relations with Damascus as an "undeclared war." Every political party in parliament signed a statement calling on Syria to cut its support for the PKK or "bear the consequences." The media went into high gear, reporting each new development in inflamed tones. Military exercises near the Syrian border began.

Then, suddenly, Assad caved, unconditionally expelling the PKK leader and ending Syrian aid to the PKK. More: this time he kept his word. Turkish officials say they are satisfied with Syria's actions and tensions have been diffused. There is now talk of increasing trade and visitors already are crossing the border in greater numbers.

All of which implies a major question for Israel: Could it be that the negotiations with Damascus, underway since 1991, are futile? That the only way to stop the violence is by emulating the Turks and making a credible threat of force? Something like: "Mr. Assad: Stop Hezbollah or else ..."

A few Israeli voices have indeed called for this "Turkish model" —prominent names including Uzi Landau, Efraim Inbar, and Eli Karmon. But theirs are still voices in the wind. Only in time, as a negotiated settlement with Damascus still does not happen or (worse) proves illusory, will Israelis realize that there is no substitute for a forceful policy toward Damascus.

Totalitarian dictators understand this language and none other.

(12 April 2000)

GETTING SYRIA WRONG

with Zachary Rentz

With Hafez al-Assad dead and his round of Syrian-Israeli negotiations now permanently defunct, it's time for a little retrospection.

During the final burst of diplomacy, lasting from December 1999 until March 2000, Western academics, journalists, and politicians made a lot of wrongheaded predictions that are worth scrutiny, for they contain some useful lessons.

Informed opinion in Israel and the West agreed that the Syrian regime had decided on peace with Israel; only the details remained to be worked out. "Peace is vital for Assad," wrote Hirsh Goodman of the *Jerusalem Report*, and almost everyone agreed. Reuters helpfully listed the three most commonly cited reasons why Assad needed to end the conflict with Israel: his ill-health and the need to pave the way for son Bashar, the Syrian economy's extreme weakness, and the humiliation of seeing the Golan Heights remain in Israeli hands. President Clinton's search for a legacy was also sometimes cited.

The start of negotiations in December inspired an orgy of optimistic prognostications. Peace is "within our grasp," Clinton averred. Itamar Rabinovich, perhaps Israel's foremost authority on Syria, deemed the renewal of talks "the most auspicious moment yet for reaching an Israeli-Syrian accommodation." Israel's ambassador in Washington declared himself "an optimist" that the talks would resolve the Syrian-Israeli dispute. Israel's Interior Minister Haim Ramon boldly announced that the government was "embarking on negotiations that will bring total peace" and "the complete acceptance by the entire Arab world that Israel can exist in the region in peace and security." Israeli businessmen spoke of opening factories in Syria and chamber-of-commerce types anticipated a big post-treaty spike in economic growth.

This good cheer persisted even after the talks broke down in early January. Undeterred, Clinton confidently announced that Assad and Prime Minister Ehud Barak both "want a peace that meets each other's needs." Foreign Minister Hubert Vedrine of France more cautiously told of being "reasonably optimistic."

Some venturous souls specified just when an agreement would be reached. Rabinovich predicted in December that Assad "must have calculated that peace must be made within the next few months." "A matter of months," echoed Barak. Osama al-Baz, a high Egyptian official involved with Arab-Israeli diplomacy since 1974, longer than anyone else, was a bit more vague, predicting "several months and perhaps a year before reaching a peace accord." Assistant Secretary of State Martin Indyk, another veteran observer, weighed in similarly: "Both

sides are committed to achieving a comprehensive peace this year."
"This year definitely," King Abdullah II of Jordan concurred.

It's striking to note that these embarrassing predictions are part of
a well-established pattern. Back in August 1994, for instance, Fawaz
Gerges of Princeton University prophesied that "a breakthrough in
the Syrian-Israeli peace talks is imminent." The Arabic press was
even more specific, reporting that Damascus and Jerusalem would
achieve "palpable progress" by the end of 1994. In 1995, France's
President Jacques Chirac publicly predicted that an Israel-Syria agreement would be signed by the end of 1995, as did his Egyptian counterpart, Hosni Mubarak. The same faulty predictions have been repeated almost every year since, up until the moment of Assad's death.

In short, almost without exception for six years, authoritative voices
ignored evident signs of Syrian recalcitrance and persisted in predicting that the Syrian-Israeli talks would culminate in a signed peace
agreement.

When nearly everyone in the know gets it wrong, and does so
year after year, what conclusions should one draw?

First, beware the herd mentality. Just because almost everyone
agrees what's about to happen, that's no reason that it will. Don't be
afraid to speak your mind, especially about the future, even when in
a tiny minority.

Second, hold political analysts accountable for their forecasts.
When a company's earnings fail to match expectations, heads roll.
But in politics, wretched predictions hardly count. To fix this, the
media should keep track of who says what, tote up the score every
so often, and (as with mutual fund managers) listen to those with a
track record of getting it right.

Third, listen with due skepticism when politicians and others make
prophecies. For instance, Barak has asserted that if the talks with
Syria failed, there would be "no way out of another round of confrontation with the Arab world." Well, maybe. And maybe Israel's
holding the Golan actually decreases the chances for war.

(21 June 2000)

WILL THE ASSAD DYNASTY LAST?

At last count, only two totalitarian leaders have succeeded in passing power on to their sons. In 1994, Kim Il Sung of North Korea

managed this unlikely feat. And precisely a year ago, in June 2000, President Hafez al-Assad of Syria repeated the trick. In both cases the youngish "revolutionary princes" have had a tough time following their formidable fathers, to the point that one wonders whether these rookies can hold on to power.

The case of thirty-five-year-old Syrian President Bashar al-Assad is particularly interesting because he tried to get out of the family business. His career in ophthalmology took him to London and to the worlds of science and hi-tech. Only after his elder brother's death in 1994 was Bashar called back and enrolled by his father in a fast-track tutorial on dictatorship. Upon the death of Hafez, the regime's grandees then flawlessly ushered Bashar to the presidency.

This background suggests on the one hand that the would-be eye doctor Bashar is cut from a very different cloth than his megalomaniac father. On the other, it points to a neophyte ruler unable to cut loose from his father's men. And Bashar's first year in office has indeed reflected this duality.

For example, he started to open the country and then backtracked. Lectures and discussion groups temporarily were allowed to convene, then organizers had to provide full details of each event (participants, subject matter, etc.) fifteen days in advance to get a government license, effectively closing down this small step toward civil society. In foreign affairs, too, Bashar wends an erratic path. One moment, he talks about resolving the conflict with Israel, the next he spouts an extreme anti-Zionism (calling Israeli society "even more racist than Nazism") and alienates Israelis with an obnoxious anti-Semitism (Israelis try "to kill the principles of all religions with the same mentality with which they betrayed Jesus Christ").

Bashar talks tough and acts weak. After Israeli aircraft hit Syrian radar stations in mid-March, killing three Syrian soldiers, his spokesman boasted that "Syria – leadership and people – will not stand idle against continued Israeli attacks against the Arab nation." But then Bashar proceeded to do exactly that—stand idly by. He even instructed his Lebanese allies to cool it.

Speaking of Lebanon, although Bashar continues to deploy an estimated 35,000 uniformed soldiers and 25,000 intelligence officers in that country, what the *New York Times* calls "the icy menace of his father" has evaporated. Even the Lebanese president, hitherto a Damascene lapdog, dared call the Syrian occupation "temporary." One wonders how long the occupation can continue. As for the United

States, Bashar asks for American sympathy toward his government, but then undercuts his standing by dramatically expanding diplomatic and economic relations with Iraqi President Saddam Hussein. In the words of one senior U.S. official, this is "a dangerous game by Syria and a big mistake."

With such a record, no one can figure out whether Bashar intends to continue in his father's footsteps or to effect fundamental changes in the system of government. Trouble is, both paths currently appear unattainable. Maintaining Hafez's perverse masterpiece of a Syria— where the leader dominates every aspect of his country's life, occupies neighboring Lebanon and plays a game of brinkmanship with Israel—is probably beyond Bashar's cunning or ruthlessness. Likewise, making a real break with the old system—by opening Syria to normal economic and political life, withdrawing from Lebanon and ending the conflict with Israel—also demands more skill and initiative than he has shown.

Foreign leaders have unusually harsh things to say about Bashar. "Garbage" is how Edward S. Walker, Jr., the recently retired U.S. assistant secretary of state for Near Eastern Affairs, described his rhetoric. "Ghastly" is how German Chancellor Gerhard Schröder characterized his talks with Bashar.

At his first year's anniversary, in other words, Bashar gives the impression of not being up to the job, but of bumbling through from one day to the next. Of course, he might evolve into a more decisive and effective ruler, but that can only happen if he manages to remain ruler. Bashar's incompetence risks frittering away Hafez's hardwon power. Unless he is a whole lot craftier than he has so far shown, the days of the Assad dynasty may well be numbered.

(6 June 2001)

10

IRAQ VS. ALL

BOTH AN ISRAELI AND IRAQI SPY?

Hussein Sumaida recounts a most remarkable story in his autobi-
ography *Circle of Fear: My Life as an Israeli and Iraqi Spy* (with
Carole Jerome, Washington, D.C.: Brassey's, 1994), and it is all the
more remarkable if true. All of twenty-six years old when he wrote it
in 1991, his personal story is interspersed with astute observations
about Iraqi and Middle Eastern politics. The result is a compelling
tale with useful information and an interesting analysis.

Here's what the author tells: His father, 'Ali Mahmoud Sumaida
(born 1935), is a Tunisian who moved to Iraq and joined with Saddam
Hussein in about 1957, then rose with the future ruler to great political heights. From childhood, Hussein (born 1965) considered his
father a psychotic tyrant and hated him with a rare passion that inspired him to go to great lengths to hurt him. In the spring of 1984,
while studying in Manchester, England, Hussein joined Da'wan, the
Iraqi Shi'i Islamist movement. Unhappy with its program ("The es-
sence of the Islamic fundamentalist movement is not religion, but
rather power through hatred"), he also worked with Iraqi intelligence.
This led to an odd but quintessentially Middle Eastern predicament:
"by day I went around with the Da'wah putting up stickers that said
Saddam was a new Hitler, and by night I went around with Saddam's
agents taking them down."

Sumaida says he soon found it repellent to work for his father or
"for the monster Saddam and his killing machine." Within a month
or two, "a strange idea began to form in the clouds of my mind:
Mossad." According to his account, he took the unlikely and drastic

step of walking cold into the Israel embassy in London and offering his services. His assignments for Mossad in Britain included scoping out an Iraqi school and a Palestinian leader. He then joined his father, now an ambassador in Brussels, and provided information about the embassy there as well as the local PLO man. He returned to England in the fall of 1984 and worked on two jobs involving Syria.

But then Mossad overreached and told Sumaida to get a job in Iraq's London embassy; his father immediately smelled a rat and began an inquiry. To preempt the inevitable, Sumaida went to an officer of the Mukhabarat (the top, most feared Iraqi intelligence force) on July 16, 1985, and confessed all about working for Israel —except that he had been a walk-in (he portrayed his service as a result of getting hooked on Israeli financial payoffs). In response, Sumaida was returned for five days to Baghdad, where he expected to be killed. But, thanks to his father's exalted status, a temporary reprieve came. He returned to England to begin serving as a double agent. Not wanting to play this role, however, Sumaida engaged in some petty theft and thereby got himself thrown out of the country

In October 1985, thanks to no less than two Iraqi presidential orders, Sumaida says he returned to Iraq and began studying at the University of Technology. There he met Ban, his wife-to-be (and the dedicatee of this book). Sometime after, the final verdict on his fate came, from Saddam himself: Sumaida was to live, but on condition that he join the Mukhabarat. The training for this career, described in some detail, began in the fall of 1986. He lived simultaneously as "a student and a junior agent for trivial affairs." By late 1987, he had proven himself adept enough to be given more serious duties, such as doing security checks on employees to be hired for confidential tasks. In October 1988, he had advanced to being part of the second layer of protection surrounding Saddam Hussein at a festival.

About this time, Sumaida began plotting ways for Ban and himself to escape Iraq. He made abortive efforts to flee to Beirut and Amman, only to make good, finally, in early 1990, on a trip to Yemen. There, for the second time in his young life, Sumaida walked into an enemy embassy, this time that of the United States, and asked for political asylum. The American response was less than warm, the British even cooler, so he ended up in Canada, where he now lives, with Ban, under an assumed identity.

Although parts of his account are inherently unbelievable (a member of the Iraqi elite volunteers to spy for Israel? A traitor pardoned in return for joining the Mukhabarat?), Sumaida's account is internally consistent, it jibes with known dates, and, to this non-Iraqi, it rings more true than false. The personal information about his own lying, stealing, smuggling, and womanizing also lends an air of authenticity. Put differently, it's hard to see why anyone would make all this up; there's a lot of dirt and no self-aggrandizement. Further, it is hard to imagine this tale's serving as anyone's disinformation. On the other hand, the odd discrepancy (such as his having played as a child with the sons of Michel 'Aflaq, a man twenty-five years older than his father) does raise questions about his credibility.

Sumaida offers information about Iraq that might be true. He reports learning that the core of the Osirak reactor survived Israel's 1981 raid and was rebuilt. He gives details about the deception pulled on inspectors visiting the factory of Munsha'at Nasr, whereby innocuous containers replaced deadly missiles. He provides a second-hand account of the 1987 meeting at which Saddam decided an Iraqi jet should attack the *USS Stark,* a bid to involve Washington more closely in the Iraq-Iran War. (This event prompts Sumaida wryly to comment that "Only in the Middle East would an attack on an American ship be considered a good way to end a war.") In the course of describing his training and activities, Sumaida reveals much about the inner workings of Iraqi intelligence. The chart detailing the structure of the Iraqi security apparatus appears sound. And throwaway lines help make totalitarian Iraq come to life: "Normally an Iraqi [college] graduate is not given any document showing his degree. This policy helps to prevent educated, skilled Iraqis from leaving the country."

No less interesting are Sumaida's alternately world-weary and idealistic observations. Repeatedly, he tries to explain the Middle Eastern mentality to Westerners, even as he thinks this an impossibility ("The key to the Middle East is understanding that you can never really understand it"). One theme concerns Middle Eastern thinking:

> In our unique system of logic, a theory believed is a fact. There is no intermediary analytical thought. My theory is my belief, therefore is a fact.... Our logic is not a straight line, but curled and twisting like our script. Our sense of life and death is not theirs [i.e., Americans']; we laugh where an American cries.

He contrasts the optimism of Westerners (they assume "that some-one looking for someone is a friend, not an enemy") with the deep pessimism of Iraqis ("Living under the Ba'th regime, my father al-ways assumed that whatever happened was for the worst"). Sumaida also offers thoughts on ways for Westerners to approach the Middle East:

> There's an old cliché about the Mideast that I get very tired of hearing pronounced by "experts" on western news broadcasts. It goes, "The enemy of my enemy is my friend." A fatuous oversimplification. Instead I prefer, "The friend of my friend isn't necessar-ily my friend." ... There are no such things as allies in the Middle East. There are only shifting sands.

Sumaida himself has escaped the Middle East and, with luck, has by now established a new life in Canada. He sums up his hopes, as well as his abiding anger, in one of the book's closing sentences: "the best revenge I can take on my father will be to love my chil-dren." Sumaida's tale confirms the possibility of good out of evil; and the superiority of Western political ways over those of the Middle East.

(March 1996)

WHY GO IT ALONE?

With the return of Americans on the United Nations inspection team to Iraq in November 1997, another crisis with Iraq appears over, and Saddam Hussein appears again to have gained strength.

The reason for his success is not hard to find: "Arabs Angry with U.S. for Iraq Crisis," reads the typical newspaper headline. And in-deed they are. From all over the Middle East, politicians, religious leaders, and Ahmad-Six Packs have harsh words for American ac-tions. In their view, Washington is "starving and besieging the Iraqi people ... without the slightest regard for their human rights."

In addition, Arab commentators seem not to find Saddam Hussein a threat to themselves. One highly placed Jordanian, for example, blandly asserts that "there is no capability of Iraq to threaten its neigh-bors for the next 20 years."

With such attitudes, it comes as no surprise that Middle Eastern governments tried to prevent the U.S. government from using force against Saddam. Neither the Saudis nor Turks agreed to the use of their territory for strikes against Iraqi targets. Secretary of State Madeleine Albright undertook an embarrassing trip to the region where she found no Arab support for using force against Iraq.

Now, all this is very strange. In the natural order of things, it should be the Saudis, Turks, and others who beseech the Americans to help fend off Saddam—the tyrant who without provocation attacked Iran in 1980, Kuwait in 1990, and Saudi Arabia and Israel in 1991. Middle Easterners, after all, are a lot closer to Saddam Hussein's missiles than Americans; and they are also a lot weaker than the United States.

Why then this topsy-turvy situation whereby the distant and strong power begs nearby and weak states to contain their mutual enemy? An answer may lie in the fact that the U.S. government has repeatedly found itself in this predicament. During the Vietnam War, Washington had to plead with the South Vietnamese to stand strong against the Vietcong and North Vietnam. During the last decade of the cold war, it had to convince the North Atlantic Treaty Organization (NATO) allies to accept modern American missiles on their territories.

In each of these cases, as in the present one, American officialdom made the same mistake: so convinced of the righteousness and importance of its cause, it shouldered the main responsibility for it, shoving aside the local parties.

This had the perverse effect of freeing up the locals; aware that what they do has almost no importance, they reverted to political immaturity. No longer having to worry about their own skins, they instead indulge in corruption (Vietnam), political opportunism (NATO), and conspiracy theories (the Middle East). The American adult renders others childlike.

The solution, then, lies in a very different American approach, one that gives significance to the allies' actions. With this in mind, I propose that President Clinton say something like this:

"It's up to you, my Middle Eastern friends. If you think you can coexist with a Saddam who possesses large armies and weapons of mass destruction, we're happy to withdraw our aircraft carriers, our soldiers in the region, and the rest of our infrastructure. If you think you can survive a Saddam who gains the proceeds of 3 million barrels of oil a day, we will lift the sanctions. In short, if you really want to return to the way things were before the Iraqi troops invaded Kuwait in August 1990, just tell us and it's yours.

"But if, to the contrary, you worry that such steps will endanger your security, we are happy to stay. However, we need you explicitly to ask us to do so. You have to pay a portion of our costs and provide soldiers and materiel to carry out the mission. Finally, so that we know that the request is deeply felt, and not just the whim of the leaders, you also must hold a referendum on the topic so that the populations of your countries can endorse our efforts."

This sensational statement would turn the politics of the Middle East right-side up and transform the United States from pariah of the region to savior.

(3 December 1997)

DESERT STORM'S FLEETING IMPACT

Iraqi forces invaded Kuwait early on the morning on August 2, 1990. This unprovoked, blatant act of aggression prompted that very rarest of phenomena: an international consensus. Almost without exception, every government publicly denounced Iraqi dictator Saddam Hussein's invasion and called for his troops to leave immediately. Prodded by Prime Minister Margaret Thatcher of Britain ("Don't be wobbly now, George"), President George H.W. Bush took advantage of this agreement to stitch together an expeditionary force made up of twenty-nine states.

Nearly everyone at the time agreed that the Kuwait War was a huge event, perhaps an epochal turning point. Bush spoke about it leading to the start of a "new world order" in which coalitions would come together to prevent Iraqi-style use of force. Pundits expected that the war assured Bush four more years of the presidency just as it meant that Saddam Hussein would soon be gone, perhaps followed by the breakup of Iraq. Analysts predicted that a new, American-oriented era had begun in the Middle East, with more democracy, human rights, and economic competitiveness. Many agreed with Henry Kissinger that victory over Iraq offered "a historic opportunity" to deal with the Arab-Israeli conflict.

In retrospect, one can only marvel at how little of this came about. Subsequent efforts to impose a new-world-order style solution on crises failed in places like Somalia and Bosnia. Saddam Hussein made a unique string of mistakes, and his futile conventional war appears to have ended an era, not started one. Other than Turkey and Israel, the Middle East continues to boast fewer real elections, fewer human rights and fewer industrial exports than almost any other region.

The Arab-Israeli conflict did change after the war, especially with the Madrid Conference of October 1991 and the Oslo process of two years later, with its seven agreements between the Palestinians and Israel in as many years. But it would be hard to characterize these as making any real progress toward resolving the conflict. While Israel has shown itself hugely flexible, giving up on one traditional position after another (especially concerning the Golan Heights and Jerusalem), the Syrians and Palestinians have basically stuck with the old outlook, showing themselves yet unwilling to accept the Zionist state. Nearly all signals betray a continuing intent to destroy Israel. This hardly counts as peacemaking.

And Iraq? The regime is far weaker and the central government no longer controls the whole country, but in its essentials—with Saddam still in power and the borders unchanged—it remains preposterously unchanged.

Looking over the past decade finds just one major consequence of the war, and it is an ironic one. Fearing a repeat of the Iraqi invasion, the other Arabic-speaking states of the Persian Gulf have nestled closer to the United States, permitting troops to be stationed on their territory, as well as many other intimate military acts.

While this new relationship has benefited both sides, it has also spurred an intense growth in anti-Americanism. Osama bin Laden epitomizes this phenomenon. A U.S. comrade-in-arms in Afghanistan against the Soviets during the 1980s, today he stands accused of sponsoring a global terrorist operation that aims to kill Americans.

In all, when one recalls how important the war was thought to be, it is astonishing to observe how minor its legacy now appears. The code name given to the war against Iraq was Operation Desert Storm. As Gulf expert Patrick Clawson notes, it is symbolically fitting. A desert storm blinds and can suffocate but, once it passes, the desert is there as ever, hardly changed. So it was with the crisis that began ten years ago. It felt hugely important, and it would have been had Saddam prevailed. But once we survived it, the whole episode left most everything in its old place, hardly changed.

(4 August 2000)

SCOTT RITTER'S STARTLING CHANGE

Scott Ritter, ex-Marine, ex-arms inspector, appears to be my kind of guy. He led the United Nations' Concealment Investigation Unit to unearth Iraqi efforts to build weapons of mass destruction (WMD). He resigned in August 1998 from UNSCOM, the United Nations group tasked with defanging Iraq, in a blaze of glory, rightly protesting UNSCOM's lack of effectiveness and correctly declaring that "the illusion of arms control is more dangerous than no arms control at all."

Now, I have to admit wondering just a bit when I read a *New York Times* page-one story in late February with the headline, "Ex-Inspector Cites Early Role of C.I.A. on U.N. Arms Teams." Why did Ritter go public with the spectacular (but totally unproven) claim that the Central Intelligence Agency had used UNSCOM in June 1996 as an instrument for gathering information to target Saddam Hussein for assassination? Still, I put doubts aside and picked up his book, *Endgame: Solving the Iraq Problem—Once and for All* (New York: Simon & Schuster, 1999), with happy anticipation.

I was not disappointed, at least not for many pages. In a well-organized and well-written account, Ritter makes his quite specific purpose clear right at the start: to establish the correct policy for stopping Saddam Hussein. He builds toward this goal in three steps.

First, he tells the story of what he calls the one Iraqi constant since 1988—the ceaseless quest to build weapons of mass destruction. In the process, Ritter reliably presents a history of Iraqi high politics over the past decade, covering such diverse subjects as Saddam Hussein's family schisms and the Iraqi security organizations. Though not a specialist on Iraq, he gained true expertise on the subject (in part by relying on Amatzia Baram, the Israel scholar of whom it is said that no two camels can meet in the Iraqi desert without his being informed).

Second, *Endgame* recounts Ritter's personal experiences and memories during his many years on the UNSCOM team. He actually reveals a good deal of insider information—headline stuff like the CIA infiltration of UNSCOM as well as details about Russian-Iraqi collusion and what defectors told UNSCOM. To take one example, a formerly very highly placed Iraqi defector implausibly quoted Saddam right after losing the Kuwait war as saying, "We are finished, sonny boy." He also describes in compelling detail about being a distinctly unwelcome guest in a totalitarian states—the shouts, the eggs, even the cocked rifles.

Third, Ritter critiques the Clinton administration for a "shallow understanding" of the obstacles to disarming Iraq and its "appalling lack of leadership." He faults the administration for its "uninspired no-endgame strategy of containment through economic sanctions of indefinite duration." Translated from jargon, he means that Washington has wrongly settled on economic restrictions against Iraq as a permanent measure, under the illusion that these in themselves will fell the regime.

Ritter objects to sanctions on several grounds: (1) They don't work, for Saddam is sacrificing his people's welfare rather than bend to American demands. (2) They lead to terrible casualty rates (Ritter finds the sanctions responsible each year for 43,000 dead Iraqis under the age of five) and inspire worldwide sympathy for the regime. (3) They cause the U.S. government to forfeit moral high ground and political advantage. (4) They render Washington reactive, for containment is inherently a passive approach, permitting key decisions to be made elsewhere. (5) They cannot last, for nearly the whole world objects to them.

These preliminaries done, Ritter finally offers his own ideas for "solving the Iraq problem—once and for all," as his subtitle puts it. He sketches out two alternatives to the present policy of containment, one military and the other diplomatic. The military option revives the "Road to Baghdad" plan of 1991: send 250,000 American soldiers to the Persian Gulf, overthrow the Saddam regime, and rebuild Iraq in our image (such as was done in Germany or Japan). Ritter foresees no military difficulties ahead (indeed, he expects American soldiers will spend "more time processing prisoners than fighting the forces of Saddam").

Ritter then thinks out the diplomatic option, suggesting the irreducible elements of a U.S.-Iraqi deal, namely: Saddam recognizes Kuwait, forswears weapons of mass destruction, gives the Kurds autonomy, ends the state of war with Israel, and works things out with the Iraqi opposition forces. In return, the U.S. government ends economic sanctions, funds the reconstruction of Iraq, rebuilds the Iraqi military, and permits peaceful nuclear research.

I'm still with the author, but just barely. For reasons I cannot fathom, he has artificially set up two extreme options—overthrowing Saddam or becoming his patron—and ignored everything in between. Of course, he will dismiss the latter option as wildly wrongheaded.... But no, he doesn't. Instead, he despairs of the military option. He says it's not feasible because U.S. policy has so badly undermined the moral and legal cause against Iraq that the conflict has irretrievably eroded into a mere "squabble" between the two countries—and that's not enough to sustain the American populace in war. Even if it were enough, the "current U.S. policy of trying to overthrow Saddam is misguided," because Saddam is a symptom of underlying problems, not their cause. Most surprising of all is this utterly un-Marine-like sentence:

> While doing business with Saddam is certainly not an attractive idea, when contrasted with the unspeakable horrors of war, or the mindless and morally corrupt policy of indefinite economic sanctions, it does present a lesser evil.

And so, with some regret but no doubts, Ritter concludes that a "bold diplomatic initiative, no matter how distasteful," is the only way to go.

These are, to put it mildly, astonishing statements. War with Saddam is worse than his continued rule? Economic sanctions are more horrible than his getting nukes?

Although this policy of capitulation would be regrettable coming from anyone, it is especially unfortunate coming from a person who reports from first-hand experience that "Iraq had lied [to UNSCOM] on every level." After experiencing the reality that "Iraq would go through the motions of disarmament, but not disarm," he now asks for more promises of WMD disarmament? Ritter wants the United States to train the Iraqi military in return for utterly meaningless assurances about recognizing Kuwait? Having learned that Iraq's "anti-terrorist school" was actually a school for terrorists, he wants the U.S. government now to pay for Iraqi economic development? In contrast to this, the much-reviled Clinton policy on Iraq looks positively brilliant.

In the end, Ritter cuts a highly erratic figure. He resigned from UNSCOM to protest its lack of effectiveness, then proceeded to do UNSCOM immeasurable harm with his revelations about CIA meddling. While vividly aware of the horrors Saddam has inflicted on the Iraqi people, from brutality to impoverishment, he nonetheless writes that they see the dictator "as a symbol of hope in their world of despair." He expresses revulsion at the Saddam regime but at one point (on learning about the CIA using UNSCOM to scout out information), he writes that he "began to understand the Iraqi point of view." He blasts the Clinton administration for fecklessness, then proposes a far worse plan of appeasement.

When Scott Ritter addressed the Senate Foreign Relations Committee in September 1998, right after his resignation, Senator Joseph Biden (Democrat of Delaware) rudely accused him of acting "slightly beyond your pay grade and saying that Secretary of State Albright had more to consider than whether "old Scotty boy" did or did not get access to a weapons site." While the senator's rudeness remains inexcusable, the full expression of Ritter's thinking makes it sadly clear that his gibe was exactly on target. This man should be dismantling weapons, not opining on foreign policy.

(14 April 1999)

SADDAM'S BOMBMAKER

Most nuclear physicists these days lead a fairly humdrum existence; but not if they live in Iraq. Khidhir Hamza, born in that country in 1939, and fascinated by electricity from a young age, attended Baghdad University before receiving a master's degree from MIT and a Ph.D. in theoretical nuclear physics from Florida State University in 1968. After beginning his teaching career at an American college, he was summoned back to teach in Iraq in order to pay off his educational debts.

Invited to join the nascent Iraqi nuclear effort in 1972, Hamza did so with some enthusiasm, considering it a wonderful professional challenge. At the time, he did not rate very highly the prospects of a bomb actually being built; and, he reasoned, even if that should somehow come to pass, surely the weapon would be used as a negotiating chip vis-à-vis Israel and nothing more. "The mission," he writes here, was in any case "breathtaking: build a nuclear bomb from scratch, starting on a dining-room table."

Hamza soon began a long march through the bureaucracy, manifesting, in addition to his talents as a scientist and scholar, a finely tuned aptitude for staying out of trouble. Of Iraq's three original nuclear scientists, he alone in those early years managed to escape the capricious wrath of Saddam Hussein, who was still making his way toward the absolute power he would gain in 1979. By 1981, Hamza was working directly for Saddam; by 1987, he had reached the position of director general of Iraq's nuclear-weapons program.

His new status inevitably brought head-turning benefits: a high salary, fancy cars, travel to the West, even a residence within the presidential compound. "All that loot was softening me up, I don't deny it," Hamza writes in *Saddam's Bombmaker: The Terrifying Inside Story of the Iraqi Nuclear and Biological Weapons Agenda* (New York: Charles Scribner's Sons, 2000). "But it was the project itself, the enormity of the task, and the pure, scientific challenge of cracking the atomic code, that excited me more."

Even as he rose through the ranks, however, Hamza worried about surviving his contact with Saddam. With time, indeed, his absorbing intellectual venture turned into a descent into a kind of Stalinist hell. Not only did colleagues begin to turn up murdered, but it was becoming increasingly clear that Saddam Hussein actually intended to use the bombs Hamza was working on developing. Though himself untouched by torture or other barbarities, and still benefiting from occasional trips abroad ("just walking down Broadway [in New York] and breathing free air was invigorating"), Saddam's chief nuclear scientist saw enough to want out.

In 1987, he began trying to extricate himself not just from building the bomb but from Iraq. He achieved the first goal three years later, leaving active administration and returning to the classroom. In 1994, although feeling "too old, too comfortable, [and] too scared," he managed to accomplish the second. After a particularly stressful year in limbo, mostly in Libya, he was finally joined by his wife and three sons. The family settled quietly in the United States, and Hamza underwent a comprehensive debriefing.

Rightly fearful that Saddam wanted him dead, Hamza began living in a semi-underground manner, partly by means of tactics taught him many years earlier for evading Israeli agents. Although well known in the circles of Iraq-watchers, *Saddam's Bombmaker* represents his most sustained effort to go public. A memoir, and a compellingly written one (thanks in large part to his co-writer Jeff Stein), it also contains important and reliable information, from a credible author, on two quite distinct topics of current interest: the inner workings of the Iraqi nuclear weapons project, and life at the highest levels of the Iraqi regime. It is hard to say which is scarier.

Hamza establishes that Iraq's nuclear-weapons program has followed two principal stages. The initial one, lasting from 1972 until 1981, involved a relatively small investment of money and depended heavily on imported (mostly French) technology. The second one began with the Israeli destruction of Iraq's Osirak reactor in June 1981, an event that spurred the regime to rethink and radically expand its whole program. Hamza thus agrees with Shimon Peres's controversial assessment that, from Israel's point of view, the attack on Osirak was a mistake.

After 1981, in any event, and proceeding more or less indigenously, the Iraqis devoted twenty-five times more resources than previously to the bomb. Their headlong effort culminated in 1990 with (in Hamza's words) "a crude, one-and-a-half-ton nuclear device"—not quite yet a bomb, and far too large to be carried on a missile, but an important step along the way.

As Hamza documents, the outside world was slow to recognize the change from stage one to stage two, and this had important consequences in the aftermath of the Kuwait war. Not realizing how much the Iraqis themselves had accomplished, those leading the disarmament efforts after 1991 focused not on Iraq's capabilities—both material and intellectual—but on actual weapons. Destroying those weapons would have made sense had Saddam's regime depended on imported material and talent; as things stood, it was a nearly futile undertaking, for they could always be rebuilt. Only in mid-1995, when the U.S. government simultaneously debriefed Hamza and his former boss (and Saddam's son-in-law) Hussein Kamil, did it realize the true scope of Iraq's program.

According to Hamza, it was his identification of the twenty-five or so key nuclear scientists in Iraq, and where they could be found, that drove Saddam to close down international inspections in mid-1998. Today, Hamza estimated at a recent presentation in New York, Iraq is "undoubtedly on the precipice of nuclear power," and will have "between three to five nuclear weapons by 2005." What it will do then is a nice question, the answer to which depends in part on circumstances but in much larger part on the designs, and the character, of its president.

This is where Hamza's second topic comes in: Saddam Hussein's personality and the nature of the regime he has built up. One thing we learn from this book is that, in common with other despots of recent times, he is a man who sees danger truly everywhere. Thus, he has "a terrible fear, perhaps paranoia, about germs"; any visitor to a room where he is present must undergo an eye, ear, and mouth inspection before entering. Stalin, one recalls, had his regime's top figures sample his food; Mao suspected his swimming pool was poisoned, and refused medical care at the hands of doctors he was sure would do him in.

Saddam also has a taste for virgins—who, among other desirable qualities, are thought to be less disease-prone. In one anecdote related by Hamza, a young woman who pleaded with the president for aid after the death of her father ended up losing her virginity after having been given a beauty makeover and left naked on a bed to await his (wordless) pleasure. Although she was let go with an envelope of money, other "young, beautiful, and flirtatious" women who have serviced Saddam find themselves retained as virtual slaves to clean the apartments of his nomenklatura. Or else not retained at all; Hamza tells of one who was discovered in a bathtub with her throat slit.

Hamza likewise confirms the picture of Saddam as someone "incalculably cruel," a man whose taste for personal brutality is exercised frequently and unpredictably. Once, listening to suggestions he considered defeatist, the president pulled out a revolver and simply shot dead the military officer making them; at a meeting with his top leadership, he abruptly had a general whisked off to the torture cells; a guard who incautiously confided the president's whereabouts —to a personal friend of the president—was shot on the spot for indiscretion. Hamza's phrase for Saddam is "an expertly tailored, well-barbered gangster"; the description fits. To the woman who told about losing her virginity to Saddam, his yellow eyes "were the eyes of death. He looked at me as if I were a corpse."

A nuclear bomb, in the hands of such a man, is bound to be cataclysmically dangerous, rendering him, as Hamza has put it in a recent television interview, all but "invincible": the "hero of the Arab world" and readier than ever to indulge his well-proven appetite for recklessness. The result—for Iran, Kuwait, Saudi Arabia, and, of course, Israel—is almost too frightening to contemplate.

What then is to be done? In Hamza's view, there are only two ways to stop the current train of events from unfolding toward catastrophe. Best by far would be to get rid of Saddam himself. But this can only happen if the U.S. government either acts on its own to bring it about or provides the necessary lethal aid to the Iraqi opposition. Second best would be to begin an emergency program to deprive Saddam of the skills of his twenty-five top nuclear scientists, preferably by getting them out of the country.

Unmentioned by Hamza but certainly valuable are such initiatives, currently being considered or implemented by the George W. Bush administration, as boost-phase missile defenses to protect our allies, energy substitutes to deprive Saddam of oil revenues, and a renewed embargo. But in the end, as this truly alarming book shows, which path we take is less important than recognizing how late the hour has grown, and how urgently we need to move the question of Iraq to the very top of our foreign-policy agenda.

(June 2001)

THE UNITED STATES FORMS A MAJORITY OF ONE

As America gets closer to initiating hostilities against Saddam Hussein's foul regime in Iraq, the Middle East is sending out a howl of protest, arguing that (as the *Washington Post* sums it up) "the risks of an attack ... far outweigh any threat he may pose."

This view is surprising, to put it mildly, ignoring as it does Saddam's record of brutality toward his subjects and aggression toward his neighbors, not to speak of his terrifying ambition to acquire nuclear weapons. The outlook derives from several factors:

- *A sense of immunity*: Most Middle Easterners "do not fear Iraq at all," observes Radwan 'Abdullah, former dean of political science at Jordan University. A twenty-year-old vendor in Cairo has the strange idea that the problem is "between America and Iraq, and we [Egyptians] don't have anything to do with it."

- *A fear of the unknown*: The prospect of Iraq splitting up or suffering total economic collapse worries its neighbors. Jordan's King Abdullah anticipates that "striking Iraq represents a catastrophe to Iraq and the region in general and threatens the security and stability of the region." Turkey's prime minister, Bülent Ecevit, fears an attack on Iraq on the narrow grounds that this "will seriously affect" his country at a time when its economy rests "on very sensitive balances."

- *An alienation from America*: Middle Easterners who want Saddam gone distance themselves from Washington's policy lest they, as the

Wall Street Journal puts it, appear to be "U.S. lackeys." This applies even to Kuwaitis.

• *An admiration for Saddam*: Radwan 'Abdullah notes: "Many Arab countries...want Iraq stronger." They root for him defying the hated West.

Middle Easterners are not unique here. Much of the world, led by the French, Russian, and Chinese governments, concurs, leaving only the British, Israelis, and Iraq's opposition firmly supporting American threats to finish off Saddam.

An anti-Saddam strategy, therefore, must accept that Washington may basically have to go it alone. This is less than ideal, but it is doable. And it prompts three observations.

First, such isolation is not new, for Washington routinely goes it alone on a host of issues. It was the lone dissenter in a 118-1 vote at the United Nations General Assembly in 1981 favoring a code to restrict the promotion of infant-formula products. More recently, the Bush administration single-handedly scuttled the Kyoto climate treaty of 1997, which called for drastic reductions in carbon dioxide emissions. The war against the Taliban last fall was nearly a solo performance, too.

As a White House spokesman rightly explained in 1996: "We may be in a minority of one, but we're going to stand by our position. Sometimes you're the only country taking a particular view on an issue but you stand by it because you have to stand by it."

Second, defeating Iraq should be militarily easy. Kenneth Adelman, a former assistant to Donald Rumsfeld, predicts that a war against Iraqis will be a "cakewalk," and offers four reasons: "1) It was a cakewalk last time; 2) they've become much weaker; 3) we've become much stronger; and 4) now we're playing for keeps."

Assuming Adelman is right, U.S. forces acting solo can take control of Iraq without needing the U.N. seal of approval, European troops, Saudi money, or Turkish bases. The task would be easier with a little help from friends, but it is not necessary.

Third, if Adelman is wrong and it's not an easy military victory, then U.S. opinion becomes decisive. When a war goes badly, U.S. public opinion can become fickle, affected by such factors as casualties, complacency, and a hostile world reaction. American disaffection hamstrung the near-solo American military efforts in Vietnam, Lebanon, and Somalia. In strategic terms, public opinion is the U.S. center of gravity, its most vulnerable point.

American planners must therefore keep a close eye on U.S. opinion. Anything that exceeds its bounds risks failure. The fate of Iraq, whether it remains subject to Saddam's depredations or is liberated, may depend as much on the mood of ordinary Americans as it will on the capabilities of American troops.

(18 March 2002)

LOOTING: AN IRAQI TRAGEDY

Who's to blame for the April 2003 destruction of Iraqi museums, libraries, and archives, amounting to what the *New York Times* calls "one of the greatest cultural disasters in recent Middle Eastern history"?*

The Bush administration is responsible, say academic specialists on the Middle East. They proceed to compare American leaders to some of the worst mass-murderers in history.

- *Hamid Dabashi* of Columbia University: U.S. political leaders are "destroyers of civilization" like Attila the Hun, Genghis Khan and Tamerlane.

- *Michael Sells* of Haverford College: They are "barbarians" whose "criminal neglect" makes them comparable to Nero.

- *Said Arjomand* of the State University of New York (Stony Brook): The U.S. government's "war crime" renders it akin to the Mongols who sacked Baghdad in 1258.

These academics overlook one tiny detail, however: It was Iraqis who, post-liberation, looted and burned, and they did so against the coalition's wishes. Blaming Americans for Iraqi crimes is deeply patronizing, equating Iraqis with children not responsible for their actions.

The academics also overlook another fact: the extreme rarity of such cultural self-destruction.

The French did not sack the Louvre in 1944. The Japanese did not burn their national library a year later. Panamanians did not destroy their archives in 1990. Kuwaitis did not destroy their historic

---

*Later assessments found these initial damage estimates to be highly inflated; nonetheless, there was destruction and it needs to be explained.

Korans in 1991. Yes, looting took place in all these cases, but nothing approached what the Associated Press calls Iraq's "unchecked frenzy of cultural theft."

And a frenzy it was. At the National Museum of Iraq, perhaps the greatest storehouse of antiquities in the Middle East, "the 28 galleries of the museum and vaults with huge steel doors guarding storage chambers that descend floor after floor into unlighted darkness had been completely ransacked," reported one eyewitness.

The devastation at Iraq's national library and archives was worse, for both institutions were purposefully incinerated. Much of the country's culture and records was destroyed; "nothing was left in the national library's main wing but its charred walls and ceilings and mounds of ash." The smoldering shell contained the charred remnants of historic books "and a nation's intellectual legacy gone up in smoke." Iraq's main Islamic library, with its collection of "rare early legal and literary materials, priceless Korans, calligraphy and illumination" was also burned.

This descent into barbarism is so unusual, it has only a single precedent—Iraqi actions in 1990-91.

- *In Kuwait*: When Kuwait was an Iraqi province, Iraqi troops plundered the national museum, set fire to the planetarium, ransacked libraries and otherwise crippled the cultural infrastructure.

- *In Iraq*: During the instability that followed Iraq's loss, anti-government elements engaged in a looting rampage, pillaging regional museums and other cultural institutions, stealing some 4,000 items. Archaeologists published a catalogue, "Lost Heritage: Antiquities Stolen from Iraq's Regional Museums," to prevent trade in these artifacts.

How to explain this possibly unique Iraqi penchant for cultural self-hatred? The inherently violent quality of modern Iraqi society is one cause.

Writing in 1968, the Israeli scholar Uriel Dann explained that a climate of violence is "part of the political scene in Iraq . . . It is an undercurrent which pervades the vast substrata of the people outside the sphere of power politics. Hundreds of thousands of souls can easily be mobilized on the flimsiest pretext. They constitute a permanently restive element, ready to break into riots."

The Kuwaiti scholar Shafiq N. Ghabra expanded on this theme in 2001 in the *Middle East Quarterly*. Noting Iraq's uneasy mix of Arabs and Kurds, Sunnis and Shiites, urbanites and tribal members, plus other divisions, he noted how unmanageable governments found this diversity, which led them to create "a state devoid of political compromise." Leaders "liquidated those holding opposing views, confiscated property without notice, trumped up charges against its enemies and fought battles with imaginary domestic foes."

The empty shell of the national library testifies mutely to the excesses of a country singularly prone to violence against itself.

The blame for the looting in Iraq, therefore, lies not with the coalition forces but with the Iraqis themselves. Yes, the coalition should have prepared better, but Iraqis alone bear moral responsibility for the cultural wreckage.

This conclusion has two implications. Middle East specialists have yet again confirmed their political obtuseness. And Iraqis have signaled that they will act in ways highly unwelcome to the coalition.

(22 April 2003)

PART 4
AMERICAN VIEWS

11

Making U.S. Policy

The Arabists' Tradition

By the time the Reverend Benjamin Weir was taken hostage on the streets of Beirut in April 1984, he had lived thirty-one years in Lebanon, where he had taught theology, done charitable work, and spread the gospel. Over the decades, he and his wife Carol came totally to identify themselves with the Muslim Lebanese while at the same time disassociating themselves completely from the U.S. government (so much so, they didn't even know the name of the U.S. ambassador in Beirut). Remarkably, Weir's kidnapping by Shi'i extremists did nothing to change the couple's views. During a March 1985 meeting with Secretary of State George Shultz, Mrs. Weir surrealistically defended the Shi'is as a sincere people with "some legitimate grievances against the United States" and blamed her husband's abduction on U.S. foreign policy. Then, on his release from captivity, Weir held a news conference at which he demanded the U.S. government fulfill his kidnappers' demands.

While the Weirs' dogmatism makes them somewhat atypical, many American teachers, missionaries, and aid workers living in Beirut or elsewhere in the Arab world share their outlook: unbounded sympathy for Muslims and loathing for the actions of the U.S. government.

Robert D. Kaplan shows two things about this outlook in *The Arabists: The Romance of an American Elite* (New York: Free Press, 1993), his pioneering, fascinating, and important study: that the Weirs are heirs to an enduring tradition of American Arabists which goes back over one-and-a-half centuries; and that tempered versions of their viewpoint have inspired much of American diplomacy toward the Middle East since World War II.

223

The Arabist tradition goes back to 1827 when Eli Smith, an upright Yankee from Yale and the Andover Theological Seminary, took off for the mountains of Lebanon to learn the Arabic language. Within a few years, Beirut had become the center of a remarkable missionary effort by American Protestants. Unlike the British Arabists, who always retained connections to their government, these Americans crossed oceans and braved terrible odds without public support or ulterior purpose; they strove only to bring their vision of Christianity to the Middle East. As Kaplan notes, "Mission work defines the American Arabist, much as imperialism defines the British Arabist."

When it became apparent that few Middle Easterners would accept their faith, the Arabists turned to good works—feeding the hungry, ministering to the sick, and establishing schools (notably the American University of Beirut, "probably the most inspired idea in the history of foreign aid" according to Kaplan). They had a vast cultural and political impact, especially in promoting Arabic as a modern literary language and in incubating the ideology of Pan-Arab nationalism. "America's first foreign aid program" certainly made its mark.

Through his readings and interviews, Kaplan beautifully evokes this exotic outpost of Americans abroad. While staunchly patriotic Americans, the Arabists pursued a strikingly non-American way of life, with households full of servants, a passion for foreign languages, and a singular sense of family continuity. Talcott Seelye, U.S. ambassador to Syria until 1981, is, for example, the fourth generation in his family to serve in the Levant; his great-grandfather arrived there in 1849. Even today, the Seelye tradition persists, as Kate, one of his daughters worked as a staff aide to Queen Noor of Jordan and more recently reports for National Public Radio out of Beirut. This is the elite and the romance of Kaplan's subtitle.

The Arabist impact on U.S. policy dates back to the late 1940s, when Washington first got actively involved in the Middle East. Like their first cousins, the "China hands," Arabists had precisely those skills the Department of State sought: language, knowledge of local culture, useful contacts. The Arabist cohort at State so dominated the Middle Eastern bureau, it managed to absorb many others to its viewpoint, including farmers' children from the Midwest and ethnics from New York City.

Trouble was, it also brought strange prejudices to the government, reminiscent of the Weirs'. Bound up in their own small world, Arabists lacked the imagination to understand either the United States or American interests abroad. They loved a pristine Middle East, and regretted its modernization. Against all evidence, Arabists quixotically sought to show the "essential harmony of Western and Arab-Islamic culture." On the negative side, they loathed Maronites and Greek Orthodox Christians, the French, and Iranians ("Scratch an Arabist and you'll find an anti-Iranian"). But most of all, they hated Israelis, whom they blamed as much for spoiling their century-old idyll as for the Palestinians' plight. Washington's increasingly strong support for Israel caused many Arabists to slide into anti-Semitism.

As one might expect, Arabists compiled a disastrous record of making policy. The "obsession with the Arabs" that Kaplan sees as their defining trait repeatedly tripped them up. Carrying old grudges, they refused to see Israel's value to the United States. On occasion, they even took the Arab side against their own government (most notably in 1973, when James Akins, the ambassador to Saudi Arabia, encouraged oil company executives to "hammer home" the Saudi line in Washington). Given a chance to run Iraq policy, they created the ill-fated policy of appeasement that encouraged Saddam Hussein to invaded Kuwait.

Fortunately, the Arabist reign in the State Department is nearing its end, as interlopers shoulder increasing responsibilities. Since Joseph Sisco took over the State Department's Middle East bureau in 1969, "peace processors" have steadily gained at the Arabists' expense. The two, Kaplan shows, could hardly be more different. Peace processors barely know enough Arabic to give directions to a taxi driver. They are hooked not on rugs but on the Arab-Israeli conflict. They love not Arab culture but policymaking. For pleasure, they don't read travel books by sand-mad British explorers but inter-office memoranda. Symbolic of the changing of the guard, several peace processors (Martin Indyk, Daniel Kurtzer, Aaron Miller, Dennis Ross) dominate the formulation of U.S. policy toward the Arab-Israeli negotiations. They're far less colorful than the Arabists, but they also make far better policy. Their dispassion and goodwill made Washington the main force behind the Egyptian-Israeli peace treaty of 1979 and the PLO-Israel agreements of the 1990s.

In bringing the Arabist legacy to light, Kaplan does more than retrieve an obscure aspect of American life. By plumbing these deep waters, he shows why America's connection to the Middle East inspires such strange views and intense passion. It's not just a matter of oil or Israel; devotion to the Arabs is also part of our history.

(16 September 1993)

THE $36 BILLION BARGAIN

Why does the U.S. government provide such generous support to Israel? Conventional wisdom points to American Jews, their votes, their political donations, and their well-organized lobbying efforts. Whole books (notably Paul Findley's *They Dare to Speak Out* and Edward Tivan's *The Lobby*) have been written to make this point.

A. F. K. Organski, professor of political science at the University of Michigan, has looked at the record of American aid to Israel and come to a different conclusion in *The $36 Billion Bargain: Strategy and Politics in U.S. Assistance to Israel* (New York: Columbia University Press, 1990). He observed a striking fact: U.S. aid was very low before 1970 and very high afterwards. Noting that American Jews exerted about the same efforts on Israel's behalf before 1970 as after that date, he asked himself why the dramatically different aid levels? Logic holds that a constant factor cannot explain a variable event; obviously, the author concludes, American Jews cannot be the decisive factor here. To clinch this argument, he points out that it was Richard Nixon, a politician singularly not beholden to Jews (according to Henry Kissinger, he "delighted in telling associates and visitors that the 'Jewish lobby' had no effect on him") who raised the levels of aid.

Organski posits a contrary argument for the turn in 1970. For him, the critical change had to do with American attitudes toward Israel's utility. From Truman through Johnson, he shows, American administrations saw Israel as a weak state that could provide no help in the Great Game versus the Soviet Union; if anything, the Jewish state was perceived as a liability. Thanks to the 1967 Arab-Israeli war, Nixon saw Israeli military power as a significant benefit to the United States. This transformation was then completed in the aftermath of the 1973 war.

As his previous books, most notably *The Stages of Political Development*, have shown, Organski has a powerful and disciplined intelligence. In *The $36 Billion Bargain*, he relentlessly applies logic to a large, amorphous body of data, and so goes far beyond the anecdotal montages that have served other authors as evidence. The result is a tour de force that actually settles a highly contentious issue. This rare accomplishment deserves to be rewarded by calling off the old and sterile debate over the Israel lobby.

The book is full of insights. Organski shows how it is in almost everyone's interest to forward the myth of the Jewish lobby. Jewish leaders clearly benefit from being perceived as having a decisive impact. Israeli leaders like to believe that they have influential friends. American policy makers exploit the Jewish lobby to explain away decisions that Arab leaders oppose. American opponents of aid love the lobby, for it strengthens their argument that close relations with Israel results from domestic considerations, not a sober assessment of foreign policy. Even Arab leaders cling to the myth, which makes unpalatable decisions made in Washington much easier for them to swallow.

Concurring with Steven Spiegel's analysis in *The Other Arab-Israeli Conflict*, Organski holds that "U.S. policy decisions with respect to Israel have, in the main, been made by presidents and presidential foreign policy elites both by themselves and for reasons entirely their own." He thereby dismisses not just the Israel lobby but the Congress, the media, the academy, and even public opinion.

Most of *The $36 Billion Bargain* is devoted to proving that the U.S.-Israel connection owes more to this American strategic perception than to the activism of American Jews. The evidence includes a review of American public opinion about Israel, a comparative look at American foreign aid, and the influence of the U.S. over Israel. A finely tabulated account of Senate votes shows that ideology has much more to do with the way senators vote than the size of their Jewish constituencies or the contributions they receive from Jewish or pro-Jewish sources. And there is another, more perverse impetus: aid to Israel provides the Congress one of those few instances of foreign policy (the Afghan rebels fighting the Soviets were another) when it can take the initiative away from the legislative branch: "It can demand that aid be increased, scolding bureaucrats and political appointees for dragging their feet, and, in so doing, claim the political credit for supporting Israel, while savoring the pleasure of driving the bureaucracy to distraction."

But why is a Congress usually skeptical about foreign aid so enthusiastic in the case of Israel? Organski does not quite explain the anomaly. He quotes a senator to the effect that the Jews are "hardworking," but that hardly suffices, especially in light of the abundant evidence from five decades that aid induces an economic and spiritual dependency. Welfare countries seem to suffer from the same debilitation as welfare mothers: lack of motivation, more interest in politics than entrepreneurship, and poverty. Or, to adopt James Bovard's graphic metaphor, perpetual assistance to poor governments "is about as humanitarian as giving an alcoholic the key to a brewery."

The reason for so much aid to Israel has to do with that country being exempt from the powerful critique about aid's unfortunate effects. As Tom Bethell so clearly pointed out in the July 1990 issue of the *American Spectator*, this has to do in part with the extremely political nature of aid to Israel; financial transfers have turned into the premier symbol of U.S.-Israeli partnership, and thereby become an end in itself. To argue against funds for Israel is tantamount to anti-Israel politics. In part too, because the motives behind the transfers are more military than economic, these are not subject to the usual analysis. But money is money; just because the U.S. Congress thinks of its funds going for F-16s rather than sugar refineries does not lessen the cost to Israel.

We are, in effect, undermining an ally's economy at considerable cost to ourselves. The only way to break this absurd situation is for some American leader with impeccable pro-Israel credentials to call for an orderly and gradual end to the aid. (Or, more shockingly, for an enemy of Israel to call for large increases in that aid!)

Looking to the future, Organski sees a decline in U.S.-Israel ties if any of three conditions obtain: the Soviet threat declines, the radical Middle East threat declines, or an Arab ally so modernizes that it becomes a tempting alternative to Israel as the United States' main ally. The author discounts the third possibility, and he is right, for other than Turkey there is no Muslim country of the Middle East on the track of true modernization, and the Turks stay as far away from Middle East imbroglios as they can.

What of the first two conditions? From the perspective of late 1990, the threat to U.S. interests from Moscow is declining at about the same speed as that of the radical Arabs, personified by Saddam Hussein, is growing. This combination of trends accounts for the perplexing sight of an American secretary of state pleading with Soviet leaders to send troops to the Persian Gulf. In other words, changes in the region cancel out changes in the world. While Israel is less useful vis-à-vis the Soviet Union, it is more so vis-à-vis the Arabs and Middle East oil, and its overall value to the United States remains fairly constant. If Organski is right about the key to U.S.-Israel relations lying in a hard-headed analysis of American interests, then changes ahead in that relationship should not be as major as many today expect.

(January 1991)

REPUBLICANS FOR ISRAEL

What do the four leading candidates for president of the United States in 2000, two Democratic and two Republican, have to say about the Middle East, now that the campaign has begun in earnest?

Perhaps the clearest insight into the candidates' positions comes from James Zogby, president of the Arab American Institute and a leading Arab-American political operative. He's a man President Bill Clinton has praised as a "remarkable voice for calm and clarity, no matter how heated the issues" and "one of the most forceful, intense and brutally honest people who ever came to the White House to see me." He's also a liberal democrat and one of Israel's most determined foes in the United States.

Zogby's recently published report, *The State of the Middle East Policy Debate*, begins with a look at public opinion. He finds that "a significant partisan split" exists on Middle Eastern issues. Specifically, Republicans are "more hard-line and pro-Israel" than Democrats.

This difference is very substantial, with Republicans three times more friendly to Israel than Democrats. Thus, in response to the question, "With regard to the Middle East, how do you feel the next president should relate to the region," 22 percent of Republicans said he should be pro-Israel, while only 7 percent of Democrats opted for this reply. (It also bears noting that among born-again Christians, the percentage on the pro-Israel side rises to 29 percent.)

Not surprisingly, the presidential candidates reflect this difference in their ranks, with Republicans far more pro-Israel than Democrats. On the key issue of U.S. policy toward the peace process, for example, Al Gore and Bill Bradley endorse the current even-handed approach of pressing Israel and the Arabs alike for concessions. In stark contrast, George W. Bush and John McCain (as well as every lesser candidate) denounce this approach and insist that, if elected president, they will not pressure democratic Israel into making concessions to the likes of Yasir Arafat and Hafez al-Assad.

Same goes with the question of moving the U.S. Embassy from Tel Aviv to Jerusalem. On one side, Zogby found, "every Republican candidate has promised to make the embassy move a priority for his administration." In contrast, both Gore and Bradley "have taken more cautious stands," not endorsing a move of the embassy outside the context of Israel's negotiations with the Palestinians.

And so too on Iraq. All four leading candidates endorse the current tough approach to Iraq, leading Zogby to describe their outlook as one of "near consensus." But Republicans take what Zogby calls "a characteristically tougher approach," with all of them advocating steps to bring down the regime of Saddam Hussein, something the two Democrats shy away from.

In all, whether the question is Israel or Iraq, the candidates agree on basics (friendly to Israel, hard-line on Iraq), with the Republicans more emphatic in their views than either Democrat. This has several important implications.

First, the Arab and Muslim lobbies remain unable to affect the policy outlook of presidential candidates. Zogby can rail against the candidates' agreement as "pandering" to Jewish voters with "worn-out clichés" and "dangerous and provocative posturing," but he can do little about it.

Second, several times more members of the Republican Party are friendly to Israel than are Democrats, and their leaderships reflect this disparity.

Third, Jews nonetheless still overwhelmingly favor the Democratic Party. This is because they care less over time about policy toward Israel and more about domestic American concerns. An insightful observer of the U.S. Jewish scene, Jonathan S. Tobin, explains that "a pro-choice stand on abortion and a willingness to vilify the National Rifle Association is the red meat that most Jewish audiences hunger for, not speeches about Jerusalem."

Finally, despite a diminished focus on the Middle East among American Jews, a consensus exists in the United States as a whole about the rights and wrongs of the Arab-Israeli conflict and Iraq, and this consensus no longer depends on a Jewish lobby to sustain it.

(15 February 2000)

How Clinton Adheres to the "Rushdie Rules"

The State Department spokesman in July 1997 launched into a tirade of a sort that may be unique in the annals of U.S. diplomacy. Asked about a woman who allegedly put up some posters in Hebron depicting the Prophet Muhammad as a pig, Nicholas Burns had this to say:

> The United States has given great thought to this over the last couple of days, and I mean at the very highest levels of our government. We condemn the outrageous, crude and sick portrayal of the Prophet Mohammed by an Israeli settler the other day. This woman is either sick or she is evil.... We are very pleased that she is going to be put on trial by the Israeli Government. She deserves to be put on trial for these outrageous attacks on Islam. We are grateful that President [Ezer] Weizman and Prime Minister [Binyamin] Netanyahu have denounced her and her actions and her sick cartoon in very clear terms.

This amazing statement deserves a close look for several reasons. First, by referring to the "very highest levels of our government," Burns is signaling that he is speaking for President Clinton. His comments are not one man's tirade but the considered and official response bearing the full authority of our leadership.

Second, the act that occasioned this fulmination was not a mass murder, nor even any sort of violent act, but the hanging of posters. I searched through weeks and weeks of State Department daily briefings and found nothing approaching this vituperative language in reference to the horrors that took place in Rwanda, where hundreds of thousands lost their lives. To the contrary, Burns was throughout cautious and diplomatic.

Third, the person who put up the posters engaged in what we in the United States would consider protected speech. Our government is supposed to endorse the right peaceably to distribute written materials, no matter how much it may execrate their contents. It seems strange that the State Department is "very pleased" that the alleged poster-distributor should be put on trial.

Fourth, Burns tried and convicted the woman accused of posting the cartoons—without waiting for her to enter a courtroom or go through a trial. Due process and the assumption of innocence, it appears, have disappeared along with free speech.

Fifth, other religious leaders get insulted all the time and no one even notices, and certainly not heads of state. To take two examples: Joseph Heller's novel *God Knows* (1984) has King David using dirty language to muse on his sexual conquests, while Martin Scorsese's movie *The Last Temptation of Christ* (1988) delves into Jesus' sexual longings. David and Jesus are fair game, but to quote the title of a book, "be careful with Muhammad!"

Finally, the outrage expressed at this press briefing fits into a larger context, what I call the "Rushdie rules." When Ayatollah Khomeini in February 1989 called for the murder of Salman Rushdie, a British subject, he opened a new era of censorship. With his death edict, he established that anyone who insults Islam, as he deemed Rushdie to have done in his magical-fantasy novel *The Satanic Verses*, puts his life on the line. True, Rushdie has survived the death sentence hurled at him from Tehran, but only by going underground and with lots of police protection. Khomeini successfully established that anyone seen as insulting Islam deserves to die.

And in fact, quite a few people, mostly Muslim, have since been killed. The most notorious incident took place in the Turkish town of Sivas, where a hotel housing a conference of militant secularists was torched in July 1993, killing thirty-seven. In Egypt the aged Egyptian Noble Prize winner Naguib Mahfouz was stabbed in the neck and another writer, Farag Foda, was killed. And the list of victims goes on.

In addition to these actual acts of violence, the Rushdie rules have also had a powerful chilling effect on writers, Muslim and non-Muslim alike, dissuading them from parodying or blaspheming Islam— or even from writing a sober critical analysis of it. The author of French-language study, *Islamisme et les Etats-Unis, une alliance contre l'Europe* (Lausanne: L'Age d'Homme, 1997), which claims a joint conspiracy of militant Islam and the United States, feared for his life so much he adopted the pseudonym Alexandre del Valle.

The Hebron incident shows that the Rushdie rules even apply in Israel, of all places. Jews there may with impunity say what they wish about their own religion, and they do, trading insults much worse than "pig"; but blaspheme Islam and they'll not only get hauled off to court but also assaulted by the full authority of the U.S. government.

This is wrong. The rules of free speech protect not nursery rhymes or paeans of goodwill but nasty, sacrilegious, and abhorrent discourse. For over two centuries, the U.S. government has consistently forwarded free speech, and did so against far more fearsome adversaries than Islamists. It must recover from Burns' very unfortunate rant and again and always stand up for this principle.

(25 July 1997)

EGYPTAIR PROBE REVEALS ANTI-AMERICANISM

The crash of EgyptAir's Flight 990 on October 31, 1999, has exposed searing differences between Egyptians and Americans. From the U.S. point of view, the inquiry seems straightforward. Figuring out what went wrong means analyzing the evidence and coming up with the best explanation for the disaster. The American public generally trusts the naval recovery squads, transportation specialists, and law-enforcement officers to do their job.

Not so the Egyptian public. Egypt's population profoundly mistrusts its government, and reasonably so given its long history of dictatorship and deception. Egyptians almost universally believe in conspiracy theories, and they nearly always blame the same three culprits: the British, the Americans and/or the Jews. In June 1967 President Gamal Abdel Nasser was caught on tape suggesting to King Hussein of Jordan that the two leaders falsely claim that U.S. and British forces had helped Israel defeat their armies. In 1990, when Egypt's tomato crop went bad, rumor had it that an Egyptian minister of agriculture who was supposedly one-quarter Jewish had engaged in sabotage by importing sterile seeds from Israel.

Conspiracy thinking can be found anywhere, but in the Middle East it dominates at the highest levels of the government, the media, the academy, and the religious establishment. And Flight 990 is a particularly inviting target for conspiracy theorists. It carried thirty-three top Egyptian military officers, plus it originated in New York, the city with the world's largest Jewish population. That's enough to convince many Egyptians that someone purposely brought down the plane to harm Egyptian interests.

Not for a second do Egyptians accept the idea that a relief pilot, Gamil al-Batouti, had intentionally nose-dived the plane. They cannot imagine that a pious Muslim and former military officer should have caused such humiliation to his family and his country. When Americans try to interpret Batouti's much-repeated statement, "I put my faith in God's hands," Egyptians see bias against Islam.

Thus Egyptians have been engaged in a surreal debate over whether the culprit was Israeli, American, or both. An Egyptian without access to Western media has almost no way of knowing that there is a serious case against Batouti.

The government mostly blames America. The managing editor of the government newspaper *Al-Jumhuriya* muses about a U.S. surface-to-air missile, or maybe a laser ray, bringing down the airliner. Mahmud Bakri explains in *Al-Musawwar*, a government-run weekly, how the airliner strayed into a no-fly zone and was instantly destroyed to keep some deadly military information secret. Or maybe, he speculates, New York air traffic controllers intentionally sent the plane in harm's way, a line of reasoning Bakri finds convincing because Jews "have strong networks of communication at U.S. airports."

Egypt's transportation minister told a parliamentary committee that Boeing, maker of the 767 that crashed, was making a scapegoat of Egypt: "It's the airline production company which tried to defend itself." Added one member of Egypt's parliament: "This 'accident' was deliberate, and the target was the large number of military [officers] onboard the plane."

Opposition dailies mostly blamed Israel. "Evidence of Mossad Involvement in Blowing Up the Egyptian Airliner," screams a huge red banner across the front page of *Al-'Arabi*. The chief editor of *Al-Wafd* writes on the front page of his newspaper that "Israel's fingers are not far away" from the crash, reasoning that the Jewish state could not pass up the opportunity to eliminate thirty-three U.S.-trained Egyptian military officers.

That a plane crash arouses such powerful and hostile sentiments in Egypt points to two conclusions. First, over twenty years of formal peace with Israel has done next to nothing to improve Egyptian attitudes toward its neighbor.

Second, although Washington is handling the crash inquiry very carefully so as to respect Egyptian sensibilities, such sensitivity cannot contain a brewing crisis. Despite what the State Department likes to calls a "long and close friendship" with Egypt that goes back a quarter century, the gap dividing Egyptians and Americans is huge and perhaps widening. In investigating the crash Washington must follow the truth wherever it leads. And given the larger troubles the investigation has exposed, the U.S. should take a close look at its relationship with Cairo, which has been on autopilot for too long.

(24 November 1999)

SUE THE SAUDIS

MEMO
To: 9/11 victims and their families
From: Daniel Pipes
Subject: Compensation

You have been engaged in an unfortunate spat with the U.S. government over the money you deserve for your losses on 9/11, prompting anger all around. Here's a solution: Forget Washington and focus on Riyadh.

The Kingdom of Saudi Arabia bears a heavy responsibility for the disaster. Osama bin Laden, Al-Qaeda, and the Taliban derived their radical ideas mainly from the Wahhabi ideology that rules in Saudi Arabia. The kingdom permitted the recruitment of some 25,000 young Saudis to wage jihad, fully aware of the danger they posed to the United States. And fifteen of the nineteen suicide hijackers hailed from Saudi Arabia.

The Saudi royal family and perhaps also the government (the two are difficult to keep apart in a country sometimes called the only family-owned business with a seat at the United Nations) donated large sums of money for years to bin Laden, Al-Qaeda and the Taliban, and perhaps arms as well.

Even post-September 11, the kingdom has been unforthcoming about cracking down on the flow of funds to jihad groups. It has not cooperated sincerely with the U.S. investigation, preferring, as one

American official complains, to "dribble out a morsel of insignificant information one day at a time."

The fact that Saudi ideology, nationals, and money play so large a role in the attacks has two important implications.

- The Saudis' own legal code is largely based on the compensating the injured party. (Hit a camel with your car and you pay compensation to the camel's owner; hit the camel's owner and you pay his family.) Saudi laws and traditions, in other words, require that the families of those harmed on September 11 be paid. You have a strong moral claim on the Saudis.

- You also have a good legal basis to demand payment from the kingdom in a U.S. court. "Although it is generally assumed that U.S. citizens can only sue governments that the State Department officially deems to be sponsors of terrorism," says Allan Gerson, an international law expert and author of *Price of Terror* (New York: HarperCollins, 2001), "that's just not true." In fact, the Foreign Sovereign Immunities Act of 1976 has permitted Americans to bring lawsuits against any foreign state "in cases involving personal injury and death as a result of the tortuous conduct of a foreign state occurring in the United States," notes another international legal expert, Leonard Garment. For example, in 1980, one court ruled the Chilean government responsible for a car bombing in Washington, D.C. In 1989, another court ruled the Republic of China (Taiwan) not entitled to sovereign immunity in connection with an assassination in California.

In theory, then, you can bring action against the deep-pocketed Saudi government.

But there's a catch. The "Air Transportation Safety and System Stabilization Act," rushed into law on September 22, 2001 offers you tax-free funds—but only on condition that you give up the right to sue. Accepting government money means that each of you "waives the right to file a civil action (or to be a party to an action) in any federal or state court for damages sustained as a result of the terrorist-related aircraft crashes of September 11, 2001."

In short, take money from the "September 11th Victim Compensation Fund of 2001" and you forfeit the possibility of suing the Saudis. Washington took this unprecedented step mostly to protect the airlines, the airports, the aircraft manufacturers, the Towers' owner and the City of New York from going bankrupt. But it also wanted to avert legal actions against foreign states like Saudi Arabia.

That's because State Department poobahs hate it when citizens initiate lawsuits against foreign governments, which they dismiss as interference in the high art of diplomacy. They'd much rather extract $6 billion from the American taxpayer than get Saudi Arabia to pay up.

This is bad policy, and immoral too. You, the victims of 9/11, should have your day in court to prove Saudi responsibility and claim whatever compensation you feel entitled to.

Please think long and hard about signing the waiver. Or, if you have already signed it, consider withdrawing your consent. The greatest service you can render those murdered in September is to establish accountability for their deaths. Pressing civil actions for damages enables you to do what your government will not do.

(18 February 2002)

Make the Saudis Pay for Terror

The Kingdom of Saudi Arabia's massive implication in the death of 3,000 Americans on 9/11, I argued above in February 2002, is reason for the victims and their families to consider suing it for compensation. Three important developments have occurred in the two months since then, all of them propelling this idea forward.

No loss of U.S. benefits: A U.S. law passed on last September 22 seemed to limit the ability of 9/11 victims and their survivors to sue the Saudis or anyone else. To share in the open-ended federal compensation fund, states the "Air Transportation Safety and System Stabilization Act," they have to waive "the right to file a civil action (or to be a party to an action) in any Federal or State court for damages sustained as a result of the terrorist-related aircraft crashes of September 11."

But Kenneth R. Feinberg, the special master in charge of dispensing the open-ended fund (which he estimates will total about $4 billion), informs me that another piece of legislation effectively reversed my interpretation of the law. On November 19, Public Law 107-71 amended the above in the following manner: "The preceding sentence does not apply to a civil action to recover collateral source obligations, or to a civil action against any person who is a knowing participant in any conspiracy to hijack any aircraft or commit any terrorist act."

In effect, the law now distinguishes between 9/11's unknowing participants (such as the airlines or airports) and knowing ones (such as the terrorists themselves or those who sponsored or financed them). It keeps the former off-bounds but permits suing the latter. In Feinberg's words, any person "in Saudi Arabia (or anywhere else) who provided assistance to the terrorists on September 11 can be sued by claimants participating in the Fund." Or, in his plain-English explanation, claimants can "have their cake and eat it too."

This amendment is wonderful news, permitting the families to accept an on-average $1.2 million from U.S. taxpayers, then sue Saudi Arabia.

More indications of official Saudi sponsorship of terrorism: Recent weeks have turned up some extraordinarily incriminating documents, such as a hard drive seized by U.S. troops in Sarajevo from a computer at the office of the Saudi High Commission for Relief of Bosnia and Herzegovina. Also, an operative was arrested carrying documents that proved Saudi funding of the Hamas terrorist group to enable it to produce a short-range missile called the "Qassam."

U.S. intelligence sources have concluded that Saudi princes are spending millions of dollars to help large numbers of Al-Qaeda and Taliban members escape the American dragnet. One source told Middle East Newsline that "the money flow to Al-Qaeda continues from members of the royal family." To stanch this flow of funds, U.S. authorities are taking the initiative, sometimes close to home. In March 2002, they raided 16 locations, mostly in the Washington, D.C. area, primarily to learn more about two high-powered individuals connected to Saudi Arabia, Khalid bin Mahfouz and Cherif Sedky, and their role in funding Al-Qaeda.

Progress against Libya: A Scottish appeals court in March 2002 upheld the conviction of a Libyan intelligence agent for the 1988 bombing of Pan Am flight 103, killing 270, a development that Allan Gerson, a lawyer for many Pan Am families, calls "a giant step" toward making sponsors of terrorism accountable.

The Scottish verdict closes thirteen years of litigation and permits families of the victims finally to press civil claims against Libya's government, with full U.S. government endorsement: "The president expects Libya to fulfill [its] obligations," says the White House spokesman. "The court has spoken. It's time for Libya to act." Negotiations are indeed under way in Paris, with the families demanding more than $10 billion (or about $40 million per death).

Together, these three developments suggest that 9/11 claimants are on solid legal, factual and political grounds in seeking compensation from the kingdom. Should Riyadh reject their claims, they can demand per death as much as the Lockerbie families, which would bring their claim to more than $100 billion.

It's hard to think of a better way for ordinary Americans to help fight terrorism than for the 9/11 families to bring home to the Saudis the costs of sponsoring this hideous behavior.

12

THE ACADEMY INTERPRETS

WHO WAS THE PROPHET MUHAMMAD?

In a well-known and oft-repeated statement, the French scholar Ernest Renan wrote in 1851 that, unlike the other founders of major religions, the Prophet Muhammad "was born in the full light of history."

Indeed, look up Muhammad in any reference book and the outlines of his life are confidently on display: birth in C.E. 570 in Mecca, career as a successful merchant, first revelation in 610, flight to Medina in 622, triumphant return to Mecca in 630, death in 632. Better yet, read the 610-page standard account of Muhammad's life in English, by W. Montgomery Watt, and find a richly detailed biography.

There are, however, two major problems with this standard biography, as explained in a fascinating new study, *The Quest for the Historical Muhammad*, edited by Ibn Warraq (Amherst, N.Y.: Prometheus, 2000).

First, the massive documentation about Muhammad derives in every instance from Arabic written sources—biographies, collections of the prophet's sayings and doings, and so on—the earliest of which date from a century and a half after his death. Not only does this long lapse of time cast doubt on their accuracy, but internal evidence strongly suggests the Arabic sources were composed in the context of intense partisan quarrels over the prophet's life. To draw an American analogy: It's as though the first accounts of the U.S. Constitutional Convention of 1787 were only recently written down, and this in the context of polemical debates over interpretation of the Constitution.

Second, the earlier sources on the prophet's life that do survive dramatically contradict the standard biography. In part, these are literary sources in languages other than Arabic (such as Armenian, Greek, or Syriac); in part, they are material remains (such as papyri, inscriptions, and coins).

Although the unreliability of the Arabic literary sources has been understood for a century, only recently have scholars begun to explore its full implications, thanks largely to the groundbreaking work of the British academic John Wansbrough. In the spirit of "interesting if true," they look skeptically at the Arabic written sources and conclude that these are a form of "salvation history"—self-serving, unreliable accounts by the faithful.

The huge body of detail, revisionist scholars find, is almost completely spurious. So unreliable do the revisionists find the traditional account, Patricia Crone has memorably written, that "one could, were one so inclined, rewrite most of Montgomery Watt's biography of Muhammad in reverse."

For example, an inscription and a Greek account leads Lawrence Conrad to fix Muhammad's birth in 552, not 570. Crone finds that Muhammad's career took place not in Mecca but hundreds of kilometers to the north. Yehuda Nevo and Judith Koren find that the classical Arabic language was developed not in today's Saudi Arabia but in the Levant, and that it reached Arabia only through the colonizing efforts of one of the early caliphs.

Startling conclusions follow from this. The Arab tribesmen who conquered great swathes of territory in the seventh century were not Muslims, perhaps they were pagans. The Koran is a not "a product of Muhammad or even of Arabia," but a collection of earlier Judeo-Christian liturgical materials stitched together to meet the needs of a later age.

Most broadly, "there was no Islam as we know it" until two or three hundred years after the traditional version has it (more like C.E. 830 than 630); it developed not in the distant deserts of Arabia but through the interaction of Arab conquerors and their more civilized subject peoples. A few scholars go even further, doubting even the existence of Muhammad.

Though undertaken in a purely scholarly quest, the research made available in *Quest for the Historical Muhammad* raises basic questions for Muslims concerning the prophet's role as a moral paragon;

the sources of Islamic law; and the God-given nature of the Koran. Still, it comes as little surprise to learn that pious Muslims prefer to avoid these issues.

Their main strategy until now has been one of neglect—hoping that revisionism, like a toothache, will just go away.

But toothaches don't spontaneously disappear, and neither will revisionism. Muslims one day are likely to be consumed by efforts to respond to its challenges, just as happened to Jews and Christians in the nineteenth century, when they faced comparable scholarly inquiries. Those two faiths survived the experience—though they changed profoundly in the process—and so will Islam.

(12 May 2000)

EMPIRES OF THE SAND

In a tour de force that offers a profoundly new understanding of a key issue in modern Middle Eastern history, Efraim and Inari Karsh review the relations between Europe and the Ottoman Empire in the final century-and-a-half of the latter's existence, and in the process nearly reverse the standard historical interpretation. According to that interpretation, from about the time of the French Revolution until World War I, a dynamic, arrogant, imperial Europe imposed its will on a static, humiliated, supine East. This framework is common to nearly every leading historian, almost regardless of era or political disposition.

Thus, in the first half of this century, when diplomatic history was in vogue, the notion of an active Europe and a passive Middle East undergirded the whole study of the "Eastern Question," that huge set of international issues created by the weakness of the Ottoman Empire and its gradual dissolution. Almost without exception, studies of this topic concentrated on decisions made in London, Paris, Berlin, Vienna, and Moscow—with little notice given to Istanbul, Cairo, and Teheran, locales that basically serve as the background for European action. Right at the start of *A Peace to End All Peace*, his excellent survey of the impact of World War I on the Middle East, David Fromkin makes this point explicit: "Middle Eastern personalities, circumstances, and political cultures," he writes, "do not figure a great deal in the narrative that follows, except when I suggest the outlines and dimensions of what European politicians were ignoring when they made their decisions."

Even scholars who focus on the Middle East itself have accepted this premise. L. Carl Brown, the distinguished Princeton historian, observes that the modern Middle East "has been so continuously interlocked with the West as to have become almost an appendage of the Western political system." In his masterful survey, *The Middle East: A Brief History of the Last 2,000 Years*, Bernard Lewis offers a more nuanced formulation, writing that after 1800, "the course of events in the Middle East [was] profoundly influenced, and in times of crisis dominated, by the interests, ambitions, and actions of the European Great Powers."

Here is where the Karshes, a husband-and-wife team, step in. In *Empires of the Sand: The Struggle for Mastery in the Middle East, 1789-1923* (Cambridge, Mass.: Harvard University Press), they characterize the standard account as "fundamentally misconceived." Middle Easterners, they assert, "were not hapless victims of predatory imperial powers but active participants in the restructuring of their region." Put more directly:

> Twentieth-century Middle Eastern history is essentially the culmination of long-standing indigenous trends, passions, and patterns of behavior rather than an externally imposed dictate. Great-power influences, however potent, have played a secondary role, constituting neither the primary force behind the region's political development nor the main cause of its notorious volatility.

Drawing on a wide range of original sources, and writing in a clearly organized fashion and in fast-paced prose, the Karshes make a very compelling case for their revisionist position, establishing it point by point and in elegant detail.

Their research has particular significance for three historical issues. First, why did the Ottomans decide—disastrously, as it turned out—to enter World War I on the German side? In the consensus view, this resulted from (in the phrasing of the historian Howard M. Sachar) a "stupendous" coup by Berlin, which pulled the wool over the eyes of the credulous Ottomans. The Karshes find this exactly wrong; they show how Ottoman leaders initiated talks with Germany to explore an alliance, and document the lukewarm reception accorded to these addresses by many German officials. Far from having been dictated by Berlin, the Ottoman decision was a supremely reckless gamble by headstrong young rulers engaged in "an imperialist bid for territorial expansion and restoration of lost glory." It was also "by far the most important decision in the history of the modern Middle East," leading as it soon did to the fall of the empire and the emergence of the strife-filled order that still prevails today.

A second point involves the modern Arab dream of a single Arabic-speaking country stretching from the Atlantic to the Persian Gulf. The standard account blames European maneuvering for the failure of this grand ambition, but once again the Karshes turn the argument on its head. Left to their own fractious politics, the Arabs, they suggest, would actually have ended up with even more, and smaller, states than was the case: "great-power interference ensured the advent of a string of Middle Eastern states that were significantly larger than the political entities that would otherwise have been created."

Finally, there is the notoriously disputed subject of Middle Eastern boundaries. Arabs routinely heap blame on the Sykes-Picot Agreement of May 1916—a secret deal by Britain, France, and Russia to divide up the Middle East—for their still-festering border quarrels. In the *Arab Awakening*, a very influential study published in London in 1938, George Antonius denounced that agreement as "a shocking document" and a "breach of faith" by the great powers. Still today, the Hafez al-Assad regime ruling in Syria denounces the long-ago Sykes-Picot deal as the source of the "false borders" that divide the Middle East and have caused so many problems. Most scholars echo this view. But the Karshes boldly present Sykes-Picot as honorable—an honest attempt by the British to reconcile their prior obligations to France with their new ones to the Arabs. In a statement bound to cause scholarly heartburn, they praise Sykes-Picot as the "first ever great-power recognition of the Arabs' right to self-determination."

On a wide range of other issues, too, this wall-to-wall revisionist account upends the conventional narrative. It establishes that Ottoman (and not Russian) aggressiveness caused the Turks to lose control of the Balkans; that Great Britain found itself ruling Egypt more on account of Ottoman mistakes than out of its own imperial desires; that the Arab Revolt of World War I was inspired less by nationalist sentiments or other "lofty ideals" than by "the glitter of British gold." More broadly, the Karshes also turn around the usual argument for British duplicity in World War I, pinning this charge instead on the Arabs. Arab leaders, they demonstrate, made fraudulent claims about the extent of their own political authority, gave empty promises of military action, and bargained continuously with the Central Powers with an eye to double-crossing the British.

In all, I can hardly remember last reading so important and daring a reinterpretation of Middle Eastern history, or one so laden with implications. Already the Karshes' radical rejection of prevailing wisdom has prompted strong reactions from the scholarly community, as anyone visiting the relevant websites can attest. In time, indeed, some of their views may end up being refuted or heavily qualified. Nevertheless, their key ideas are likely to prevail, and even to become the new standard account. And who knows? This book could eventually affect the academic study of other areas of East-West contact, including Africa, India, and East Asia.

Conceivably it could affect political attitudes as well—and much for the better. *Empires of the Sand* shreds the main reason for Europeans to feel guilt ridden toward the Middle East. If Sykes-Picot was not a "breach of faith," and if the British and French generally behaved with at least as much honor as their Middle Eastern counterparts, might not the British, the French, and other Europeans begin to rethink their stock responses to the issues that currently bedevil the region?

And why stop with Europeans? Arab Middle Easterners have long sought comfort in the notion of their victimization at the hands of the perfidious, conspiratorial West. By coming instead to accept that they themselves largely created their own destiny and made their own history in the twentieth century, they might persuade themselves they can do the same in the twenty-first—only this time by throwing off their habitual sense of grievance, reigning in their autocratic rulers, reforming their moribund economies, and overcoming their radical ideologies.

(January 2000)

THE FAILURE OF POLITICAL ISLAM?

Will Islamists manage to take power, or will the mostly non-Islamist autocrats now in power stay there?

The answer has enormous importance primarily to the Muslims involved, but also to Israel and the West. Should Islamists win power, the Middle East is in for a long and dark era. Weapons of mass destruction will proliferate; warfare will become more common; and economies will contract. All-out hostility with Israel will likely be the case again; Americans will be targeted for terrorism and other violence.

The Islamists could well take over several governments in a short period. In Algeria, the Islamic Salvation Front (FIS) has launched a virtual civil war. In Egypt, Islamists control parts of the cities and countryside. Militant Islamic parties have done impressively well in nearly all the Muslim countries with electoral politics (Turkey, Lebanon, Jordan, Kuwait, Pakistan, Malaysia). By any measure, the militant Islamic challenge to the established order is growing. Much of the Muslim world is currently at risk.

It therefore comes as something of a surprise to learn that Olivier Roy, a leading French analyst of Islam, has written a book titled *The Failure of Political Islam* (Cambridge, Mass.: Harvard University Press, 1994; trans. by Carol Volk from the French: *L'Echec de l'Islam politique*. Paris: Seuil, 1992). He believes political Islam to be a failure? Roy knows all about Algeria and the other countries, of course, so "failure" for him must refer to something other than conventional political power.

The failure he alludes to follows from an elaborate argument that distinguishes between militant Islam and neofundamentalism. For Roy, the former means the drive for political power, and the latter means focusing on the family and the mosque. Instead of taking over the state, neofundamentalists try to create their own miniature versions of the just society. What the government of Iran furthers is militant Islam, while the Saudi authorities sponsor neofundamentalism. In Roy's view, neofundamentalism represents a "degradation" and an "enfeeblement" of militant Islam, for it challenges "the political, economic, and social realms ... only in words."

Outside of Iran itself, he argues, militant Islam has failed and the weaker cause of neofundamentalism has flourished. This "watering down" of Islam means that Islam has but limited political force. Its impact, aside from the parenthesis of the Iranian revolution and the war in Afghanistan, is essentially sociocultural: it marks the streets and customs but has no power relationship in the Middle East. It does not influence either state borders or interests. It has not created a "third force" in the world. It has not even been able to offer the Muslim masses a concrete political expression for their anticolonialism.

The challenge of militant Islam, in brief, is overrated. Roy grandly declares, "the Islamic revolution is behind us." This is so even in Iran: "the Tehran of the mullahs," he asserts in an astonishing passage, "has a very American look." (To which this reader replies: Check carefully the next photograph you see from Tehran and decide how much it brings to mind Peoria, Illinois.)

For these reasons, Roy concludes, militant Islam poses no great challenge to the West. It "is not a geostrategic factor: it will neither unify the Muslim world nor change the balance of power in the Middle East." We can relax. "Degraded" and "enfeebled" as it is, neofundamentalism would mean no serious changes even should it stagger to power: "Today, any Islamist political victory in a Muslim country would produce only superficial changes in customs and law."

Roy is a very knowledgeable student of Islam, even a brilliant one, whose (well-translated) book is replete with fine insights and memorable epigrams. (My favorite: "There are happy Muslims; there are no happy Islamists.") His analysis contains some important kernels of truth. He is right to note, for example, that militant Islam is a form of modernization. Contrary to the usual assumption, it is not medieval in spirit at all but an acutely modern form of protest. In Roy's elegant formulation, it "is the shari`a [Islamic sacred law] plus electricity."

Roy also makes the important point that militant Islam cannot work: there's no possibility that its program will serve Muslims well or that they will stick with it over the long haul. As Muslims recognize it to be dysfunctional, they will abandon it. Here, however, Roy misses the point: the realization that militant Islam does not work could be years or decades off; in the meantime, as the Marxist-Leninist precedent shows, regimes can do a great deal of mischief to their own populace and the rest of the world. The mullahs in Iran have tasted power and appear to like it; we must assume they will make great efforts to retain control of their country.

But the stunningly wrong-headed notion in Roy's book is his thesis about the failure of militant Islam. He seems to assume that because Islamists have not swept the Muslim world, they cannot do so in the future. This is comparable to an analyst's looking around in 1933, sixteen years after the Bolshevik revolution, and deciding that because communism came to power in only two countries (Mongolia being the second), and even there did not live up to its socialist ideals, therefore "the revolution is behind us." That would have been a profoundly mistaken conclusion; and so is Roy's today, sixteen years after the Iranian Revolution.

Indeed, Roy has already been proven wrong. The French version of *The Failure of Political Islam* appeared in October 1992, and the three years since have exposed his complete misunderstanding of the situation in Algeria. He expected a "watered down" movement not to amount to much; if FIS reaches power in Algeria, he predicted, it "will not invent a new society.... the FIS's Algeria will do nothing more than place a chador [women's headdress] over the FLN's Algeria."

Well, FIS is yesterday's organization, surpassed by the Armed Islamic Group (GIA). As its name implies, the GIA is not a gentle band of preachers urging moral self-improvement but a deadly gang of murderers. News of their work comes almost daily out of Algiers. They specialize in murdering the children of police officers, women without veils, unsympathetic journalists, and non-Muslim foreigners. They kill their victims in particularly horrifying ways, slitting throats and cutting off heads. As in Cambodia, where the Khmer Rouge attacked all those educated and Western-oriented, so in Algeria is anyone speaking French or wearing a business suit a potential victim. In comparison to the potential deaths in the culture war building in Algeria, the revolution in Iran was child's play. The GIA on its own repudiates Roy's prediction of militant Islam's becoming tame.

Which raises the question: How can someone who knows so much be so completely wrong? Roy seems to write in the French tradition of intellectual virtuosity—taking an implausible point and making a brilliant argument for it. He also indulges in the intellectuals' sin of *épater la bourgeoisie*; fears of militant Islam being particularly severe in middle-class France these days, he perversely must insist on their being illusory.

But whatever games Roy is playing in his own circles, his book has potentially real importance in the United States. Enlightened opinion already tells us not to worry about militant Islam: leading American specialists on the subject, such as John Entelis, John Esposito, and John Voll, argue that we should look beyond militant Islam's rough edges and bristling rhetoric. If we do so, we will find a movement that is democratic in spirit, capitalist in orientation, and prepared to co-exist with the West. To this, Roy adds: militant Islam has degenerated into a quietist movement seeking to create nothing more than "authentically Muslim microsocieties."

Coming at a time when FIS and the GIA are within striking distance of taking power, his words suggest that Americans need not worry about events in Algeria. Unfortunately, Roy and his ilk have the ear of our policymakers, for it is U.S. policy in Algeria (but less so in Egypt and Iran) conspicuously not to condemn the Islamists' ideas and goals. Instead, it seeks them out to engage in dialogue.

As Algeria stands today on the threshold of becoming the last great tragedy of the twentieth century, leading intellectuals find ways, yet again, to lull Westerners into false hopes. Let us at last learn from history and this time not be fooled.

(June 1995)

THE JEWISH DISCOVERY OF ISLAM

A fierce intellectual debate broke out in October 1976 when Edward Said, the Palestinian-born Parr Professor of English at Columbia University and a partisan of trendy French post-modernists, wrote an essay for the *New York Times Book Review* arguing that Western scholars of the Middle East represented "an unbroken tradition in European thought of profound hostility, even hatred, toward Islam." In his diatribe, Said singled out Bernard Lewis, then the Cleveland E. Dodge Professor of Near Eastern Studies at Princeton, as the de facto leader of this nefarious school of "Orientalism." Hardly one to shrink from a challenge, Lewis, one of the century's most eminent scholars of Islam, responded by defending vigorously the moral integrity and intellectual successes of the Orientalist tradition, that unique effort by members of one civilization to comprehend and appreciate another.

A witness to this debate might have expected Lewis's colleagues in the field to stand by him, not just because he was defending their work but because Said, for his part, clearly lacked the academic credentials that specialists of any kind usually demand of one who opines on their subject. But they did not; to the contrary, Middle East specialists overwhelmingly accepted Said's critique, and even expanded on it. Whole new sub-fields were developed to flesh out his arguments (for example, by applying them to gender, something

Said barely mentioned); and Orientalism acquired a meaning so intensely pejorative that "neo-orientalist" is today the worst insult one can hurl at a scholar in the field.

Still, the battle is not entirely over. Martin Kramer, a highly talented former student of Lewis's who now heads the Dayan Center at Tel Aviv University, continues the not-entirely-lonely effort to preserve and extend several centuries' worth of Western scholarship. In *The Jewish Discovery of Islam: Studies in Honor of Bernard Lewis* (Syracuse, N.Y.: Syracuse University Press, 1999), Kramer has brought together a collection of nine essays by Middle East scholars to which he has added his own insightful introduction, all focusing on a neglected aspect of this tradition.

In helping to develop nineteenth-century European attitudes toward the Middle East, Jewish scholars, Lewis has pointed out, brought a very different sensibility to bear from that of their Christian counterparts. Unaffected by "nostalgia for the Crusades," and untouched by the bitterly hostile feelings toward Islam and Muslims that prevailed in Europe, Jews, in Lewis's words, played "a key role in the development of an objective, nonpolemical, and positive evaluation of Islamic civilization." More broadly, they were "among the first who attempted to present Islam to European readers as Muslim themselves see it and to stress, to recognize, and indeed sometimes to romanticize the merits and achievements of Muslim civilization."

Kramer quotes these words in his introduction as he offers his own survey of illustrious Jewish figures—scholars and non-scholars alike—who had a major impact on Europe's perception of Islam. Again and again he is able to point up the dramatic contrast between them and the often crabbed, racially charged, and theologically hostile attitude toward Islam taken by many Christians. Seen from today's vantage point, indeed, when Muslim-Jewish relations are so often tense and even violent, the almost joyously positive tenor of this older Jewish encounter seems nothing short of astonishing.

Benjamin Disraeli (1804-81), for example, later to become prime minister of Great Britain, once thought of volunteering for the Ottoman army. Ignaz Goldziher (1850-1921), perhaps Europe's single most influential student of the Middle East, went so far as to pray as a Muslim in Cairo, recounting that "never in my life was I more devout, more truly devout." Some actually converted: Muhammad Assad, né Leopold Weiss of Lvov and Vienna (1900-92), advised the Saudi king and served as Pakistan's ambassador to the United Nations before settling down to publish an influential English-language translation of the Koran.

The facts established by Kramer and his contributors have a number of implications. For one thing, as Jacob Lassner writes here, by presenting Islam more objectively, not to say empathetically, Jewish scholars turned the whole field of comparative religion "from religious apologetics ... into a respected discipline." And this empathetic approach has prevailed until this very day, making a mockery of Said's grand theory of Orientalist hostility to Islam. One Arab scholar goes to far as to credit Goldziher with creating "a kind of orthodoxy which has retained its power until our own time." By contrast, the more "Christian" approach—which did indeed see Islam as a rival and regard Middle Eastern culture as inferior, and on which Said focused to the utter neglect of the German-Jewish school—has long been not just defunct but despised and repudiated.

Ordinary Muslims now living in the West also owe much to the Jewish scholars. As Kramer puts it, "the respect for Islam which Jews had done so much to disseminate not only survived in Europe, but served as the basis for Europe's tolerance of Muslim minorities" after World War II. And he goes on to make the same point in symbolic terms, "The mosque-like synagogues erected by Jewish communities in the nineteenth century prepared Europe to accept the real mosques which Muslim communities erected across the continent in the twentieth."

But there are also a number of unpleasant ironies lurking in this tale. One hope of the early Jewish scholars of Islam was to generate sympathy for Jews as well as Muslims. As Kramer writes in his introduction, a corollary of their celebrations of medieval Islamic civilization—a civilization in which Jews had played no small role—was the implicit suggestion that, were contemporary Jews allowed to participate fully in European society, they would enhance it no less than they had enhanced Baghdad or Cordova, peaks of human achievement worthy of anyone's admiration. But even as they helped lay the groundwork for tolerance of Muslims and respect for Islam, these "pro-Islamic Jews" (the term is Bernard Lewis's) failed when it came to improving attitudes toward their own people. This can be seen still today, when the ideology associated with Western multiculturalism and third-worldism—two ostensibly outward-looking movements whose lineage can be traced in part to the work of the pro-Islamic Jews—remains inimical to Israel and Jews alike.

Muslims themselves have played a critical role in this process. Having adopted the romantic conceptions propagated by Jewish scholars, and having incorporated them into the Islamic self-image, they then turned them into weapons against Zionism and Jews. As Lewis has written, the myth of a time when Jews enjoyed equal rights with Muslims "was invented by Jews in nineteenth-century Europe as a reproach to Christians—and taken up by Muslims in our own time as a reproach to Jews," particularly the Jews in the state of Israel who have declined to assume their "rightful"—i.e., subordinate—place in the Islamic Middle East. It is an old story, this story of good will rewarded with enmity, but seldom has it been illuminated with such bitter clarity.

(March 2000)

THE DREAM PALACE OF THE ARABS

Fouad Ajami, the Majid Khadduri Professor of Middle Eastern Studies at Johns Hopkins University, has found two niches that are all his own, one scholarly and the other journalistic.

As a scholar, Ajami focuses not on the usual questions of statecraft and foreign policy, but on intellectual developments in the Arabic-speaking world. By making issues and personalities come alive, he manages to interest an impressively large American audience in debates conducted by Egyptians, Lebanese, and Saudis. As a public commentator, Ajami has regular access to leading television and magazine outlets, making him the Middle East specialist with probably the greatest public reach. Though English is not his first language, Ajami's command of language has few rivals in the world of political analysis. Whether speaking on CBS News or writing for the *New Republic*, *U.S. News and World Report*, or *Foreign Affairs*, he dazzles with his metaphors and panache.

He's a poet who happens to do politics. Just as T. E. Lawrence (from whom, incidentally, the title of his most recent book, *The Dream Palace of the Arabs*, is drawn) wrote so distinctively that a single line of his prose is often enough to identify him as the author, Ajami's writing has a unique quality. No one else could have written this passage:

Temperamentally, Iran has been a land susceptible to the power of ideas, to political and philosophical abstraction, to the pamphleteer…. The culture of the Arabian Peninsula and the Gulf states has in contrast always been thoroughly empirical and raw, its politics the struggles of clans and determined men, tribal affairs to the core.

His aphoristic style boils complexities down to their essentials. Middle East politics he describes as "a world where triumph rarely comes with mercy or moderation." Pan-Arabism he characterizes as but "Sunni dominion dressed in secular garb."

Ajami has two other noteworthy qualities. As a native Arabic speaker, he has many advantages over we foreigners who spend years cutting our teeth on his difficult language, and even then know it only imperfectly. "It has been the besetting sin—and poverty—of a good deal of writing on the Arab world," he points out, "that it is done by many who have no mastery of Arabic." Second, unlike so many other prominent Arab-Americans—Khalil Jahshan, Rashid Khalidi, Mohammad Mehdi, and James Zogby—Ajami is a political moderate and an American patriot. He neither apologizes for Arab dictators nor spins anti-American conspiracy theories. He likes the United States and seeks to pursue its interests.

To make matters complete, he is blessedly free of the common Arab obsession with Israel. His outlook on the Arab-Israeli conflict seems to be roughly that of any liberal observer—except that he knows the subject much better. This leads to interesting results. On the question of Iraq, Ajami gently berates President George H.W. Bush for stopping too soon against Saddam Hussein: "A strong case could have been made for remaking the Iraqi state," something the Iraqi people would have gratefully thanked him for. On the peace process, he brings a skeptical eye to Yasir Arafat's antics. If Shimon Peres hailed the PLO's decision in April 1996 as an annulment of its charter calling for Israel's destruction, proclaiming this "the greatest revolution that the Middle East had known in the last hundred years," Ajami knows better. "Arafat had obliged," he writes, "or so it seemed. True to his past, he was to be in this episode all things to all men. He left enough ambiguity in what he had done to give himself plenty of cover." He's a liberal, yes, but nobody's fool.

Predictably, this robust, blunt-spoken approach to Middle Eastern issues sits badly with Arab-American colleagues, who respond with resentment, shrillness, and peevishness. They have engaged in a more-or-less systematic campaign to make him miserable, denouncing him in public and harassing him in private. After appearing at a Jerusalem Fund event in the company of Henry Kissinger some years ago, Ajami came under a barrage of abuse. One would-be rival, Edward Said of Columbia University, accuses Ajami of offering "unmistakably racist prescriptions" toward the Arabs. Another, Assad AbuKhalil of California State University-Stanislaus, calls him "neo-orientalist" (a huge insult in Middle Eastern studies circles). Whatever the internal price Ajami pays for this slander, he soldiers on, unintimidated and seemingly undaunted.

Which brings us to *The Dream Palace of the Arabs: A Generation's Odyssey* (New York: Pantheon, 1998), a four-part inquiry into the past quarter-century's experience with the "intellectual edifice of secular nationalism and modernity...the rupturing of the secular tradition in the era now behind us." Individual chapters trace the biography of an Iraqi-born intellectual, Khalil Hawi, who symptomized this problem, assess the impact of the Iranian revolution, look at Egyptian public life, and interpret the response of Arab intellectuals to peacemaking with Israel.

The book's recurrent theme is mistaken hopes and misplaced faith. Hawi committed suicide in 1982. The Iranian revolution's struggle with the dominant order "led down a blind alley." Arab nationalism "hatched a monster" in the Iraqi bid for Kuwait in 1990. Egypt's experience with revolution under Gamal Abdel Nasser "ran aground." The Oslo accords degenerated into "a grim wave of terror" against Israelis. Generalizing, Ajami finds that "What Arabs had said about themselves, the history they had written, and the truths they had transmitted to their progeny had led down a blind alley" (that metaphor again).

To this reader's taste, the early chapters are a bit contrived. Ajami's use of poets and intellectuals to represent their eras sometimes gets mired in detail. As the book goes along, though, the analysis becomes more direct, culminating in a remarkable final chapter on "The Orphaned Peace," where Ajami explains what went wrong with the Arab-Israeli negotiations. "No sooner had the peace of Oslo [been announced] than the new battle began, the fear of Israeli military supremacy now yielding to the specter of Israeli cultural hegemony." Ajami locates a few intellectuals who scorn this fear ("I can assure my Arab brethren," writes a Syrian, "that Israel does not have culture richer than ours and intellectual achievements deeper than ours") but finds them to be an excruciatingly small minority.

Instead, the great majority of the Arab intellectual elite repudiated Oslo as "not their peace but the rulers' peace." For these many, enmity with Israel served as the "one truth that could not be bartered or betrayed, the one sure way back to the old fidelities." The peace process even had the surprising effect of making writers, journalists, and professors yet more determined in their opposition to Israel. Muhammad Sid Ahmad, an Egyptian who favors the peace, explains: "The diplomats and military men have to follow rules and talk to Israel. But with intellectuals nothing has changed. It's even become more radical than before."

Ajami rightly ascribes much importance to the intellectual class rejecting Oslo: it "did not govern, but it structured a moral universe that hemmed in the rulers and limited their options." Bereft of its support, the Egyptian, Jordanian, and other rulers found they could not sell the idea of peace to their civil societies—the professionals, voluntary groups, religious elements, and other leaders. Generally, "the most articulate sections of the society, among the professionals and the enlightened," most resisted normalization. Governments, unsure and cowardly, deferred. "Diplomatic accommodation would be the order of the day," Ajami observes, "but the intellectual class was give a green light to agitate against the peace." The author pays homage to "the rulers who dared break with the culture's prohibitions and the few traders eager for a new order of things," but sees them losing to "the centurions of Arab political orthodoxy."

Ajami's assessment of Peres's "new Middle East" holds particular interest. Caught up with the demise of their pan-Arab, pan-Syrian, Third Worldist visions, Arab intellectuals were in no mood for his sunny vision of economic expansion. "Peres had walked in—exuberant, wordy, and hopeful—during a funeral." The Israeli politician "arrived trumpeting a world that held out nothing but the promise of cultural alienation. Instead of an Arab world that was whole and true, the popular Syrian poet, Nizar Qabbani, lamented, 'we now get a supermarket with an Israeli chairman of the board.'" Qabbani and his ilk shed no tears for Peres when he lost to Binyamin Netanyahu in 1996. Quite the reverse: Peres's defeat was a gift that got them "off the hook."

Ajami confesses he finds this outlook of his intellectual peers "strange," then soberly explains why their seemingly perverse attraction to failure:

In an Arab political history littered with thwarted dreams, little honor would be extended to pragmatists who knew the limits of what could and could not be done. The political culture of nationalism reserved its approval for those who led ruinous campaigns in pursuit of impossible quests.

Extremism and failure, in other words, beget more of the same. Ajami closes his book with a forlorn prediction: "The day had not come for the Arab political imagination to steal away from Israel and to look at the Arab reality, to behold its own view of the kind of world the Arabs wanted for themselves." If Ajami is right, Arab intellectual life will continue to exalt irrationality and aggression.

We may not like that but at least, having read *The Dream Palace of the Arabs*, we can at least begin to understand it.

(February 1998)

A LESSON COURTESY OF THE TURKS

How can Israel staunch its wounds in southern Lebanon where about a thousand of its soldiers have been killed over two decades

SOURCES

The essays presented here are substantially as they were originally published; most changes concern verb tenses, references to
dates, spellings, and terminology. On occasion I have adjusted facts
when improved information came out later (for example, adjusting
down the number of those killed on September 11, 2001), made re-
placements where information duplicated from one article to another,
or made slight stylistic adjustments. The following bibliography lists
when and where the articles first appeared and their original titles.

PART 1: WAR ON TERRORISM

1. BEFORE 9/11

"Death to America." *New York Post*, 8 September 2002.
"Khomeini, the Soviet and U.S." *New York Times*, 27 May 1980.
"The New Enemy." *Wall Street Journal Europe*, 27 August 1998.
"A New Way to Fight Terrorism." *Jerusalem Post,* 26 May 2000.
"The New Global Threat." *Jerusalem Post*, 11 April 2001.
"Terrorism on Trial" (with Steven Emerson). *Wall Street Journal*, 31
    May 2001.
"Bin Laden and Herndon, Virginia." *Jerusalem Post*, 20 June 2001.
"Rolling back the Forces of Terror" (with Steven Emerson). *Wall
    Street Journal*, 13 August 2001.

2. AMERICAN RESPONSES POST-9/11

"Mistakes Made the Catastrophe Possible," *Wall Street Journal*, 12
    September 2001.
"War, Not 'Crimes': Time for a Paradigm Shift." *National Review*, 1
    October 2001.

"What Bush Got Right—and Wrong." *Jerusalem Post*, 26 September 2001

"State's Terror Untruths." *New York Post*, 28 May 2002.

"Terror & Denial." *New York Post*, 9 July 2002.

"Border Agencies in Denial." *New York Post*, 16 October 2002.

"What's True Islam? Not for U.S. to Say." *New York Post*, 26 November 2001.

"Aim the War on Terror at Militant Islam." *Los Angeles Times*, 6 January 2002.

"A Deadly Error." *New York Post*, 21 January 2002.

"A War Against What?" *New York Post*, 1 October 2002.

"The Enemy Within." *New York Post*, 24 January 2003.

3. MILITANT ISLAM POST-9/11

"A Middle East Party." *Jerusalem Post*, 14 September 2001.

"Muslims ♥ Bin Laden." *New York Post*, 22 October 2001.

"Victory Shifts the Muslim World." *New York Post*, 19 November 2001.

"Arabia's Civil War: The Saudis vs. the Extremists." *Wall Street Journal Europe*, 14 May 2003.

"Militant Islam's New Strongholds." (with Jonathan Schanzer). *New York Post*, 22 October 2002.

"Terrorist Profs." *New York Post*, 24 February 2003.

"Al-Qaeda's Limits." *New York Post*, 28 May 2003.

PART 2: ISLAM AND MUSLIMS

4. WRIT LARGE

"The Evil Isn't Islam." *New York Post*, 30 July 2002.

"Islam's Future." *New York Post*, 13 August 2002.

"Islamists—Not Who They Say They Are." *Jerusalem Post*, 9 May 2001.

"Where Does Religious Freedom Exist?" *Jerusalem Post*, 23 September 1999.

"What Is Jihad?" *New York Post*, 31 December 2002.

"The Jihad Menace." *Jerusalem Post*, 27 July 2001

"A Father's Pride and Glory." *Jerusalem Post*, 15 August 2001

"Arafat's Suicide Factory." *New York Post*, 9 December 2001.

5. IN THE WEST

"How Many American Muslims?" *New York Post*, 29 October 2001.

"It Matters What Kind of Islam Prevails." *Los Angeles Times*, 22 July 1999.

Review of Ibn Warraq [pseud.], "Why I Am Not a Muslim." *Weekly Standard*, 22 January 1996.

"An American Rushdie?" *Jerusalem Post*, 4 July 2001.

"Crisis of Illegal Immigration." *Jerusalem Post*, 5 September 2001.

"Something Rotten in Denmark?" (with Lars Hedegaard). *New York Post*, 27 August 2002.

6. PRESENTING AND REPRESENTING ISLAM IN AMERICA

"Think Like a Muslim." *New York Post*, 11 February 2002.

"Become a Muslim Warrior." *Jerusalem Post*, 3 July 2002.

"PBS, Recruiting for Islam" *New York Post*, 17 December 2002.

"Harvard ♥ Jihad." *New York Post*, 11 June 2002.

"Islam's American Lobby." *Jerusalem Post*, 20 September 2001.

"CAIR: 'Moderate' Friends of Terror." *New York Post*, 22 April 2002.

"'Mainstream' Muslims?" *New York Post*, 18 June 2002.

"U.S. Arabs' Firebrand." *New York Post*, 25 March 2002.

PART 3: THE ARAB-ISRAELI AND OTHER CONFLICTS

7. OSLO DIPLOMACY

"Imagine a Palestinian State: A Nightmare for the Arabs and for Israel." *New York Times*, 25 April 1988.

"Dim Prospects for Palestinian State." *Indianapolis Star*, 26 December 1988.

"Arafat Said Yes, But Most Palestinian Leaders Say No." *Wall Street Journal Europe*, 22 September 1993.

"Implications of the Rabin-Arafat Accord." *Forward*, 24 September 1993.

"The End of the Reign of Optimism in the Middle East." *Washington Times*, 16 March 1994.

"The Word on the Arab Street on Israel" (with Tonya Ugoretz Buzby). *Wall Street Journal*, 8 June 1995.

"Two-Faced Yasir" (With Alexander T. Stillman). *Weekly Standard*, 25 September 1995.
"..Too Bad Their Minds Are Made Up." *Forward*, 25 December 1998.
"This Pivotal Moment." *Jerusalem Post,* 7 June 2000.
"They Had a Name for It" (with Mimi Stillman). *Jerusalem Post,* 5 July 2000.
"A Perverse Dynamic at Work." *Jerusalem Post*, 2 August 2000.
"Oslo's Nine Lives." *Jerusalem Post*, 25 October 2000.
"Winds of War." *Jerusalem Post*, 20 December 2000.
"The Oslo Process—An Israeli Choice." *Jerusalem Post*, 3 January 2001.
"Land for What?" *American Spectator*, March 2001.

8. The Oslo War

"Lift the 'Siege'?" *Jerusalem Post*, 14 March 2001
"The Left's Ongoing Oslo Delusion." *Jerusalem Post*, 25 April 2001.
"Israel's Lebanon Lesson." *Jerusalem Post*, 23 May 2001
"Preventing War: Israel's Options." *Jerusalem Post*, 18 July 2001
"Arabs Still Want to Destroy Israel." *Wall Street Journal*, 18 January 2002.
"The *Only* Solution Is Military." *New York Post*, 25 February 2002
"To End the Violence." *New York Post*, 7 January 2003.

9. Syria vs. Israel

"Assad, the Spoiler." *Forward*, 24 December 1993.
"Just Kidding: Syria's Peace Bluff." *New Republic*, 8 & 15 January 1996.
Review of Itamar Rabinovich, "The Brink of Peace: The Israeli-Syrian Negotiations." *Weekly Standard*, 16 November 1998.
"Assad Isn't Interested." *Jerusalem Post*, 29 August 1999.
"True Syrian Intentions." *Jerusalem Post*, 17 March 2000.
"A Lesson Courtesy of the Turks." *Jerusalem Post,* 12 April 2000.
"Getting Syria Wrong" (with Zachary Rentz). *Jerusalem Post,* 21 June 2000.
"Will the Assad Dynasty Last?" *Jerusalem Post*, 6 June 2001.

10. Iraq vs. All

Review of Hussein Sumaida, with Carole Jerome, "Circle of Fear: My Life as an Israeli and Iraqi Spy." *Middle East Quarterly*, March 1996.

"Why Go It Alone?" *Washington Post*, 3 December 1997.

"After 'Desert Storm,' Barely a Footprint Was Left in the Sand." *Los Angeles Times*, 4 August 2000.

Review of Scott Ritter, "Endgame: Solving the Iraq Problem— Once and for All." *Washington Times*, 14 April 1999.

Review of Khidhir Hamza with Jeff Stein, "Saddam's Bombmaker: The Terrifying Inside Story of the Iraqi Nuclear and Biological Weapons Agenda." *Commentary*, June 2001.

"A Majority of One." *New York Post*, 18 March 2002.

"An Iraqi Tragedy." *New York Post*, 22 April 2003.

Part 4: American Views

11. Making U.S. Policy

Review of Robert D. Kaplan, "The Arabists: The Romance of an American Elite." *Wall Street Journal*, 16 September 1993.

Review of A. F. K. Organski. "The $36 Billion Bargain." *Commentary*, January 1991.

"The Friendly Republicans." *Jerusalem Post*, 15 February 2000.

"How Clinton Adheres to the 'Rushdie Rules,'" *Forward*, 25 July 1997.

"EgyptAir Probe Reveals Anti-Americanism," *Wall Street Journal*, 24 November 1999.

"Sue the Saudis." *New York Post*, 18 February 2002.

"Make the Saudis Pay for Terror." *New York Post*, 15 April 2002.

12. The Academy Interprets

"Who Was the Prophet Muhammad?" *Jerusalem Post*, 12 May 2000.

Review of Martin Kramer, ed., "The Jewish Discovery of Islam: Studies in Honor of Bernard Lewis." *Commentary*, March 2000.

Review of Efraim Karsh and Inari Karsh, "Empires of the Sand: The Struggle for Mastery in the Middle East, 1789-1923."*Commentary,* January 2000.

Review of Fouad Ajami, "The Dream Palace of the Arabs: A Generation's Odyssey." *Commentary*, February 1998.

Review of Olivier Roy, "The Failure of Political Islam?" *Commentary,* June 1995.

Index

265